WORDS

FOR ROBERT BURCHFIELD'S
SIXTY-FIFTH BIRTHDAY

WORDS

FOR ROBERT BURCHFIELD'S
SIXTY-FIFTH BIRTHDAY

EDITED BY E.G. STANLEY AND T.F. HOAD

D. S. BREWER

First published 1988 by D. S. Brewer
240 Hills Road, Cambridge
an imprint of Boydell & Brewer Ltd
PO Box 9, Woodbridge, Suffolk IP12 3DF
and of Boydell & Brewer Inc.
Wolfeboro, New Hampshire 03894-2069, USA

ISBN 0 85991 259 0

British Library Cataloguing in Publication Data
Words : for Robert Burchfield's sixty-
    fifth birthday.
    1. English language
    I. Stanley, E.G.,   II. Hoad, T.F.
    III. Burchfield, R.W.
    420   PE1072
    ISBN 0-85991-259-0

Library of Congress Cataloging-in-Publication Data
Words : for Robert Burchfield's sixty-fifth
birthday.
    1. English language — Lexicography.
2. Burchfield, R.W. I. Burchfield, R.W.
II. Stanley, Eric Gerald. III. Hoad, T.F.
PE1611.W68   1988   423'.028   87-32576
ISBN 0-85991-259-0

Printed in Great Britain by
St Edmundsbury Press, Bury St Edmunds, Suffolk

CONTENTS

FOR ROBERT BURCHFIELD

Words are like children, they will not keep still
But grow and change, challenge, betray, turn shrill
Or old and useless, no more telling truth
As once they did in their springtime of youth,
Proliferating in profligacy
To drunk slang's rootless desert anarchy.
Others grow wise beyond our wildest hope.
To understand we need a telescope,
So far beyond our daily thoughts they soar.
Others are heard but once, and then no more.
Innumerable on the sands of time
These shells of meaning, commonplace, sublime,
Through which we hear the voices of the dead.
What's read we modify into what's said,
And so in turn pass on a living tongue
To babes unborn and lyrics yet unsung.
With words we whisper from our deepest heart,
Give praise to God, beg anguish to depart,
Lighten a journey with a well-made jest,
Corrupt a virgin, or become most blest
With thought-filled nuances we did not choose.
You this unruly crowd did not refuse
To catalogue, define, tame, welcome in
Between new sheets to find each origin,
Parent or scapegrace, till all meaning's plain
In the four ordered volumes which contain
Completion of our language to this day
From earliest times. What would your tutor say
(For he was mine too) were he here once more
New-come from Narnia, striding on our floor,

1

Words

His pipe in mouth? He would salute and praise,
And say 'Not only poets win the bays.'
But in a lower and a humbler kind
May I thank you for friendship unconfined?
You understood why, in my poetry
I turned from urban, drab cacophony
To value nature and true company,
Let the between-wars formlessness depart —
Those ironies that masquerade as art,
Thin, songless intellects who could not scan,
With rhymes uncertain, and with thoughts no man
Would teach his children — to return to form,
Perfection of technique touched to transform
Discretion, balance, and a joy in life,
The growing children and the loving wife,
Into a music that could hold daylight
Inside first dew of morning all through night
For ever and beyond, or so we thought.
Yes, you perceived, encouraged, gently taught
Your younger colleague, him who here reveres
His daily friend for more than twenty years.
Your monuments do not know how to die.
Their roots lie deep in human mystery,
Flower through thoughts to words, in friendship, love,
Rich scholarship below, conscience above,
Higher still, laughing generosity
Of spirit, which irradiates the free
And patient art of lexicography.
Oxford has lived a golden age, sustained
Through to completion while Macmillan reigned
Under Elizabeth. Your work's complete,
Beyond the reach of envy or defeat.
And though our little lives soon pass, soon fade,
The cricket field yields to the yew tree's shade,
Your world of order, virtue, and repose,
Of thinking, reading, teaching, writing, shows
A life of quiet conquers more than war:
But we shall look upon your like no more.

Francis Warner

R. W. BURCHFIELD AND EARLIER DAYS

J. B. Trapp

Memory — probably fallible — suggests that my first acquaintance with Bob Burchfield — first sight of him, rather — must have been in March 1943. It was in one of the smaller lecture rooms of Victoria University College, the Wellington constituent college of what was then the federal University of New Zealand. Bob had come up in 1940 from Wanganui Technical College, the day school of a small city, but his studies had been disrupted by the War. Just arrived from a country high school, I was sitting at the back of the room in the hope, fulfilled as it happened, of remaining unnoticed. From there I could watch the thirty-odd second- and third-year B.A. students and — even more at their ease — the more advanced Honours M.A. people taking their places for one of Ian Gordon's twice-weekly literature lectures. That year we were hearing about the Romantics. Next year the wheel would dip down to the Elizabethans, next rise again to the seventeenth century, then the eighteenth and so back to the Romantics. So in your three-year first degree, if you followed the course of action recommended to me by a canny elder sister and requiring special professorial permission you could, by joining the advanced literature course in your first year, find yourself exposed to a fuller selection of special periods of modern literature, rounding them out with the missing one of the four and with papers on Shakespeare and on the Victorians in your fourth, M.A. year. Nothing medieval in the 'literature' part of course. Nothing twentieth-century, let alone contemporary, either — except incidentally in the 'language' component of your first year. This last was really a rather well-planned adaption to Antipodean conditions of H. J. C. Grierson's Edinburgh rhetoric course. Medieval texts were in those days taught largely from a linguistic standpoint in the second, third and fourth years only: progressing from Wyatt's *Anglo-Saxon Reader* and Sisam's *Fourteenth-Century Verse and Prose* to *Beowulf, Troilus and Criseyde* and *Sir Gawain and the Green Knight*. Only in that final year was some attempt made to deal with Chaucer and the Gawain poet as supreme

3

literary masters.

As you passed through this course of instruction in the subject you had chosen for Honours you made up, by annual examination, a degree on what is now called the course-unit system. New Zealand education was based on the broad, general Scottish pattern and acquired through lectures rather than tutorials. When, a few years later, tutorials were introduced, they were not one-to-two-or-three affairs, still less one-to-one, but one-to-twenty or so, especially in the first year. The few essays we wrote were conscientiously read and commented upon by our teachers, but not individually discussed. No chance of that, with some 450 students in the English Department, more than 400 of them in the first year. First-year English was compulsory for arts, commerce and law degrees — as Latin and mathematics had formerly been for arts. It was a solemn sight that later confronted Bob and me, as raw young teachers, at the raw hour of 8 a.m. in the steeply raked chemistry lecture theatre: 400 assorted students, aged from 17 to 50 and intent, not always very willingly, on a first-year examination pass. In 1943 the Department's teaching staff, depleted by one-third because of the Second World War, was two: a Professor and a Senior Lecturer. New Zealand believed in education and in self-help. School standards were good and anyone who had passed the public university entrance examination was admitted to read for a degree. As a new, thinly populated country, dependent on overseas markets for its primary produce it had, however, little money to spend. Indeed, when Victoria College was founded in 1896, it engaged four professors, one to teach English and philosophy, one classics and modern languages, one physics and chemistry and one — by a brilliant piece of opportunism — mathematics and law. The occupant of the last-named chair stayed the shortest time, leaving to become head of MIT; and other recruits, some of them the College's own students returning from postgraduate studies overseas, in due time made a more rational deployment of scholarly labour possible. Three of the foundation professors stayed long: both Bob and I were taught classics by one of them, then in his 80s, who retired only at the end of the War.

In our day, the chair of English was held by Ian Gordon, who had been appointed at 29 less than ten years before. Gordon was a brilliant teacher of literature who has also done a great deal for New Zealand writing. He was then probably at the top of his bent. Though he could convey real enthusiasm for literature, his method was down to earth: a few biographical and publication facts on the blackboard as an orientation and he would launch into a clear and well-formed lecture, with copious readings, a strong emphasis on the necessity of reading the texts and little concern for critical theory and critical stance. Was it not enough that we were to take a special option later on Aristotle's *Poetics* and a paper on the history of criticism? What Gordon did supremely well was to send one to the texts and — the College and other libraries being well stocked with these — you could read widely and discriminate as you chose.

That at least is how it remains in memory. And Bob's place in it, first as student of the course and then teacher of it? The sight of that already thick-set, fair-haired, smiling figure, affable and unconcerned, battle-dressed, sergeant-striped (I think), attaché case swinging as he walked to take a seat towards the front of the lecture room, is etched clearly on recollection. A couple of years and more older than I, he was already serving in the Royal New Zealand Artillery and able somehow to keep up his work and come in for lectures. Lectures, it should be said, tended to be clustered at the beginning and end of the day for the convenience of part-time students. You might find yourself being instructed or, worse, instructing at 8 a.m. and at 8 p.m. on the same day.

As far as I remember, we did not then meet. In those days you were conscripted for service at home at 18 and overseas at 20, so that Bob departed for service in Italy that same year. I continued a full-time student, preserved from local conscription by vacation labour in cheese-factory and freezing works — and from overseas service by the end of the War in August 1945. We really got to know each other well early in 1946 when Bob, with two slightly older contemporaries returned from Navy and Air Force respectively, came virtually straight out of uniform to be again a student. It was an enormous benefit for those of my age and inexperience to be thrown together with such men. We read our Honours year together with enjoyment, and I had my first close experience of Bob's industry, application and self-discipline, and of the rock-like evenness of temper and sense of purpose that took him through what must have been a difficult transition. Even his hand-writing: small, well-proportioned, firm, unfussy, legible, precise, seemed — and still seems — to reflect a temperament, a character, an intelligence that asks clearly to be valued only as it deserves, without concealment or arrière-pensée. Not priggish: no-one who laughed and still laughs so easily and well could be that.

So we sat our finals and went our ways. Somewhat to our joint surprise, since we had expected to train for school teaching, each of us found himself more agreeably situated, he as a junior lecturer in an English Department at Victoria College which could now allow itself such appointments, I in an excellent scholarly library in the city. Later when Bob, steered by James Bertram, had departed for Magdalen with his Rhodes Scholarship, I took his place as teacher and, at one remove, Warden of the College's only men's hall of residence. Meantime, since·I was teaching part-time in the Department and contributing to the fiftieth anniversary number of the College magazine which he was editing — a first appearance in print for both of us — we saw a good deal of one another. Again, I was struck by that passion for labour and for detail, for doing things himself, which has always been his trademark. No New Zealander, it has been truly said, will ever believe that s/he does not have to do everything him/herself, or that anybody, even another New Zealander, can do it so well.

At about the time when Bob began his stint as a lecturer at Victoria College, one part of its English Department's teaching was transformed by the arrival, after his retirement from Auckland, of P. S. Ardern. Ardern was quite in another class as a medieval philologist from anyone else in Australasia, with an assured mastery of Old and Middle English and of Old Icelandic. I have always assumed that it was he who confirmed Bob in what was probably a natural gravitation towards philology and the Middle Ages, the language side. Language has, I think, always held his interest rather than literature. Certainly it was Ardern who gave Bob a thorough re-grounding, to the extent even of lending him the large, calligraphic, bound volumes into which he had transcribed the definitive texts of his lecture-commentaries on *Beowulf*, *Gawain* and the sagas.

Of Bob in Oxford I can say little, being innocent of that university as of Cambridge. I was one of his correspondents during the year in which he preceded me to England and we visited each other afterwards, both of us eventually *en famille*. He was, I knew, a pupil of J. A. W. Bennett and had won the confidence of C. T. Onions — awesome figures to wide-eyed provincials. Onions, Bob once told me, had demanded help from him with 'these dreadful New Zealand *p*- and *t*- words' in his lexicographical work. He taught for Magdalen, then for Christ Church, later as Fellow of St. Peter's and always gained and kept the respect and friendship of those he taught. You soon began to suspect that when Oxford philology had a difficult, thankless and laborious job to be done, it called for Burchfield. On his own account, too, he began to edit the *Ormulum*. He became editorial and administrative Secretary of the EETS, whose editors' prefaces over many years pay uniform homage to his thoroughness, generosity, tact and effectiveness. It was a life of huge, grinding labour. I never heard him complain of this, however, or of other people, except those whom he thought idle and careless — his two worst indictments — in their scholarship or their profession. Later, when he had taken over, re-organized and reactivated the Supplement to the *OED*, he was lenient with at least one of the more erratic of those who read for him. How he managed not only to produce that monument in good time and also to act as editor of *Notes and Queries* and chief editor of Oxford dictionaries simultaneously with carrying a full load of college and University teaching I cannot imagine. Surely it cannot have been as much a matter of course as he made it seem. Patient, unremitting application must be the answer; 'patience passe science' as the old saw goes.

It is not for me to characterize Bob Burchfield's achievement. I intend only that these few pages, mainly about a briefly shared early background, should stand as a token of affection and admiration, as well as of gratitude for a friendship of more than forty years.

THE OLD, THE NEW AND THE STRANGE:
ON SOME DICTIONARIES FROM THE REIGN OF
WILLIAM AND MARY (1688—1702)

Janet Bately

> Whoever considers the present State of Philological Literature, and what small Improvements and Acquisitions have been made therein of late Years, especially in that Part which relates to *Spelling-Books* and *Dictionaries* . . . must needs confess the Fortune of this Science far less considerable, and more inauspicious than that of any other whatsoever. The Article of *English Dictionaries* especially has been so far from any thing of a Progressive Improvement, that it is manifestly retrograde, and sinks from its low Apex; from bad, to very bad indeed. So far have our Dictionaries been from answering the End or Purposes of such a Book, that little more Use can be made of them than barely to know how *to spell*, and what is the Meaning of a Word *in the gross*; nor are they sufficient for this small Purpose neither.

So wrote Benjamin Martin in the Preface to his *Lingua Britannica Reformata* (1749). And he proceeds to specify and enumerate 'the proper Requisites of a genuine English Dictionary' as Universality, Etymology, Orthography, Orthoepy, a 'Critical and accurate Enumeration' and a reasonable coverage of learned terminology, ending with 'those Words and Phrases which have found Admittance into our Tongue, and yet appear like Aliens, in their native foreign Dress'.

In spite of Martin's ambitious plan[1] and his strictures on his predecessors, his dictionary, in the words of Osselton, 'appears as a final attempt to adapt an obsolete technique of lexicography to . . . changed conditions and attitudes to language'.[2] And even Samuel Johnson, who in the preface of his English Dictionary of 1755 was to condemn the deficiencies of earlier works and their failure 'to *collect* the *words* of our language', had to admit that he himself had neither always executed his

---

[1] For useful discussions of Martin's dictionary see DeWitt T. Starnes and Gertrude E. Noyes, *The English Dictionary from Cawdrey to Johnson, 1604 – 1755* (Chapel Hill, 1946), 146 – 163, and N. E. Osselton, *Branded Words in English Dictionaries before Johnson* (Groningen, 1958), 102 – 119.
[2] Osselton, *Branded Words*, p. 119.

own scheme, nor satisfied his own expectation, though, as he hastened to add, 'it may repress the triumph of malignant criticism to observe, that if our language is not here fully displayed, I have only failed in an attempt which no human powers have hitherto completed'. The purpose of this paper in honour of the editor of the Supplement to the *Oxford English Dictionary* is to explore the achievements of lexicographers in the period leading up to the publication of the dictionaries of Martin and Johnson and in particular the extent to which the lexicographers of the reign of William and Mary provided an adequate account of the vocabulary of that time.

In the reigns of James the First and Charles the First, which spanned the first half of the seventeenth century from 1603 to 1649, lexicography flourished in this country. Robert Cawdrey's *A Table Alphabeticall* (1604), generally recognised as the 'first' English dictionary,[3] was followed by John Bullokar's *An English Expositor* (1616; repr. 1621, 1641) and by Henry Cockeram's *The English Dictionarie* (1623; 2nd edn 1626; repr. 1631, 1632, 1637, 1642). The period of the Commonwealth and the Protectorate (1649 – 1659) saw the publication of Thomas Blount, *Glossographia* (1656) and Edward Phillips, *The New World of English Words* (1658) and in addition a new edition of Bullokar by W. S. (1656) and four reprints of Cockeram (1650, 1651, 1655, 1658). All the above-mentioned works were 'hard-word' dictionaries, reflecting a growing interest in specialist vocabulary which found an outlet also in publications such as the 'Physical Dictionary explaining Hard Words', attached to Culpeper, Cole and Rowland's translation of Riverius, *The Practice of Physick* (1655),[4] John French's *New light of Alchymie. Also a Chymical Dictionary* (1650),[5] Henry

---

[3] For the development of the English dictionary, see Starnes and Noyes, *The English Dictionary*, Jürgen Schäfer, 'The Hard Word Dictionaries: A Reassessment', *Leeds Studies in English* 4 (1970), 31 – 48, and James A. Riddell, 'The Beginning: English Dictionaries of the First Half of the Seventeenth Century, *Leeds Studies in English* 7 (1974), 117 – 55, and *idem* 'The Reliability of Early English Dictionaries', *The Yearbook of English Studies*, ed. T. J. B. Spencer, 4 (1974), 1 – 4. See also Gabriele Stein, *The English Dictionary before Cawdrey*, Lexicographica: Series Maior (Groningen, 1983).

[4] This short work has entries such as '**Attest**, witness, declare', '**Ascent**, Going up', '**Precede**, go before', '**Wild-Poppies**, Red-Poppies which grow among Corn, called likewise Corn-Rose', as well as definitions for terms such as **Gangren, Glandules, Glutinous, Livid, Nitre.**

[5] The head-words of this dictionary are mainly Latin. However, see, e.g., **Alcol** ('**Alcol, Alcool**, or **Alcohol**, is a most subtil powder of any thing'), **Cist** ('**Cist**, or **Kist**, is the quantity of two Gallons of Wine'), **Wismodt** ('**Wismodt** in [sic] Tin that is foule and immalleable, and cannot be wrought upon'), **Necromancy, Pyromania** and **Succubus.**

Manwayring's *Seaman's Dictionary* (1625), John Cowell's *The Interpreter* (a work dealing with the terms of the law, 1607), John Minsheu's *Ductor in Linguas, The Guide into Tongues* (a polyglot etymological dictionary, 1617; 2nd edn 1625), William Somner's *Dictionarium Saxonico-Latino-Anglorum* (1659), and Richard Verstegan's *Restitution of Decayed Intelligence in Antiquities* (containing a list of 'old words', Antwerp, 1605, first London printing 1655). An attempt to cater for what seems to have been a rapidly growing interest in foreign languages[6] was the production of the first Dutch-English dictionary, by Henry Hexham (1647), and the publication of Randal Cotgrave's French-English dictionary (1611), a work which in 1632 was extended by the addition of a dictionary English-French by Robert Sherwood, Londoner. Giovanni Florio's *A Worlde of Wordes; or most copious and exact Dictionarie in Italian and English* (1578, 1591, 1598), reprinted in 1611 as *Queen Anna's New World of Words*, was similarly extended by Giovanni Torriano in 1659. At the same time, the tradition of the sixteenth century Latin and French lexicographers was carried on in the form of new editions of the Latin dictionaries of Rider (ten editions between 1606 and 1659, mainly by Francis Holyoke), Thomas Thomas (seven editions between 1606 and 1644) and John Withals (four editions between 1602 and 1634).[7]

Lexicographical activity continued during the reign of Charles II (1600 – 1685). However, in spite of vociferous demands for an authoritative work on the lines of the dictionary published by the French Academy,[8] only one new 'English' (i.e. hard-word) dictionary, Elisha Coles' *An English Dictionary* (1676, repr. 1685), was published in his reign, the lexicographers' efforts now being directed mainly to the producing of bigger and better versions of Bullokar (revision 'by a Lover of the Arts', 1663, also 1667, 1676, 1680, 1684), Cockeram (12th edn, revised and enlarged by S. C., 1670), Blount (1661, 1670, 1674, 1681) and Phillips (1662, 1671 and 1678), and to the compilation of new bilingual dictionaries. Fresh efforts in this direction were Christopher Wase, *Dictionarium Minus. A compendious Dictionary* (1662 and 1675), Francis Gouldman, *A Copious Dictionary in Three Parts* (1664, 1669, 1674, 1678), Thomas Holyoke, *A Large Dictionary* (1676 – 7), Elisha Coles, *A Dictionary, English-Latin, and Latin-English* (1677 and

---

[6] See further R. C. Alston, *A Bibliography of the English Language from the Invention of Printing to the Year 1800* (Ilkley, 1974).
[7] For a useful survey of Latin dictionaries of the Renaissance, see DeWitt T. Starnes, *Renaissance Dictionaries English-Latin and Latin-English* (Austin, 1954).
[8] See, e.g. Dryden, Epistle Dedicatory to *The Rival Ladies*.

1679), and Adam Littleton, *Linguae . Latinae Liber Dictionarius Quadripartitus. A Latine Dictionary in Four Parts* (1677 – 1678, 2nd edn 1684). James Howell produced his *Lexicon Tetraglotton* in 1660, following it by a major revision of Cotgrave-Sherwood's *French-English Dictionary* in 1673, while a *New Dictionary French and English* by Guy Miège appeared in 1677. A feature of all these dictionaries was the inclusion of English glosses to English headwords and the itemisation of individual senses.[9] In addition we find a new law dictionary, by Thomas Blount (1670),[10] alongside a revision of Cowell's *Interpreter* by Thomas Manley (1672 and 1684), while the development of the etymological dictionary continued with Stephen Skinner's *Etymologicon Linguae Anglicanae* (1671). Other reissues and revisions included Henry Manwayring's *Seaman's Dictionary* (1670).

The major innovation of this period was the dictionary of non-standard usage, with Richard Head's *Canting Academy* appearing in 1673[11] and the first edition of John Ray's *Collection of English words not generally used* in 1674. At the same time there appeared the first edition of John Worlidge's *Dictionarium Rusticum* (1668/9),[12] also Thomas Houghton's *Rara Avis, or The Compleat Miner*, a work containing an explanation of miners' terms of art (1681), and three books of idioms in Latin and English, that is, William Walker's *Phraseologia Anglo-Latina* (1672) and *Idiomatologia Anglo-Latina* (1673) and William Robertson's, *Phraseologia Generalis* (1681).

New specialist dictionaries and works containing glossaries included a translation of Stephen Blancard (or Blanckaert)'s *Physical Dictionary*

---

[9] A practice foreshadowed in fifteenth and early sixteenth dictionaries. See, e.g., '**Abacted**. v. Driven away' (Gouldman, following Rider-Holyoke) and see Starnes' comment, *Renaissance Dictionaries*, p. 276, that 'An innovation for English-Latin dictionaries is Wase's method of distinguishing the different meanings of certain English words by the use of explanatory words or phrases'.

[10] See also *Les Termes de la Ley*, reprinted, 'corrected and enlarged by T. B.', 1667. This lacks many of the terms in Cowell and Blount.

[11] For a survey of the development of cant lexicography see Starnes and Noyes, *The English Dictionary*, pp. 212 – 227, where Head's *Canting Academy* is described as transitional between earlier glossaries and the cant dictionary proper. Definitions include '**Kidnapper**. A felow that walketh the streets, and takes all advantages to pick up the younger sort of people, whom with lies and many fair promises he inticeth on board a ship and transports them into foreign plantations'.

[12] Attached to his *Systema Agriculturae*. 'The date given on the title page of the *Dictionarium* is 1668; however, that for the *Systema* is 1669, and the book itself is noticed in the *Term Catalogues* for Hilary Term 1668 – 9. Typical entries are '**Aumbry**, a Country Word for Cup-board to keep Victuals in', '**Frith**, underwood, or the shroud of Trees', '**Germins**, young Shoots of Trees', 'A **Jug**, a Common Pasture or Meadow'.

(1684),[13] Joseph Moxon's *Mathematical Dictionary* (1679),[14] Thomas Willis's *Remaining Medical Works*, with its 'Table of all the hard words derived from the Greek and Latin, of all Terms of Art and other works not vulgarly received, with the explanation of them' (1681),[15] and Robert May's *The Accomplisht Cook*, with its glossary of terms of carving (1660, fifth edn 1685),[16] while a number of scientific works written in Latin — as, for instance, Walter Charleton's *Onomasticon Zoicon* (1668) and John Ray's *Catalogus Plantarum Angliae* (1677) — incorporated vernacular equivalents for the names of plants, animals etc. under discussion.[17]

In contrast, the period that accompanied the accession of William and Mary (1688 – 1702) might at first sight seem to have been a relatively quiet one for lexical studies, a lull before the great burst of activity in the eighteenth century. Thus, we find the now almost statutory cluster of new editions of older works — a revision of Ray's *Collection of English Words* in 1691, a re-issue of the 1687 printing of Worlidge's *Dictionarium Rusticum* in 1697, new editions of Blount's *Law Dictionary* ('with the Addition of above Six Hundred Words') in 1691,

[13] The majority of the head-words are Latin or Greek terms (e.g. '**Glandula**, a Glandule'); however, see the entry for **Gas**, quoted below, n. 87.

[14] *Mathematics Made Easie: or, a Mathematical Dictionary, explaining the Terms of Art, and Difficult Phrases used in Arithmetick, Geometry, Astronomy, Astrology and other Mathematical Sciences.* Entries include '**Axiom**, Gr. A Common Sentence, Principle, or Ground of any Art, generally taken for granted', and '**Autumn**, Harvest, or Fall of the Leaf; one of the four Quarters of the Year . . . Called so from the Latin Verb *Augeo*, which signifies, to Encrease, because then the Fruits of the Earth are encreased to full maturity, and the Husbandman's Gains augmented thereby'.

[15] 'Englished by S. P. Esq.'. Entries include **Acid** ('sharp'), **Adjuted** ('Helped'), **Adust** ('Burnt or parch'd'), **Atoms** ('Small little Bodies, such as Motes in the Sun-shine'), **Crass** ('thick'), **Elixir** ('An Arabian word for Quintessence, high Cordials so called'), **Ganglioform, Gesticulation** ('a wanton moving up and down of the legs and Arms or other parts of the Body, like a Tumbler or Mimick'), **Grumous, Spine** and **Vernal**.

[16] E.g. 'Break that Deer', 'Disfigure that Peacock', 'Leach that Brawn', 'Tusk that Barbel'. Terms of carving are also given by Randle Holme. Their first appearance in the English dictionary is in Kersey's revision of Phillips, where they are described as terms used by 'Skilful Carvers'.

[17] See, for instance, *Onomasticon Zoon* 'long-shanks or crane legs', and Ray, *Catalogus* 'Acer Majus . . . The great Maple, commonly, yet falsely, the Sycomore-tree'. See also Ray's *Nomenclator* or *Dictionarium Trilingue* (1685), with English words given not only their Latin and Greek equivalents but occasionally also their native synonyms, as 'Anemony or Windflower', 'Asparagus or Sperage', 'Brushwood or Bavin', 'Coperas or Vitriol', and Culpeper's *English Physitian* (1652, rev. edn 1691), with entries such as 'Cuckoo pint or Wake Robin', 'Money-wort or Herb Two-pence' and 'Sope-wort or Bruise-wort'.

of Moxon's *Mathematical Dictionary* in 1692 and 1701,[18] of Skinner's *Etymologicon* in 1701 and of Blancard's *Physical Dictionary* in 1702, a fifth edition of Phillips in 1696, reissued in 1700; a revision of Cowell's *Interpreter* by White Kennet in 1701, and an apparently new work entitled *Linguae Romanae Dictionarium Luculentum Novum*, which was to all intents and purposes a third edition of Littleton's Latin dictionary, in 1693.[19] Florio's Italian dictionary reappeared in a revision by J. Davis in 1688 and a new Dutch dictionary was published by William Sewel in 1691.[20] The provision of etymologies was continued in *Gazophylacium Anglicanum* (1689)[21] and the collection and explication of technical terms in works such as Edward Hatton's *Merchant's Dictionary*, appended to his *Merchant's Magazine* (3rd edn 1699, 4th edn 1701),[22] and John Evelyn's *Compleat Gardner* (1693),[23] while cant was the subject of *The Fop Dictionary*, in John and Mary Evelyn's *Mundus Muliebris* (1690) and B. E.'s *A New Dictionary of the Terms Ancient and Modern of the Canting Crew* (1699?).[24] Another new compilation of technical terminology was Randle Holme's *The Academy of Armory, or a Storehouse of Armory and Blazon* (1688), which, despite its title, contains lists of words and phrases dealing with an extraordinary range of subjects, from terms used by Anglers, Barbers, Farriers, Joyners, Printers, Tallow-Chandlers and Seamsters to the names of plants and

[18] 'Revised by Hen. Coley, Teacher of the *Mathematics* in *Baldwins Gardens*'. Coley's new material includes entries such as '**Gorge**, Is a Term in Fortification . . .'

[19] See Starnes, *Renaissance Dictionaries*, pp. 317 – 22.

[20] For the tradition behind Sewel, and in particular the achievements of his predecessor Hexham, see N. E. Osselton, 'The Sources of the First Dutch and English Dictionary', *MLR* 64 (1969), 355 – 62.

[21] 'Containing the Derivation of English Words Proper and Common'. The author states that he has 'forebore, as much as possible, the setting down such as are purely of a *Latin* Original'. This work combines etymologies with definitions, as, for instance, '**Gossemeer**, a word found in a book entituled The *French Gardener*; where it is expounded, *the light down that is blown off the Sow-thistle*. The Author of an English Dictionary giveth this name to the morning dew; which like to a cob-web, it spreads all the fields over, especially in the time of drought; which in the Teut. is called **Unser Frawen haar**, (*i.e.*) the hair of the Virgin *Mary*; from the Fr. G. *Gossampine*; and this from the Lat. *Gossypium*, Cotton, for the Similitude of it.'

[22] *A Merchant or Trader's Dictionary*, added to Hatton's *Merchant's Magazine*. Entries include '**Copes-Mate**. A Partner in Merchandizing', '**Immunity**. Privilege or freedom', '**Gare**. Very course Wool', '**Naufrage**. Shipwreck' and '**Ork**. A Butt for Figgs or Wine'.

[23] See, e.g., '**Devils Gold Ring**, in French, *Lisette*, a sort of Worm or Caterpillar infesting the young shoots of Vines'.

[24] For a brief description of B. E.'s dictionary see Starnes and Noyes, *The English Dictionary*, pp. 221 – 2.

animals.[25] *The Ladies Dictionary* of 1694, sub-titled 'a general entertainment for the fair-sex', combining dictionary-entries with material of a very different kind,[26] is in the tradition of Blount (named along with Blancard as a source) and Coles and includes etymologies, old words, dialect words and cant.[27]

However, a handful of works produced during this reign not only were, in their own way, essentially new contributions to lexicography but also foreshadowed the major achievements and innovations of the eighteenth century. The first of these is Guy Miège's *Great French Dictionary* of 1688, a work which was to form the basis of the second, Abel Boyer's *Royal Dictionary* 1699 (abridged edn 1700); a third is J. K.'s *New English Dictionary* of 1702. In the Preface to his *Great French Dictionary*, Guy Miège describes not only his practice in the Dictionary, but also the years of work that lay behind it.

When I made my first Attempt of this Kind (I must confess) I did it under great Disadvantages. Then the Publick was in haste for a FRENCH DICTIONARY; and they had it accordingly, hurried from the Design to the Composition, and from under my Pen to the Press. Nothing was prepared for it, and That which should have been the Work of many Years was both conceived and brought forth in less than two. Neither was I then so well versed in either Language, as I

[25] See, e.g. '**Augury**, telling of Fortune by flying of Birds', '**Coelestial**, Heavenly', '**Poler**, an ancient term used for the cutter of hair', '**Irrigation**, is a aspersion of moisture on things to be dissolved, to make them more liquid', '**Gradation**, is an exaltation of mettles to the height of their fineness and purity' and 'The **Pewit**, or **Black Cap**, called also the **Sea Crow**, or **Mire Crow**; it is a kind of cinereous or **Brown Gull**'.

[26] Subjects dealt with in such entries include Fornication (and how to avoid it), 'The Husbands Duty towards his Wife', and '**Husband Indifferent**, or how to make your Life easie and pleasant with him'.

[27] See, e.g., entries such as '**Blower**, one Mans particular Lass', '**Bobtail**, a kind of short arrow-head; also a Whore', '**Burnet**, *o*. Wollen, also a Hood', '**Churle** (*Sax. Ceorle*) a Country Clown, a Bumpkin; in the North a *Carle*', '**Eye-bite**, to bewitch with the Eyes', '**Lactary** (*Lactarium*) a dairy-house; and may be used for a dairy-man, milk-man or Cheese-monger. *Br.*', '**Pregnant**, big with Child; also fully copious, ripe', '**Scoundrel**, a sorry base Fellow', '**Sympathy** (*sympathia*) natural consent or combination, mutual passion, affection or disposition', '**Trigamist**, *g*. having three wives'. Another work 'accommodated to the use of Ladies, Gentlewomen, and such other Persons, whose Station requires their taking care of a House', William Salmon's *The Family Dictionary or Household Companion* (1696), is wholly encyclopedic, with entries dealing with the properties of herbs (e.g. 'Adders Tongue. This herb is used successfully in Wounds new or old . . .'), salves, recipes, and instructions for laundering etc.

have been since I made it my Business. All this, together with the dangerous Concurrence of *Cotgrave*'s long-settled Reputation, and the Want of Barbarous Words, so much wanted at first, (and as much nauseated at last) was more than sufficient to run down the Book, to baffle its Author, and disappoint the Bookseller. But Something there was, by good Providence, that made it strangely work it self into the World, and become Acceptable, even beyond my Expectation.

Which was no small *Inducement* for me, greater indeed than all the weak Temptations of an *Empty Name*, to go on, and neglect nothing that might make the next Impression a complete and absolute Piece in its Kind. Accordingly I took my Notes, and made Collections ever since. The Multiplicity whereof, with the Thoughts of a new Method, put me at last upon the Necessity of making That a New Piece of Work which I had proposed to my self but as an additional Improvement to the former. So that I don't present you here with a patched Impression, augmented with many Thousand Words, &c, but with a new Production of my Pains and Industry, writ all over with my own Hand, and the Result of many Years Study.

The result, he claims complacently but not inaccurately, 'exceeds considerably any Thing that has been done in this Kind; whether we consider the Copiousness of *Words*, the several *Senses* of such as are Homonymous, or the *Phrases* which are brought in to shew the Vse thereof.' And turning to the second part, in which English is the 'leader' he comments, that, ''tis so much beyond any English Dictionary extant, that I have often wondered, in the Composing of that Part, that this Nation should be so much wanting in this respect.'[28]

Boyer's dictionary is highly derivative in comparison with that of Miège (its major source), but none the less worthy of attention in that it expands both Miège's collection of ordinary words and illustrative quotations and the more specialist elements drawn from the hard-word dictionaries. It follows Miège in a generous use of the obelisk, adding the mark D + for 'A *Dubious* Word or Expression, *that is*, an Expression of no general use, and about which authors are divided', and it introduces the asterisk to indicate a figurative word or expression.[29] As for the abridged edition of Boyer, this includes in the second part the accentuation of all the English words and is, in R. C. Alston's words, 'the most important source extant for the accentuation of English (and

---

[28] For a study of Miège's achievement, see Janet Bately, 'Miège and the Development of the English Dictionary', *Five Hundred Years of Words and Sounds*, ed. E. G. Stanley & Douglas Gray (1983), 1 – 10.
[29] For the obelisk in Miège and Boyer see Janet Bately, 'Dryden and Branded Words, *N & Q* 210 (1965), 136f.

consequently the quantitative value of stem-vowels) before the advent of dictionaries of English pronunciation in the second half of the eighteenth century'. And Alston goes on to claim that 'as a lexicon it is of considerable value to students of both French and English lexicography and provided a model for bi-lingual dictionaries which has seldom been improved on'.[30]

J. K., in his *New English Dictionary*, is also derivative in so far as he takes the bulk of his material from English-Latin and English-French dictionaries but is totally original in that he was the first English-dictionary maker to include 'ordinary' words of the language as head-words in the main body of his work.[31] His dictionary, which earned the praise of Isaac Watts,[32] is sub-titled 'A compleat Collection of the Most Proper and Significant Words, Commonly used in the Language, with a Short, Clear Exposition of *Difficult Words* and *Terms of Art*'.

In order to demonstrate the extent of the coverage of English vocabulary that these dictionaries provided for the contemporary reader, I propose to compare a number of the lexical items that they contain, selected more or less at random, with the corresponding entries in the *Oxford English Dictionary*, Kersey's revision of Phillips' *New World of English Words*, and the dictionaries of Martin and Johnson, looking at the handling of archaisms as well as of new and strange items and the everyday words of the language.

1. Old words.

The recording of archaic and obsolete terms is a feature of English dictionaries from Bullokar's *An English Expositor* onwards, with an initial one hundred and thirty five entries swelling to over one thousand by 1721.[33] Bullokar not only included 'sundry olde words now growne

[30] Note prefaced to the reproduction of Abel Boyer's *The Royal Dictionary Abridged* (London, 1971).
[31] See N. E. Osselton, 'John Kersey and the Ordinary Words of English', *English Studies* 60 (1979), 555 – 61. Of course Cockeram's dictionary gives 'hard word' definitions for ordinary words, as, for instance, 'Godless, atheistical'.
[32] Isaac Watts, *The Art of Reading and Writing English* (1720). I am indebted to Starnes and Noyes, *The English Dictionary*, p. 75, for this reference.
[33] Figures from Johan Kerling, *Chaucer in Early English Dictionaries* (Leiden, 1979), 233. Kerling detects two stages in this tradition, the first down to 1671, when Skinner's *Etymologicon* was published, and the second stage from then on until 1721 and the appearance of Nathan Bailey's *An Universal Etymological English Dictionary*, 'the last in a tradition to include old words for the common reader' (*ibid.*, p. 231). Benjamin Martin drops obsolete words, while Johnson admits them 'when they are found in authours not obsolete, or when they have any force or beauty that may deserve revival' (Preface).

out of use' but identified the category to which they belonged by means of an asterisk.[34] His contemporary Cockeram adopted the same practice in his second edition of 1626.[35] However, their successors Blount and Phillips discarded this method of indicating the status of word, with Phillips using instead labels such as 'old word', 'an Old English word', 'an old Saxon word' or, more specifically, 'Chaucer', and employing an obelisk (†) to denote words which he 'would not recommend to any for the purity, or reputation of them'[36] and Blount similarly referring to 'old words' or to 'Chaucer'.[37]

J. K. did not attempt to include 'old words' in his *New English Dictionary*, though (if the identification with John Kersey is correct) he was subsequently to enter large numbers of them in both his revision of Phillips's *New World of English Words* of 1706 and his *Dictionarium Anglo-Britannicum* of 1709.[38] In a detailed study of the old-word tradition in English lexicography down to 1721, Johan Kerling has recently sought to evaluate Kersey's contribution to the 1706 edition of Phillips, observing that 'a number of old words found in the edition of 1696 are not taken over; a number are taken over unmarked; a number of entries previously not marked as old are now marked as such; of some old words it is now indicated why they are old or unusual, and therefore now belong in one of Kersey's "specialised" categories, and a collection of old words

---

[34] Most of Bullokar's 'old words' seem to have come directly or indirectly from Thomas Speght's Chaucer glossaries: see Kerling, *Chaucer*, pp. 50 – 77. In later editions the obelisk is also used. See, e.g., the edition of 1684 with '†**Abarstick**, An old word Signifying insatiable', beside '***Lectorn. A Desk**'.

[35] Also all subsequent editions except the last revision of 1670, apparently under the influence of Bullokar: see Kerling, *Chaucer*, pp. 79 – 80.

[36] Preface to first four editions.

[37] Kerling, *Chaucer*, pp. 87 – 8, quotes Blount's expressed intention to shun old words and says that 'because no old words were marked in it, the *Glossographia* will not be discussed further here, in spite of its importance in the English lexicographical tradition' (see also p. 97). However, a number of words are in fact so marked in the first edition, as for instance, **Cresset** (see below, p. 27), while a number of entries make specific mention of Chaucer: see, for instance, **Barbican** ('Chaucer used the word Barbican for a Watch-tower') and **Lodemanage** ('Chaucer makes this word to signifie the skill or art of Navigation'). Another entry '**Algebra** . . . *Chaucer* calls it *Algrim*' is a possible source for Phillips' entry '**Algrim** (old word) the same as **Algebra**', which Kerling (*Chaucer*, p. 276) includes in a list of words 'undoubtedly taken directly from Speght's glossaries', on the grounds that it is 'not found in the dictionaries of Bullokar, Cockeram, Blount and Minsheu.

[38] For lists of 'old words' in these two dictionaries, see Kerling, *Chaucer*, pp. 174 – 205. For justification for the identification of J. K. with John Kersey (made already by the editors of the *Oxford English Dictionary*), see, e.g., Christian Heddesheimer, 'The Authorship of "A New English Dictionary" (1702)', *N & Q* 213 (1968), 444 – 5.

are now included for the first time'.[39] 'The impression this list of old words gives is that of a reviser carefully considering which words in earlier editions of the dictionary are no longer in common use and should be marked as obsolete . . .'[40] Instances of more precise marking, such as 'an old law-term', 'Saxon', 'in old statutes' are seen as reflecting the reviser's own reading: 'In a small number of cases words are no longer marked as merely old . . . Their small number makes it difficult to conclude that Kersey went through the old words systematically and tried to be more specific about them: it would rather seem that he was only more specific about them when he happened to know the word from his own reading'[41] and again, 'All the words now marked as Chaucerian occur in Speght's glossary. The impression we get here is that Kersey did not systematically mark words as Chaucerian, but rather marked them as such when he happened to know them to be in Chaucer. At times, indeed, he will refer to a passage in Chaucer.'[42]

And Kerling concludes, 'the selection of old words he does include . . ., his categorising of old words on a small number of occasions, and his 'updating' of the dictionary by marking as old a number of words that had become obsolete suggest very careful and interested work'.[43]

Careful and interested Kersey's work may have been, but in his treatment of old words he owes more to the lexicographers of the late seventeenth century than Kerling allows. Thus of the five added 'Chaucerian' words in the revision of Phillips[44] — **to appeal**, **to defend**, **divinistre**, **rouncy** and **wangs** —, three go back to one or more of Miège's *Great French Dictionary*, and the law dictionaries based on Cowell's *Interpreter*. So we find:

Rouncy a Word us'd in *Chaucer* for a Cart-Horse (Kersey-Phillips)[45] beside

†**Rowncy**, a Word used by Chaucer for a Cart-horse, *un Cheval de Charette* (Miège),[46] with which compare

Runcilus & Rucinus, Is used in *Doomsday* (says *Spelman*) for a Load-Horse . . . or a Sumpter-Horse; and sometimes for a Cart Horse, which

[39] *Chaucer*, pp. 175 – 6.
[40] *Chaucer*, p. 179.
[41] *Chaucer*, p. 180.
[42] *Chaucer*, p. 181.
[43] *Chaucer*, pp. 193 – 4.
[44] *Chaucer*, p. 180.
[45] This word is placed between the entries **Rowland** and **To Rowze**.
[46] Boyer does not have a comparable entry, neither does J. K. *OED*, which gives the definition 'A horse, especially a riding-horse', describes the word as *obs. exc. arch.*, and has no illustrative quotations from authors between Skelton and Browning.

Chaucer in the Seamans Tale calls a Rowncy
He rod upon a Rowncy as he could (Cowell-Manley, 1684)
and
Rucinus (from the Ital. *Runcino*) Is used in *Domesday* for a Load-horse,
or Sumpter-horse; and sometimes a Cart-horse, which *Chaucer* calls a
Rowney (Blount, *Law Dictionary*, 1670);[47]
similarly
To **Defend** To stand in Defence of, to protect or support, to uphold or
bear out, to maintain or assert; to justify: Also in our ancient Statutes and
Laws, to prohibit, or forbid: In the same Sense, *Chaucer* uses it in these
Verses:
Where can you say, in any manner Age,
That ever God defended Marriage? (Kersey-Phillips),
beside
To **Defend**, *defendre*, *appuyer*, *soutenir*, *proteger*. As, To defend a
Place . . . a Cause, or the Truth . . . To defend (assert, or maintain) an
Opinion . . . Heretofore this Verb was also used for to forbid, or to
prohibit. And in that Sense Chaucer uses it in these Words,
Where can you say, in any manner Age,
That ever God defended Marriage? (Miège)
and
Defend, *Defendere*, Signifies in our ancient Laws and Statutes as much
as to forbid and prohibit . . . In the same sence *Chaucer* uses it in these
words,
Where can you say, in any manner Age,
That ever God defended *Marriage* . . . (Cowell-Manley, 1684);[48]
and
Wang, an old *Saxon* Word signifying a Field.
Wangs, or **Wang-Teeth**, the Cheek, or Jaw-Teeth according to these
Verses in *Chaucer*.
In witness that this is Sooth,
I bite the Wax with my Wang-Tooth (Kersey-Phillips),
beside
‡**Wang.** an old Saxon Word anciently used to express a Field . . .
†**Wang-teeth**, for the Cheek (or Jaw) Teeth. In which Sense Chaucer
uses it in these Verses of his,
And in witness that this is Sooth,

---

[47] Similarly the edition of 1691, which adds 'Also a Colt'. cf. Coles '**Rowney**,
o. a Cart-horse' (edn of 1701 **Rowny**).
[48] Similarly Blount, *Law Dictionary*. Although in the sense 'to prohibit, to
forbid' To **Defend** is described as an old word, the law dictionaries cite the
expression 'God defend', for 'God forbid', as still current, while Johnson
includes this sense with quotations from Milton and Temple (a. 1698).

I bite the Wax with my Wang-tooth (Miège)

Wang, Properly signifies in the Saxon Tongue a Field, but we use it also for the Cheek and Jaw-teeth, which *Chaucer* calls *Wangs* and *wang-teeth*, according to these Verses,

> *And in witness that this is Sooth,*
> *I bite the Wax with my Wang-tooth* (Cowell-Manley 1684).[49]

Only the references to Chaucer in the entries To **Appeal** ('to make an Appeal: Also an old Word, signifying to Dismay or Daunt; but *Chaucer* uses it for to Decay') and **Divinistre** ('a Word us'ed by *Chaucer*, for a Divine or Doctor of Divinity') are not to be found in either Miège or the law dictionaries. However, in this case Kersey appears to be drawing direct on earlier English hard word or etymological dictionaries: thus, the entry **Divinistre** occurs in Blount (1681) with the comment 'so *Chaucer* calls an inferiour Divine, a smatterer in Divinity',[50] and not To **Appeal**, but To **Appal** is found in *Gazophylacium*, with the comment '*Chaucer* useth it for **Decay**'.[51]

Similarly, of the one word marked as old in 1696 but 'now marked as Chaucerian'[52] — **Frith** — and the three words not marked at all in 1696 but now marked as Chaucerian — **Cope**, **Dulcarnon** and **Paraments** — the majority again seem to owe their label to older dictionaries. Thus, **Dulcarnon**, a certain Proposition found out by *Pythagoras*; upon which account he offered an Ox in Sacrifice to the Gods in Token of Thankfulness, and call'd it *Dulcarnon*. Whence the Word is taken by *Chaucer*, and other old *English* Writers, for any hard knotty, Question, or Point

To **be at Dulcarnon**, to be at one's Wits ends (Kersey-Phillips),

corresponds to

Dulcarnon, a proportion found out by Pythagoras, for which happy invention, he sacrified [sic] an Oxe to the gods in thankfulness, which

---

[49] Similarly (but with some significant variation) Blount, *Law Dictionary*. Blount, *Glossographia*, and Bullokar also refer to Chaucer in their entries for **Wang-tooth**, although they do not quote from him. *OED* separates the entries **Wang**, 'field' and **Wang**, 'cheek, molar tooth', describing both as '*obs. exc. dial.*'

[50] Cf. Coles, '**Divinistre** *o.* a smatterer in Divinity'. *OED* cites the word only from Chaucer's *Knight's Tale* and gives the meaning as 'A diviner'.

[51] Cf. Phillips 1696 'To **Appeal** (*old word*) to dismay or daunt', beside similar entries in Cockeram and Blount under the head-words **Appale** and To **Appall**.

[52] Kerling, *Chaucer*, p. 180. Kerling also cites here the word **Acheked**. However, Phillips 1696 in fact has a reference to Chaucer with the entry '**Acheked**, *Chaucer* choaked'.

sacrifice he called *Dulcarnon* (Phillips 1658);

‡**Dulcarnon**, an old Word used by Chaucer, and other old English Writers, for any hard Question or Point.

I am at Dulcarnon, that is at a Dilemma, or at my Wits end . . . Dulcarnon, you must know, in the original Sense, was a Proportion found out by Pythagoras, after a whole Years Study (Miège),

beside

Dulcarnon I am (says Chaucer) tell God me better mind send, at Dulcarnon, *i.* at a *Dilemma*, at my wits end. For *Dulcarnon* was a Proportion found out by Pythagoras after a years study . . . (Blount, 1681);[53]

while

Parament (Fr.) an Ornament for an Altar: *Paraments* is us'd by *Chaucer* and other ancient Writers for Robes of State (Kersey-Phillips)

corresponds to

Paraments, robes of state (Phillips 1658),

‡**Paraments**, or Robes of State (a Word used by Chaucer) (Miège)[54]

and

Paraments Robes of State, or the Place where they are kept, *Chaucer* (Blount, 1681)

Similarly, the entry **Frith** in Kersey-Phillips is anticipated by Miège, who in his turn is using material found also in the law dictionaries: thus,

Frith, anciently signify'd a Plain between Woods, and in *Chaucer* a Wood: Also all Hedge-wood except Thorns. The *Saxons* made use of the Word to express Peace or Liberty; but it is now taken, especially in Scotland, for an Arm of the Sea, or Mouth of a great River. (Kersey-Phillips),

beside

Frith . . . a Strait Sound or Narrow Sea

Fryth, (*old word*) Wood (Phillips 1696),

is indebted to the earlier,

Frith, a Word most used in Scotland for an Arm of the Sea . . .

This is the common Acceptation of the Word, at this time. But in Doomsday it is used for a Plain between Woods, and Chaucer uses it for a Wood. Smith, in his *England's Improvement*, makes it signify all Hedgewood, except Thorns. Whereas the Saxons of old used it, to

---

[53] The last instance of the word cited by *OED* dates from 1577.

[54] Boyer uses only the single obelisk. cf. Martin **Paraments**, 'the robes of state'. The last instance of the word cited by *OED* in sense (a) is from l'Estrange, 1654. Chaucer is quoted for sense (b).

express Peace or Liberty (Miège)[55]

beside

Fryth, [Coke] . . .Expounds it a Plain between two Woods, and so it is used in *Doomsday*; *Chaucer* uses it for a Wood. *Camden* in his *Brit.* for an Arm of the Sea, or great River, and so we frequently use it at this day. *Smith* (in his *Englands Improvement*) makes it signifie all Hedgwood, except Thorns. It is a task to reconcile this, when they all disagree with the Saxon, with whom we know *frid* or *frith* signifies Peace (Cowell-Manley, 1684).[56]

Only two words described as Chaucerian by Kersey-Phillips remain 'unsourced'[57] — **Chevesal** and **Cope**. **Chevesal** is 'a word marked as Chaucerian in all the earlier editions of the *New World*', and retained by Kersey but now defined as 'the cargo, or fraight of a ship. *Chaucer*', instead of the earlier 'a Gorget. *Chaucer*',[58] while **Cope**, 'cloak', entered in Phillips as an 'old word' is also ascribed to Chaucer. Phillips 1696 does give the old meaning 'cloak' for cope, but does not indicate either that this is 'old' or that it is found in Chaucer.[59]

The dictionaries of the reign of William and Mary also anticipate Kersey-Phillips in their marking as 'old' or obsolescent of a number of words which earlier dictionaries had entered without such a designation. Thus of the thirty four words listed by Kerling as first marked as old in Kersey's revision,[60] six have an obelisk in Miège, to indicate that they are 'only used in a burlesk, jocose, or comical Sense; or else, that [they are] not current in any Style, but [are] either forced, or Provincial, or such as [grow] out of date', and four the double obelisk, to denote 'an obsolete, or antiquated Word, hardly fit to be used in any manner of Style'.

---

[55] Boyer ‡**Frith**. In his entries for ‡**Wang**, ‡**Dulcarnon**, †**Paraments** and ‡**Frith**, Boyer follows Miège, but omits all reference to Chaucer.

[56] Blount, *Law Dictionary*, though providing similar information, is less close here, having, for instance, no reference to Domesday. Cf. *Gazophylacium* 'Frith, from the Lat. *Fretum*, the sea; *q.d.* a place which the tyde overfloweth'.

[57] Kerling, *Chaucer*, pp. 180 – 181.

[58] *OED* defines †**Chevesaile** as 'the collar of a coat, gown or other garment' and adds that 'by late antiquaries . . . etc., it is apparently often taken for a gorget'. Cf., e.g., Camden, 'a gorget called a Chevesail' (1605).

[59] **Cope**, in the sense of 'cloak' is given no illustrative quotations from the period between 1575 and 1745.

[60] Kerling, *Chaucer*, pp. 178 – 9. Three of these words, **Baleful**, **Bawdrick**, **Jewise**, were in fact already being marked as old by Coles, two, **Latimer** and **Pascage** (**Pascuage**), have entries in Cowell-Manley which suggest obsoleteness.

So Miège places an obelisk beside the head-words **Blatant**,[61] to **Bourd**; **Gaunt**;[62] **Griff-graff**; **Guerdon**; **Hort-yard**; **Scathe**; and double obelisk against **Cot**; **Greese**; **Lectern**; **Leman**.[63] We may compare Boyer's practice, with a single obelisk against **Blatant**, to **Bourd**, **Griff-graff** and **Scathe**, a double obelisk against **Cot**, **Gaunt**, **Greese**, **Hort-yard**, **Lectern** and **Leman**, and no mark against **Guerdon**. To **Bourd**, **Greese** and **Hortyard** are omitted from the abridged version. J. K., significantly, has an entry only for **cott**, which is unbranded.[64] As for Kersey-Phillips' entry '**Yare** (old Word) prompt, ready, eager or sharp upon a Thing . . .', this seems to owe something to Boyer's unmarked entry 'eager or sharp upon a thing', while the designation 'old word' is paralleled not only in Phillips 1678 and Coles, but also in *Gazophylacium*.[65] Johnson's dictionary has entries for all the above words except to **Bourd**, **Greese**, **Hortyard**, and **Lectern**.[66]

Some of the more specific labels used by Kersey, such as 'an old law term' or 'in old statutes', can also be traced back to this period. Thus, for instance, **wastel bread** is given by a double obelisk by Miège and his comment, 'This is a Word used in the Statute for Bread made in the Reign of Henry the Third, by which is meant the finest sort of Bread', (itself drawing on older law-dictionaries) anticipates the entry in Kersey-Phillips: **Wastel-bread**, (in old *Statutes*) the finest sort of white Bread

---

[61] Miège's illustration ('As, a blatant Writer') is an expression found in Marvell, *Reh. Transp.* II. 371. Bullokar quotes Spenser, while Johnson quotes Dryden, giving the meaning 'bellowing as a calf'.

[62] Although Kerling cites Gaunt as 'entered but not marked as old in the 1696 edition of the *New World*' (p. 178), there is in fact no such entry.

[63] Bullokar marks **Lectorne** with an asterisk, to denote an 'olde word, onely used of some ancient writers, and now growne out of use'; Littleton has the obelisk, while the second edition of Blount has the entry '**Lectern** or **Lectorn**, with *Chaucer's* Interpreter, is a Desk. I suppose he means a Reading-Desk in a Church, which in old Latin is called *Lectrinum*' (so also later editions). **Cot**, in contrast, is said by Cowell-Manley (following Verstegan) to be used 'still in many places of England'.

[64] **Gaunt** also has an obelisk in Martin; **Cot**, **Guerdon** and **Scathe** in contrast are entered unmarked.

[65] See *Gazophylacium*, '**Yare**, an old word signifying desirous, or covetous . . .', and Miège, '**Yare** or sharp upon a Thing' and cf. Martin '**Yare**, eager, ardent, sharp upon a thing'.

[66] The last instance of to **Bourd** cited by *OED* is dated 1703. **Cot**, or cote, is said to have become 'obs. or merely dial.' about 1625, and to have been revived as a poetical and literary term. Instances include a quotation from Dryden's Virgil (1697). **Skathe** is described as now arch. and dial., **Yare** as obs. or arch., **Leman** as arch. Seventeenth century illustrations of the word **Lectern** almost all have spellings without *c*, as, e.g., *lettren*, *latron*. **Hortyard** is described as 'an affected alteration of *orchard*, frequent in the sixteenth and seventeenth centuries'. Illustrative quotations include one from Evelyn (1699).

or Cakes, such as were sopped in the Wastel-bowl'.[67] Similarly '**Await**, (in ancient Statutes) Way-laying, or lying in Wait to do a Mischief' goes back to Cowell-Manley's entry '**Awayte** . . . Seems to be that which we now call **Way-laying**, or lying in **wait** to do a Mischief', while '**Covenable** or **Convenable**, (old *Law-word*) convenient, suitable, or fit; as **Convenably endowed**, i.e. endowed as is fitting' echoes Cowell-Manley '**Covenable** . . . Is a French word denoting fit or convenient. So 4 H. 8, *cap.* 12 *covenably* endowed, that is, endowed as is fitting. It was also written *convenable*'. We may compare Miège's entries †**Convenable** and †**Covenable**.

The dictionaries of the reign of William and Mary also seemingly confirm the continued currency in the English language of a number of words marked as old in the fifth edition of Phillips but unmarked in both Kersey-Phillips and Martin.[68] Although in this case Kersey may well have removed Phillips' marking independently of the seventeenth century dictionaries, verbal resemblances suggest that he had at least some of their entries before him as he made his revision. Thus, for instance, we may compare

Cosset, a Lamb, Colt, Calf, &c. fallen and brought up by hand without the Dam (Kersey-Phillips)

with

Cosset (old word) a Lamb, Colt or other Creature brought up by hand without the Dam (Phillips IV and V)

A **Cosset**, Lamb or Colt, or *Cade* Lamb or Colt, that is, a Lamb or Colt fallen and brought up by hand (Worlidge 1681 and 1697)

A **Cosset** Lamb or Colt, &c, i.e. a cade Lamb, a Lamb or Colt brought up by the hand. Norf. Suff . . . (Ray),

and

Cosset (a Lamb, Calf &c. brought up without the Dam) (Boyer),[69];

similarly we may compare

Croe or Crome, an Iron-bar, or Leaver, with a flat End: Also a notch in the Side-boards of a Cask, or Tub, where the Head-pieces come in (Kersey-Phillips)

with

Crome or Cssom, (*old word*) a Crow of Iron. (Phillips 1696)

and

---

[67] Cf. Phillips 1696, '**Wastel-bread** (*old word*) fine Cimnel' and Cowell-Manley, '**Wastel Bread** (Anno 51 Hen.3), Statute of Bread . . . seems to be the finest Sort of Bread . . .'; similarly Blount, *Law Dictionary. OED* describes **Wastel** as obs. exc. hist.

[68] For the changes in Kersey-Phillips see Kerling, *Chaucer*, p. 177.

[69] The first instance cited by *OED* (which gives the word as still current) is from Spenser's *Shepheard's Calendar*.

A **Crow or Crome** of Iron; an Iron Bar with an end flat (Worlidge), beside

Croe, *Pince, Levier de fer; Jable, petite Entaillure (ou petit Creux) à cinq or six doits au bout des Douves pour mettre les pieces du fond du Vaisseau* (Miège),

Croe (a Leaver of Iron) (Boyer),

and **Croe** 1. an iron leaver 2. a notch in the stays of a cask, where the head-pieces come in (Martin),[70]

while Miège sheds interesting light on the status of the pronunciation of the word 'vat':

Fat, **Fate**, or **Uat**, a great wooden Vessel . . . (Kersey-Phillips);

Vat, or (as it is vulgarly pronounced) Fat . . . A Cheese-vat, or Chese-fat (Miège);

cf. **Fat** . . . This is generally written *Vat* (Johnson).[71]

One of the words cited by Kerling as 'marked as old in the edition of 1696' and 'now included, but not marked' in Kersey-Phillips is **Binne**. However, in this case there is in fact no real change in designation, since Phillips' term 'old word' applies to the obsolete sense 'manger', and that sense has been omitted by Kersey. Thus, we may compare

Binne (old Word) a manger, also a place to put Bread in (Phillips 1696),[72]

Binne, or **Bin**, in the old *Saxon* signified a *manger*, we use the name now most commonly for a place to put bread or oats in (Blount 1681) and

Binn, a sort of Cup-board or Hutch, to lock up Bread and other Provisions; a Bread-basket: Also a Place boarded up to put Corn in

---

[70] Cf. Gazophylcium, 'A **Crome**, **Cromb**, or **Crom** of iron', with a separate entry for 'A **Crow** of iron. v. **Crane**'. *OED* describes **Crome** as 'now local.' and gives the meaning as 'hook, crook'; it has no entry corresponding to Kersey's second part. Miège and Boyer also have unmarked entries for all the other words listed in this category by Kerling (*Chaucer*, pp. 177 – 8) and J. K. has all except **Bereft** and **Queest**, making it unnecessary to speculate with Kerling as to 'what the principles were behind Kersey's decision to "unmark" these words'. Of **Keen** Kerling (*Chaucer*, p. 178) comments that in the sense of 'sharp', this 'was probably a common enough word, with, however, a restricted collocation-pattern as it is usually found only in the context of swords and razors'. But see the wide range of sub-entries in Miège and Boyer.

[71] Kerling, *Chaucer*, pp. 177 – 8, '**Fat** was probably gradually replaced by the Southern form *vat*'. Cf. J. K. 'A **Vat**, or fat, a kind of vessel', and Martin **Fat**, sense 3 'a vat, or vessel'. Cf. *OED*, where **Fat** sb. is marked as obsolete, but is given illustrative quotations from both the late seventeenth and the early eighteenth centuries.

[72] Cf. Baret's *Alvearie* (1573) 'A **Binne** or place to put bread in'.

(Kersey-Phillips),[73]
with
Binn, *Reduit où l'on serre le Pain, l'Avoine, des Bouteilles, &c*
(Miège),[74]
and
A **Binn**, a place made of Boards to put Corn in (Worlidge).
The *Oxford English Dictionary* similarly indicates its sense 2, 'the manger', as the only one that is obsolete.

On two other occasions Kersey does not brand or otherwise categorise words marked old by Phillips and entered with a double obelisk in Miège. However, one of these, **Cresset**, is also entered without comment by Boyer, Martin and Johnson and is accepted as still current by the *Oxford English Dictionary*.[75] In the case of the other, **Domesman**, carelessness may be responsible for the absence of the designation 'old'. Thus, compare

Cresset, (*old word*) a Lanthorn, a Beacon (Phillips 1696),
Cresset, an old word used for a Lantern or burning Beacon. *Min.* (Blount 1681),
Cresset or **Cresset-light**, a great Lanthorn hanged on a Pole, or a burning Beacon (Kersey-Phillips),
†**Cresset**, or **Cresset Light**, for a burning Beacon . . . (Miège),
Cresset, *Subst.*, (*or* Cresset-light for a burning Beacon) . . . (Boyer),
A **Cresset-light**, or burning Beacon (J. K.),
Cre'sset or Cresset Light, a burning beacon (Martin)
Cre'sset. A great light set upon a beacon, lighthouse, or watchtower. Hanmer. They still raise armies in Scotland by carrying about the fire-cross (Johnson, with a quotation from Milton).

In the case of **Domesman**, on the other hand, there is no evidence that the word was indeed still current at the beginning of the eighteenth century. We may compare the entry
Domes-man or **Doomsman**, a Judge or Person appointed to doom or

---

[73] The use of the word 'bread-basket' as a possible meaning for **binn** in Kersey-Phillips is of interest in view of Osselton's comment on J. K.'s entry A **Bread-basket**: 'The case of *bread-basket* is instructive. The compound is recorded in actual use in the O.E.D. only from the year 1753, but it had had a shadowy existence in the world of Latin-English, English-Latin dictionaries for 200 years before that as an explanation of the Latin *panariolum*. From Huloet in 1552 it passed through a succession of other dictionaries into Littleton, where it appears . . . for Kersey to take over' ('John Kersey and the Ordinary Words', p. 559). It should be noted that Boyer also has the word, though not Miège.
[74] Cf. Johnson, '**Bin**, A place where bread, or corn, or wine, is reposited'. *OED* **Bin** sense 4, 'a partitioned case or stand for storing bottles in a wine-cellar', gives its first quotation from 1758.
[75] However, **Cresset-light** is described as obsolete.

determine Suits at Law, or Differences: Also a Confessour or Priest that hears Confessions (Kersey-Phillips)
with
Domesman, (*old word*) one that passeth Sentence, a Judge, or Confessor (Phillips 1696),
‡**Domesman**, a Word anciently used for a Confessor.
Doomsman, Juge, ou Arbitre (Miège),
and
†**Domesman**, Subst. (an obsolete word for a Confessor) . . .
Dooms-Man, Juge ou Arbitre (Boyer).[76]

However, Kersey is not anticipated by the dictionaries of the previous reign merely in the relabelling of words in his main source, Phillips's *New World of English Words*. A number of the old words in his revision which had not previously been included in the *New World* were already to be found, as Kerling has shown,[77] in seventeenth century dictionaries other than Phillips, including Miège's *Great French Dictionary* and the second edition of Thomas Blount's law-dictionary (1691). To the list provided by Kerling I would add the words **Delf** and **Treet**, from his list of words with 'unidentified sources'.[78] Thus, the entry 'Delf, or Delfe (old Word) a Mine or Quarry; from the Saxon, delwan to delve or dig' combines material from Miège ('‡**Delf**, or **Delfe**, an old Word signifying a Mine, and a Quarry') and the law dictionaries (e.g. **Delfe** (from the Sax. delfan to dig or delve,) Is a Quarry or Mine, where Stone or Coal is dug . . .', Blount 1691).[79] The entry '**Treet**, an old Word for Wheat. In *Stat. 5 H.3. Bread of Treet* seems to be that sort of Bread which was made of fine Wheat', combines Miège '‡**Treet**, and (sic) old Word for Wheat . . .' and Cowell-Manley 'Treete, . . . Wheat; In the Statute *5.H.3.* Bread of *treete* seems to be that Bread which was made of fine Wheat . . .'.
And whereas Kerling finds it 'difficult to prove Kersey's use of Ray',[80] I would use the evidence of the late seventeenth century dictionaries to reject completely the suggestion of 'The Collection of English Words' as

[76] Another word cited by Kerling as 'marked as old in the edition of 1696' and 'now included, but not marked' — **Entreate** — is in fact marked old in respect of that meaning which is described as old by Phillips. Thus, compare 'To **Entreate**, (old word) to handle' (Phillips 1656) and 'To **Entreat** . . . also formerly, to treat of, or handle' (Kersey-Phillips).
[77] Kerling, *Chaucer*, pp. 182–186.
[78] Kerling, *Chaucer*, p. 187.
[79] Similarly Boyer ‡**Delf**, ou **Delfe**, *Subst.* (an obsolete Word for a Mine, or a Quarry'. *OED* gives **Delf** sb.1 as 'the ordinary word for a quarry in the northern counties'.
[80] Kerling, *Chaucer*, p. 186.

a source.[81]

Thus, of the two words cited by Kerling as possibly derived from Ray, one, '**Scrat** (old Word) an Hermaphrodite, one that is of both Sexes' is, as he observes' also found in Coles (and indeed in Miège, where it is given an obelisk and defined as 'a kind of Hermaphrodite, that is male and female').[82] The other appears rather to be drawn from White Kennet's revision of Cowell:

Arval, **Arvil**, or **Arfal**, (old Word) a Burial, or Funeral Solemnity.
Arvil-Bread, the Loaves distributed to the Poor upon such Occasions.
Arvil-Supper, a Feast of Entertainment given at Funerals; a Custom still observ'd in some of the North and North-West Parts of *England* (Kersey-Phillips);
Arvill-Supper: A Feast made at Funerals; in part still retained in the North (Ray);
Arvil Supper. Feast of Entertainment given at Funerals, which Custom is still retained in some of the N and NW parts of England. see **Arvil bread** the loaves distributed to the poor at such Funeral Solemnities. **Arvil**, **Arval**, **Arfal** are used for the Burial or Funeral Rites . . . (Cowell-Kennet 1701).[83]

As for **Collock** 'an old Word for a Pail', which Kerling reports as occurring in White Kennet's *Parochial Antiquities attempted in the History of Ambrosden, Burcester and Adjacent Parts in Oxford and Bucks* (1695) and in Ray, *Collection of English Words*,[84] this word is found also with a double obelisk in both Miège and Boyer.[85]

2. The Strange, the New and the Familiar.

The seventeenth-century English dictionary-makers were assiduous in their collection of specialist vocabulary, but were not interested at all in recording the ordinary words and idioms of the language. However, the compilers of the bilingual dictionaries had every-day vocabulary as their

---

[81] See Janet M. Bately, 'Ray, Worlidge, and Kersey's Revision of *The New World of English Words*', *Anglia* 85 (1967), 1 – 14.
[82] Boyer 1700 also uses the obelisk here. Cf. *OED* **Scrat** 'obs. exc. dial.', with illustrations from standard usage up to 1634.
[83] Cf. *OED* †**Arval**, 'obs. exc. dial.' None of the non-dialectal uses cited by *OED* are from obviously accessible sources.
[84] Kerling, *Chaucer*, p. 187. Cf. White Kennet, *Parochial Antiquities*, '**Colerus**, A great piggin, or pail, with a wide neck, is called a collock in the North'.
[85] Martin has unmarked entries for **Scrat** and **Arval**.

primary concern and it was to them and not to the English dictionaries that J. K. turned, when in 1702 he came to publish his collection of words 'commonly' used in the English language.[86] In the second part of this article I wish to examine the extent to which both the every-day and the specialist vocabulary of the reign of William and Mary was available to dictionary-users and how up-to-date the information provided was. A full examination of all the material available is not of course possible here. So I have arbitrarily confined myself to a scrutiny of those words that begin with the letter G and of a selection of other items from among the branded words in the dictionaries of the period. Not surprisingly, a large number of entries in the *OED* are absent from these works. Many of the books consulted by the teams of scholars who compiled the *OED* would not have been available to the seventeenth century dictionary makers, and a very large proportion of the words in this section seem to have been specialist words of very limited currency. A number of these remain unfamiliar today; others have become more generally accepted, as for instance, **Gas** (*OED* 1658-),[87] **Generic** (*OED* 1676-), **Gesticulator** (*OED* 1693-), **Gland** (*OED* entry 2, 1692-),[88] to **Granulate** (*OED* 1666-), and **Gregarious** (*OED* 1668-). Three of these words are recorded by Kersey-Phillips and two by Martin.[89] Dr Johnson has five.[90]

The words just cited seem first to have entered the language in the second half of the seventeenth century, and therefore a lexicographer of the time of William and Mary, if not his eighteenth century successors, might be forgiven for omitting them. However, other words found in the *OED* but not Miège, Boyer, J. K. or the hard word dictionaries of the time are known to have entered the language at a much earlier date. Some seem to have had their first dictionary entry in Kersey-Phillips: thus, for instance, **Gerundive** (*OED* 1483-), **Gymnasium** (*OED* 1598-), **Gypsum** (*OED* 1646-). However, a significant number do not appear in English dictionaries until much later in the eighteenth century: thus, for instance, **Gangrenous** (*OED* 1612-), **Gargoyle** (*OED* 1412-), **Garrotte** (*OED* 1622-), **Generator** (*OED* 1646-), **Geniality** (*OED* 1609-), **Genuflect** (*OED* 1630-), **Germ** ('rudiment of a new organism', *OED*

---

[86] See Bately, 'Miège and the Development of the English Dictionary', and Osselton, 'John Kersey'.

[87] The entry in Kersey-Phillips is itself derivative, going back ultimately to definitions such as that in Blancard's *Physical Dictionary*: '**Gas**, a term used by *Helmont* and signifies a Spirit that will not coagulate, or the Spirit of Life, a Balsom preserving the Body from Corruption'. The modern sense first appears at the end of the eighteenth century.

[88] Cf. Kersey-Phillips, '**Gland**. See *Glandula* and *Mucilaginous Glands*'.

[89] Cf. Martin **Gas**, **Gland**, Kersey-Phillips **Gas**, **Gland**, to **Granulate**.

[90] No entry for **Gesticulator**.

1644-), **Goitre** (*OED* 1625-), **Gradient** (adj., *OED* 1641-), and **Grava-men** (*OED* 1602-), only one of which (**Gradient**) is found in Martin, but four are in Johnson.[91]

Of the words which today might be classified as 'ordinary' and which are absent from the dictionaries of this time a number are occasionally apparently relatively new words, as **Galore** (*OED* 1675-), **Gangway** (*OED* 1688-),[92] **Giggle** (*OED* 1677-), **Global** (*OED* 1676-), to **Gobble** (of a turkey-cock, *OED* 1680-), **Goldfish** (*OED* 1698-). However, others are of much greater antiquity, as, for instance, to **Gambol** (*OED* 1507-), to **Garden** ('to work in a garden', *OED* 1577-), to **Garner** (*OED* c. 1375-), **Garnet** (the semi-precious stone, *OED* c. 1310-),[93] **Gate-post** (*OED* 1522-), **Gauntness** (*OED* 1607-),[94] **Genially** (*OED* 1661-), **Genuine-ness** (*OED* 1647-), **Geranium** (*OED* 1548-), **Gingham** (*OED* 1615-), to **Gleam** ('to shine', *OED* c. 1225-), to **Glimpse** (*OED* c. 1400-), **Glitter** (*OED* 1602-), to **Gloat** (*OED* 1575-),[95] **Gloating** (*OED* sb. 1593-, adj. 1602-), **Gloom** (*OED* entry 1, 1596-), **Glossy** (*OED* 1556-), **Go-between** (*OED* 1598-), **Godlessness** (*OED* 1553-), to **Grab** (*OED* 1589-),[96] **Grade** (*OED* c. 1511-), to **Grade** (*OED* entry 2, 1563-), **Greed** (*OED* 1609-), **Greenhouse** (*OED* 1664-), **Greensward** (*OED* 1600-), **Grime** (*OED* 1590-), **Griminess** (*OED* 1650-), **Grimy** (*OED* 1612-), **Grin** (*OED* sb. 2, 1635-), **Grip** (*OED* Old English onwards), to **Grip** (*OED* OE onwards),[97] **Grittiness** (*OED* 1711-), **Grouse** (*OED* 1531-), and **Gutless** (*OED* 1605-).[98]

Since Kersey-Phillips' dictionary does not include 'ordinary' words, only a handful of the items listed above — **Gangway**, **Geranium**, **Greenhouse**, and **Grouse** — are found there, and the definitions given show that almost without exception their presence is due to the fact that at the beginning of the eighteenth century these were 'specialist' words.

---

[91] Johnson has entries for **Gangrenous**, **Generator**, **Germ** and **Gradient**. In the entries for **Generator** and **Germ** ('a sprout or shoot') he quotes Sir Thomas Browne. Strangely he includes neither **Gerundive**, nor **Gymnasium** nor **Gypsum**.

[92] Johnson, '*Dict.*'

[93] Cf. the entries **Granate**, **Grenate** in the seventeenth-century dictionaries and Kersey-Phillips.

[94] Cf. **Gaunt**, with an obelisk in Kersey-Phillips, although the word is used by Dryden. See further above, p. 24.

[95] See *OED*'s comment on the currency of this word in the seventeenth and eighteenth centuries.

[96] Rider's Dictionary cites this word as a variant of To **Grabble**.

[97] The dictionaries of the period have noun and verb **Gripe**.

[98] *OED* cites instances from the period 1605 – 1625 only. For the modern usage see *OED* Supplement, with an instance dating from 1929.

Thus, for instance, **Greenhouses** are 'certain Houses built in Gardens for Ornament, and necessary for many choice Greens that will not bear the Winters Cold abroad in our Climate'.[99] Martin, including both ordinary and hard words in his dictionary, also has, somewhat surprisingly, only three — **Garnet**, to **Gobble**, and **Greenhouse** — while Johnson has twenty.[100]

It is, of course, possible that some of the words recorded in the *Oxford English Dictionary* as current both before and after the reign of William and Mary had fallen out of use at this time, to be revived at a much later period. So, for instance, the *Oxford English Dictionary* has no entry for **Gentlefolk** between 1594 and 1732, while **Gargantuan** is illustrated from works published between 1596 and 1630 and then once again from 1893. Dr Johnson has an entry for **Gentlefolk** (which he illustrates from Shakespeare), but not for **Gargantuan**.[101] Miège and his contemporaries have neither.

At the same time, carelessness — or at least non-comprehensiveness — is responsible for the absence of entries for some words and phrases. For intance, a number of words entered in the hard-word dictionaries of the period are not found in Miège or Boyer — thus, for instance, Phillips 1696 has entries for **Galaxy** (*OED* 1384-), **Ganglion** (*OED* 1681-), **Gemination** (*OED* 1597-), **Gestation** (*OED* 1533-), **Glaciation** (*OED* 1646-), **Glaucoma** (*OED* 1643-), **Gossamer** (*OED* c. 1325-), **Grandiloquence** (*OED* 1589-), **Gusto** (*OED* 1647-), **Gyration** (*OED* 1615-). Blount, but not Phillips, has **Garrulous** (*OED* 1611-), **Gelid** (*OED* 1606-), **Go(u)rmand** (*OED* 1491-), **Graduation** (*OED* 1477-), **Grandiloquent** (*OED* 1593-) and **Gymnasticks** ('books treating of exercise', *OED* 1652-).[102]

Other words are absent from Miège, but are recorded in either Boyer or J. K. or both. Thus, Boyer has entries for **To Await** (*OED* c. 1230-), **Gamekeeper** (*OED* 1670-), **Gaze** (*OED* c. 1430-), and **Guiltlessness** (*OED* 1571-), while J. K. records **Gannet** ('a bird'), and **Gladdon** ('Gladdon, gladdin or gladwin, an herb'), both found from the Old English period onwards, **Gaol-bird** ('or lewd wretch', *OED* 1603-),

---

[99] *OED*'s first example is from Evelyn, *Kal. Hort.* In 1712 J. James was still finding it necessary to explain the term.
[100] **Gangway**, to **Gambol**, to **Garden**, to **Garner**, **Garnet**, **Genially**, **Genuineness**, to **Gleam**, **Glitter**, to **Gloat** (misunderstood), **Gloom**, **Glossy** (quoting Browne, Milton and Dryden), to **Gobble**, **Gobetween**, **Greenhouse**, **Greensward**, **Grime**, **Grin** (quoting Dryden), **Grittiness** and **Grouse**.
[101] Cf., e.g., Blount 1656 **Gargantua**.
[102] All but two (**Grandiloquence**, **Grandiloquent**) are recorded by Johnson, who includes **Gymnasticks** under **Gymnastick**, Adj., 'Pertaining to athletick exercises'.

Glasswort ('an herb', *OED* 1597-), **Grumbler** (*OED* 1633-), **Guelder-rose** ('or elder-rose'; *OED* 1597-) and **Gut-wort** ('an herb', *OED* 1597-), and both dictionaries have the entries **Gamesomeness** (*OED* 1727-) and **Gruff** (Boyer 'grim-fac'd, sowr-look'd', J. K. 'grum, dogged or surly'; *OED* 1690-).[103] Personal preference may be responsible for the inclusion by Miège of the salutation 'good morrow' (*OED* c. 1386-) to translate French 'bon jour', but not of 'good day' (*OED* c. 1205-).

However, since Miège's aim is two fold, that is to promote understanding of a literature written in a foreign language, and to enable the users of his dictionary to be able to speak idiomatically and 'properly', he — like Boyer after him — includes not only many unusual words but also a large number of words which either have apparently only just come into use or are not normally recorded in literature — including some that were later to be omitted by dictionary makers through a sense of delicacy.[104]

So, for instance, the *Great French Dictionary*, published in 1688, has a number of entries which are roughly contemporaneous with first entries in *OED*, such as the colloquial †A **Beau** ('or pretty Fop', *OED* 1687-); †**Brown George** ('or Ammunition bread', *OED* 1688- 'a loaf of coarse brown bread, hard coarse biscuit'), and the technical **Glacis** (term of fortification, *OED* 1688-). All of these entries are also in Boyer and Johnson, two in Martin and one in J. K. and Kersey-Phillips.[105] Not in Miège, but recorded by Boyer in his dictionary of 1699, are a number of other 'new' words such as **Group** ('a Term of Painting', *OED* 1695-).[106]

Yet other entries actually antedate the material in the *OED*.[107] Some of these are slang, or at least essentially colloquial expressions, and are usually marked with an obelisk: thus, for instance, the use of **Bacon** in

---

[103] Phillips 1658 has **Gladin**, **Gromel**, *Gazophylacium* has **Gaunt**.

[104] Even four-letter words are solemnly provided with etymologies by the author of *Gazophylacium*, while the *Ladies Dictionary* discourses on a number of subjects which would have seemed indelicate to the Victorians. For an important study of coverage in *OED* see Jürgen Schäfer, *Documentation in the O.E.D.: Shakespeare and Nash as Test Cases* (Oxford, 1980).

[105] Martin has **Beau** and **Glacis**, J. K. and Kersey-Phillips have **Beau**.

[106] 'The Figures in the Grouppes ought not be to like each other in their Motions, any more than in their Parts'.

[107] A number of words and phrases with 'first instances' in *OED* that post-date Miège's *Great French Dictionary* are in fact found already in the hard-word and bilingual dictionaries of the reign of Charles II or even before; so, e.g., To **Agglomerate** ('or to roll it self up into a round shape, as a Hog-louse', Miège, beside Phillips' 'to roul up together', *OED* sense 1, 1692-); He looks as big as **bull-beef** (Coles, Latin Dictionary 1677, *OED* 1690), a **Newgate Bird** (Walker 1672, no entry *OED*). See also A **Clot-head** (Littleton 1677, *OED dial.*, 1878-); **Durgen** (Littleton 1677, *OED* 1706-, quoting Kersey-Philips); **Flimsy** (Littleton 1677, *OED* 'first recorded in 18th c.', with 1702 J. K. as the first example).

the idiom 'To save his Bacon, to take care of himself', (*OED* 1691-);
Bellarmin ('a burlesk Word used amongst Drinkers to express a stout
Bottle of strong Drink . . . To dispute with Bellarmin, *vider la Bouteille*'
(*OED* 1719-, without the phrase); **Brusher** ('A brusher, or brimmer',
OED 1690-); **Carot** ('A Carot, or red-haired Man', *OED* 1690-); **Doddle**
('To Doddle along, or to Doddle about', *OED* 1761-); To **Gee** ('As, the
Business wont gee', *OED* 1700-), and To **Grease** ('To Grease a fat sow in
the Arse or in the Tail, that is to give to those that dont want it' [reading
from Boyer], *OED* Suppl. 1785-). Of these entries one, A **Brusher**, is
found also in B. E.'s dictionary of cant, and in J. K., while Johnson
quotes 'to save his bacon' from Pryor; none is in Kersey-Phillips or
Martin.

Other instances of antedatings in Miège's dictionary are of words
which might be described as learned or specialist, or refer to some new
concept or thing: thus, †**Effrontery** (*OED* 1715-, but already in Phillips
1658), **Gatherers** ('The fore-teeth of a Horse', *OED* 1696-), **Gavot** ('a
sort of Dance', *OED 1696-)*, **Gemelliparous** (*OED* 1727-), and
Vaudevil ('or Lay, a Country-Ballad', *OED* 1737-, but already in Blount
1656).

Antedatings of special senses include **Gallery** ('A covered Gallery, in a
Siege', *OED* 1704-), **Galley** ('The Admiral Galley', *OED* 1770-),[108] **Gout**
(venereal disease, *OED* 1694-), to **Grapple** ('with ones Stubborness',
OED 1830-), †**Blue** ('Twill be a blue Day for him', *OED* sense 1783-),
Hero ('of a Comical Romance. He that makes the Subject of it', *OED*
1697-), while Boyer has **Daiz** ('Canopy of state', *OED* 1863-).[109]

Some of these terms are now fully-established as 'ordinary' words of
the language, as are other antedatings, such as To **Gabble** (transitive,
'As, d'ye hear how they gabble French?', *OED* 1758-), **Gagged** (*OED*
1839-) and **Gagging** (*OED* 1817), **Gawze** (in combination, as 'a Gawze
Hood, or Peticoat'; *OED* 1759-), **Goldhammer** ('a sort of Bird'; *OED*
1706-), to **Groul** ('or mutter', *OED* 1707-), **Guessing** (adj., 'Physick is
but a guessing Science; *OED* 1703-).

A number of other 'ordinary' words found in the three dictionaries are
not recorded at all in *OED*, a fact which may suggest that they either had
but limited currency and were overlooked, or were deliberately rejected
by the Victorian lexicographers.[110] Words from this category — almost
all of which are marked with an obelisk in Miège and Boyer — include
Chum ('Tobacco to chew'), **Dor** ('at Westminster-School, *Congé de*

---

[108] Already found in Torriano's revision of Florio.
[109] Miège has the French head word **Dais**, but not its English form.
[110] For the practice of *OED* see the Introduction and, especially, *A Supplement
to the Oxford English Dictionary*, ed. R. W. Burchfield (Oxford, 1972 – 86), pp.
xiv – xv.

dormir'), A **Galligaskin** 'or old fashion Taylor', **Glovestick**, **Gold-wire-drawer**, **Grumporters** ('heavy Dice'), and **Catch-fart** ('*Surnom burlesque que l'on donne aux Pages qui portent la Queue de leurs Dames*'); and the expressions 'A **beard** in folio (*une barbe in folio*)', and 'a Rogue in **grain** (*un franc Coquin*)'. Colloquial and slang expressions include 'The **Barn** is full, she has got a great belly', 'To **beshit** or disgrace himself, *se decrediter*', 'An unlucky **Bird**', *un mechant Garnement*',[111] 'to **broach** a Virgin' (described as *Dans un Sens burlesque*), 'He is faln into a **Cow-turd**, that is, he has married meanly', 'To be **double**, or to be married; a double Man, or a married Man'. As Miège and Boyer indicate by their use of the obelisk and other devices, some of these terms have been included on the grounds that the reader may wish to know of their status in order to avoid them. Other words considered 'improper' have been omitted altogether. However, these are far fewer in number than the deliberate omissions in eighteenth, nineteenth and early twentieth centuries.[112]

3. The Significations

Martin, writing in 1749, considered that 'A Critical and accurate Enumeration and Distinction of the several Significations of each respective Word must be allow'd by all to be indispensably the chiefest Care of every Writer of Dictionaries'. And yet, he continued, 'nothing is more certain, than that all our *English Dictionaries* are more notoriously deficient in this important Particular than in any other; indeed it has never been attempted in any one of them that I have seen'. This criticism is certainly a pertinent one. However, already in the reign of William and Mary ample coverage of the range of senses of individual words was being provided by the bilingual dictionaries. Indeed, Martin himself acknowledges his debt to Boyer's Royal Dictionary and to an eighteenth century Latin dictionary by Ainsworth, which was heavily indebted to its seventeenth century predecessors.[113] In the English part of these dictionaries, 'the Authors were obliged to consider every different Sense of an English Word, in order to make a proper Translation thereof into each respective Language'. So, for instance, under the head-word To **Go** Miège has more than three columns of entries. **Gate** is defined *Porte, grand' Porte; demarche; air, ou mine*

---

[111] For **Bird** in the jocular sense of 'man' (1853-) see *OED* Suppl.
[112] See Bately, 'Miège', p. 5, n. 18.
[113] See Starnes, *Renaissance Dictionaries*, pp. 325 – 40.

and its illustrative quotations include 'To keep the Gate', 'To have a portly (or majestick) gate', and 'Her gate shewed her to be a Goddess'. **Parasite**, in the English section is defined as 'a Smell-feast, a Spunger, or Hanger on . . . A flattering Parasite, one that feeds a rich Man's Humour with flattery, that he may be welcome to partake of his good Cheer . . . A Parasite, of all Trades, is the basest, like an Echo, he is all Voice and Words, and speaks only what he hears others'. In the French section we are given a slightly different gloss: **Parasite**, . . . a Parasite, Spunger, or Smell-feast, a Trencher-friend, a Shark, a Hanger on, one who for a Meals meat will say, or do, or indure any Thing'.

Although complaints about the lack of a good English dictionary were to continue well into the eighteenth century, the existence of dictionaries like those of Miège, Boyer and J. K., along with a wide variety of specialist word-lists and glossaries, ensured that the ingredients were there in the reign of William and Mary not only for a prescriptive dictionary such as Dryden was seeking, but also for a more comprehensive work recording the language of the age, of a type which was not to reach its ultimate form until the publication of the Supplement to the *OED*. In the words of Boyer, 'the Architect [was] only wanting, and not the Materials for such a Building'.

IRISH ADOPTIONS IN THE ENGLISH OF TIPPERARY, CA. 1432*

Michael Benskin

Richard Stanyhurst, a man of old Dublin family, published his *Description of Ireland* in 1577.[1] Like many other writers of his time, interested in Irish affairs, he has much to say about language and its political significance. A long line of colonial administrators would have agreed with his observation (f. 3r, col. b)

> that a conquest draweth, or at the least wyse ought to drawe to it, three things, to witte, law, apparayle, and languague. For where the countrey is subdued, there the inhabitants ought to be ruled by the same law that the conquerour is gouerned, to weare the same fashion of attyre, wherewith the victour is vested, & speake the same language, that the vanquisher parleth. And if anye of these three lacke, doubtlesse the conquest limpeth.

In the early days of the English settlement, the pace of conquest was anything but limping: in spite of the frontier fixed by the Treaty of Windsor, in 1175, Henry II's freebooting vassals continued to carve out fiefdoms for themselves, submitting to the crown's dominion only after the event. At its greatest extent, in the late thirteenth century, the area of effective colonisation included about half the country — most of Meath and Leinster, much of Munster, and Ulster east of the Bann. In the words of its most eminent historian,

* For discussion of various matters relating to this article, I am indebted to Professor William Gillies (Edinburgh), Mr Kenneth Nicholls (Cork), and Hr Jan Erik Rekdal (Oslo); but none of them has had opportunity to criticise the draft, and they are not to be blamed for its shortcomings. Thanks are due also to Dr Inger Moen (Oslo), for improvements to part of the text. For supply of a microfilm, I am grateful to Dr Keith Williamson and Edinburgh University Library, and to the National Library of Ireland for approving the arrangement.
[1] Richard Stanyhurst, *Description of Ireland*, in Rafael Holinshed's *Chronicles* (1577; *Short Title Catalogue* 13568).

the Norman settlement of Ireland was no mere military occupation
supported by the settlement of English and French burgesses in a few towns,
but a part of that great movement of peasant colonization which dominates
so much of the economic history of Europe from the eleventh to the
fourteenth century . . .[2]

The feudal order of this *terre engleis*, subject to the common law and
ruled from Dublin by representatives of the English crown, is readily
contrasted with the archaic society of the Irishry that lay beyond. Yet
the boundary between them, no matter the provisions of treaties, can
never have been absolute. From the first, there was intermarriage: many
of the *conquistadores* fathered children as much Irish as English, whose
children in turn were heirs to two languages and cultures. In some of the
marcher lordships, the inheritance was long maintained.

'English' is a complex term here. The named heroes in the chronicles
of invasion were French-speaking, as were the English upper classes in
general at that time; and the Irish vocabulary still bears a French stamp.[3]
The immigration of peasantry and artisans, by contrast, is of itself
evidence for the establishment of English speech in Ireland; in those
parts where the English political order prevailed, it eventually displaced
French much as it did in England. As a written language, however,
Hiberno-English is scarcely known from before the early fourteenth
century, and it is poorly documented until the fifteenth.

By then, the *terre engleis* was shrinking rapidly: local war in the
marches, piecemeal reconquest by the dispossessed, had begun even in
the late thirteenth century, and through the fourteenth they gathered
momentum. Edward Bruce's invasion of 1315 – 18 brought ruin in its
train, from which parts of the colony never recovered. His defeat was
the end of any cohesive nationalist movement, but the litany of local
devastation and desertion continued, accompanied variously by famine
and plague. No stream of new immigrants repaired the colonial loss.
Great lordships fell divided among co-heiresses, and descended to the
absentee. In an account of the *State of Ireland, and Plan for it's
Reformation*,[4] written ca. 1515, it was held that the king's laws were
obeyed only in half the county of Louth, and so much of Meath, Dublin,
Kildare, and Wexford; and in these, 'all the comyn peoplle . . . for the

[2] A. J. Otway-Ruthven, *A History of Medieval Ireland* (1968), 109.
[3] Cf. H. Risk, 'French loan-words in Irish', *Études Celtiques* 12 (1968 – 71),
585 – 655, and 14 (1974), 67 – 98.
[4] Printed in *State Papers. King Henry the Eighth*. Part III. *Correspondence
between the Governments of England and Ireland* (1834). Vol. ii, 1515 – 1538;
vol. iii, 1538 – 1546. See ii. 1 – 31.

more parte ben of Iryshe byrthe, of Iryshe habyte, and of Iryshe langage' (p. 8).

The list of 'obedient shires', Wexford omitted, is common currency in writings of the time, but the picture is somewhat misleading. The counties of Tipperary and Kilkenny, to speak only of these, are included among 'thEnglyshe Countyes, that bere trybute to the wylde Iryshe' (p. 9); they appear also as counties ruled by English nobility who follow the Irish order, part of the land of war (pp. 6 – 7; see below, p. 45). It would be easy to conclude that here too the colony had failed, been absorbed into Irishry as much by the defection of its lords as by reconquest. The archives, as opposed to the chroniclers and the politicians, tell a rather different story.

Tipperary *de jure*, and Kilkenny *de facto*, were part of the lordship of the Butler earls of Ormond.[5] Their records survive, in the National Library of Ireland, as the largest single collection of muniments relating to the mediaeval colony; the material dating from 1172 to 1547 takes up the first four volumes of Edmund Curtis' *Calendar of Ormond Deeds.*[6] The mere fact of its existence is evidence for lordship exercised along English lines. Government by assembly, proclamation, and the sword, had no need of written instruments: administrative archives are not a legacy from the land of war. Moreover, the forms of the documents and their modes of script keep pace with English practice; the later mediaeval material wears no old-fashioned look, nor does it betray the influence of written Irish. Mostly the mediaeval items are in Latin, but so much is true of almost any natural collection from England; in the Butler lordship, English comes into documentary use at about the same rate as in most counties of England. The form of English, again as in England, is variously local in character, but here there are obvious marks of contact with spoken Irish. Mainly these are phonological, the product of a bilingualism that was perhaps extensive; but phonology is not to the present purpose. Rather, this essay attends to vocabulary, to Irish words adopted as English, and English words adapted to Irish use; implicitly, it is as much about social institutions as about words. The essay takes the form of a commentary on a single text, known generally as 'The Statutes of the White Earl'.

James, fourth — 'White' — earl of Ormond (1405 – 52) was the last of

[5] For a map showing the original grants to Theobald Butler, see Otway-Ruthven, *History*, p. 68. The later boundaries of the lordship appear in maps 43 – 4 of *A New History of Ireland* vol. ix, p. 42 (see n. 11 below). On the settlement, see [A.] J. Otway-Ruthven, 'The character of Norman settlement in Ireland', *Historical Studies* 5 (1965), 75 – 84 (esp. 81 – 2).

[6] *Calendar of Ormond Deeds*, ed. E. Curtis (Dublin, 6 vols, 1932 – 43; Irish Manuscripts Commission).

the fifteenth-century earls of Ormond resident in Ireland. He was a national figure, and served repeatedly as chief governor. Mr Nicholls[7] refers to him with good cause as 'surely the most astounding figure in fifteenth-century Irish history . . . a patron of Gaelic as well as of English litterateurs', a man who straddled two cultures that were for the most part antagonistic. Yet when the same writer describes the Statutes as reflecting 'in general a purely Gaelic system of government', consideration of the diplomatic should perhaps give pause. The Statutes are entered on the dorse of a roll of the court of the liberty of Tipperary,[8] substantially a copy of a writ with the sheriff's return, dated 1432. Writs and sheriffs and court rolls were not a part of the Gaelic order. The Statutes affirm that the earl shall hold court sessions annually in his *franchise* — the very term acknowledges English royal authority — and in the same way as the king holds his parliament. The earl claims a subsidy, but it is to be granted by the people — and as a sum of money, not in the Irish fashion.

The manuscript is D 1647 in the National Library of Ireland, and is reproduced with the kind permission of its custodians. It has been printed twice before, but inaccurately, by Curtis (with observations from Charles McNeill, *Cal. Ormond Deeds* iii, no. 102, pp. 97 – 9) and by Canon Empey.[9] The script of the Statutes has been identified with that of certain additions to the writ, datable to 1447 – 9, and the Statutes have accordingly been referred to the same years;[10] but close palaeographical analysis gives no ground for believing them to be by the same hand. The items entered below the Statutes, relating to the outlawry of Donatus More Okyally, all belong to 13 Henry VI (1434 – 5); there is no reason to think them a later copy, or that the Statutes were added above them on the roll. Moreover, the wording of lines 28 – 32 arguably creates a presumption that James Gallda Butler was still alive when the Statutes were composed; his death is usually given as 1434.[11] The manuscript, could, of course, be a later copy, but there is so far nothing

---

[7] K. W. Nicholls, 'Anglo-French Ireland and after', *Peritia* 1 (1982), 370 – 403 (see p. 400).

[8] The court was held at various towns in south Tipperary, including Clonmel, Lisronagh, and Crumpstown.

[9] In C. A. Empey and K. Simms, 'The ordinances of the White Earl and the problem of coign in the later middle ages', *Proceedings of the Royal Irish Academy* 75 C (1975), 161 – 87 (see p. 186). The paper offers a valuable survey of the historical background.

[10] Empey and Simms, 'Ordinances', p. 168, following McNeill in *Cal. Ormond Deeds*.

[11] So *A New History of Ireland* ix (*Maps, Genealogies, Lists*), ed. T. W. Moody, F. X. Martin, and F. J. Byrne (Oxford, 1984), p. 169; cf. T. B. Butler, 'Seneschals of the liberty of Tipperary', *Irish Genealogist* 2 (1943 – 55), 294 – 302, 326 – 36, 368 – 76 (see p. 368).

to indicate that it belongs outside the years 1432 – 4.

In what follows, repeated reference will be made to two other documents from the Ormond Deeds. NLI D 1517 (*Cal. Ormond Deeds* ii, no. 440) is a survey of the agricultural and grazing land in the Ormond lordship, and contains two entries in English. One is completely illegible, even with ultra-violet, but the other, 'vsagis and constitutis of the Count*ray* Tip*erare*', is clear; it is of about the same date as the Statutes, to judge by the hand. The second document is no. 267 in *Cal. Ormond Deeds* iv, the complaint addressed to the crown by the gentleman inheritors and freeholders of the County Tipperary in 1542. Citations are from the facsimile in part iii of *Facsimiles of National Manuscripts of Ireland.*[12] no. lxxv.

The English of mediaeval Ireland is hereafter called 'mediaeval Hiberno-English', abbreviated 'MHE'.[13] In phonetic representations, the standard IPA symbols are used, save that the Irish palatalised consonants are indicated by a trailing diacritic '. (In Irish, the opposition between palatalised and non-palatalised variants is phonemic.) Antedatings in respect of the *OED* and *MED* citations are duly noted, though not in the belief that they are important in themselves: some are trivial, a matter of just a few years. With terms adopted from Irish, it is largely a matter of chance whether the surviving manuscripts reflect the real chronology; in some cases, as *keheryn* (*tye*) below, they clearly do not.

Note: abbreviations are expanded conventionally, and italicised (-*is* so printed is superscript *s* in the MS). Letters enclosed in < > are insertions above the line. Hyphens are editorial. Word spacing is very variable; some words in no sense compounded yet run into one another.

---

[12] *Facsimiles of National Manuscripts of Ireland*, ed. Sir John T. Gilbert (Southampton, 4 vols, 1874 – 84).

[13] For some account of its dialectal character and external history, see W. Heuser, *Die Kildare-Gedichte* (Bonner Beiträge zur Anglistik 14 [1904; repr. Darmstadt, 1965]), 20 – 55; A. J. Bliss, 'The inscribed slates at Smarmore', *Proceedings of the Royal Irish Academy* 64 C (1965), 33 – 60; Brian Ó Cuív, *Irish Dialects and Irish-Speaking Districts* (Dublin, 1967); A. McIntosh and M. L. Samuels, 'Prolegomena to a study of mediæval Anglo-Irish', *Medium Ævum* 37 (1968), 1 – 11; Michael Benskin and Angus McIntosh, 'A mediæval English manuscript of Irish provenance', *Medium Ævum* 41 (1972), 128 – 31; M. Benskin, 'Local archives and Middle English dialects', *Journal of the Society of Archivists* 5 (1977), 500 – 514 (see 505 – 506, 511 – 512); Alan Bliss, *Spoken English in Ireland 1600 – 1740* (Dublin, 1979).

Text

De statut*is* & correct*ion*ibus & dom*i*nijs dom*i*ni Comit*is*
Ermon*i*e in / Com*itatu* Typerar*ie*

Item ther shall no man breke þᵉ pees in Counte typ*er*are wᵗ
oute þᵉ lord ys leve neþ*er* ryde wᵗ ban*er*ys dysplayd to prey

5   to barne to rauusse apon non ffrend ne neybor*e* of þᵉ
countr*e* Typerar*e* And ȝyf any so dothe he shall fall
in þᵉ lorde ys m*er*cy aftyr þᵉ form*e* of lave. And so
har recetto*ur*s & maynten*our*s in þᵉ same m*er*cy.

It*em* ther shall non Ientyll ma*n* ne ravaynno*ur* ne

10   non oþ*er* folke Spen þᵉ Countre wᵗoute þᵉ lord ys
leve apan þᵉ peyn of forfete of all har godys

It*em* þ*er* shall non chieften in þᵉ Counte Typerar*e*
aske non Coydhyhe ne forhogr*e* apon [? non]
freholer in þᵉ lyb*er*te of þᵉ counte typ*er*ar*e* mute

15   he be aman þᵗ þᵉ lorde ȝav [?f.te ?*cancelled*] leve by p*re*uelege
of h*is* Sele to hy*m* Apan þᵉ peyn þᵗ may fall

It*em* ther shall no keheryn tye walke þᵉ
countre neþ*er* Spen þᵉ pepyll neþ*er* rere non
vrlawus þ*er* yn mut þᵉ lord ys keheryn ty

20   Item þᵉ lord shall hole hys Sys-honys eu*er*y ȝer*e* & call
all h*is* lib*er*te of þᵉ contre Typerar*e* to þᵉ seyd Sysen in h*is*
owyn ffranchys to hy*m* bothe spyrytuall & temp*or*all
lyke as hᵗ ys wᵗyn þ*is* same roll as well as þᵉ kyng
may hole hys p*ar*lement. And aftyrwar<d> þᵉ countr*e*

25   shold graunte þᵉ lord h*is* Subsedy þᵉ whych was oþ*er* ys
vsyde thyrte marke & oþ*er* whylys lx marke whan
nede wer*e*.

It*em* þᵉ lord graunte to Iames Galde botiller h*is* owy*n*
brodyr*e* þᵗ he shold be keper*e* of all þᵉ countr*e* vndyr*e*

30   hy*m* Sylfe & sett forogr*e* & <haue> Coydhyhe in eu*er*y fre
holer*e* ys hous as wyd as all þᵉ countre of Typerar*e*
And hath graunt hy*m* xxiiij fote men to Serve
hy*m* wher he wolde go oþ*er* walke & c'
And al so whan þᵉ lord wold go to any porc*i*oun

35   he wold Sett h*is* horssyn & knawys & oþ*er*s to Connyw
awarle þᵉ Countre aboute hy*m* & þ*is* by h*is* marchall
of horse þᵉ whyche was Olyf*er* Comyn & Emond
travers & c'

It*em* Emond ketyng & laynagh botyller was þᵉ

40   lord ys chyefteyn*is* of h*is* keheryn ty & c'

counte (3, 12, 14) 'county'.

As a name-element, *shire* (OE *scīr*) was never established in Ireland: county-names are either in the form exemplified by *County Wexford*, or are unqualified, as in *Kerry*. The *County* prefix, in ordinary speech, is largely optional, though it serves in many cases to distinguish the county from the county town: *County Kildare* and *Kildare* can be contrasted as *Kerry* and *County Kerry* can not. With particular names, the use or non-use of *County* may be habitual, but in written form the prefix *Co.* is commonly applied to all. Of the English county-names, *Durham* is the only one that is used freely in this way. Otherwise, a connecting *of* is obligatory, and a definite article precedes, as in 'the County of Leicester'. Even with the definite article, however, the Irish county-names exclude *of*: 'the County Kildare', 'the County Cork', and so on, are idiomatic in Ireland. These differences seem not to have attracted philological attention before, and neither of the distinctively Irish usages is exemplified in the dictionaries.

The Statutes of the White Earl illustrate both types, the earliest instances I have found: 'in Counte typ*erare*' (3), 'þ^e Counte Typ*erare*' (12).

In Latin texts from mediaeval Ireland, county-names are either *comitatus de* followed by a proper name in the ablative, or *comitatus* followed directly by the proper name in the genitive. That is also the pattern in texts from England. In French texts, from 15th-century England and Ireland alike, the form is *le counté de* followed by a proper name.[14] It is possible that the Latin construction with the genitive is the basis for the *County Wexford* pattern; but in spoken usage French is likely to have been more influential, and so far as I can ascertain, it affords no basis for the *of*-less construction. Moreover, MHE *country* can be used in the same way: so in the Statutes of the White Earl (6 & 21, contrast 31), and in the co-aeval 'vsagis . . . of the Count*ray* Tiperare' (NLI D 1517). On present evidence, the appositional style could as well have begun with *country* as with *county*, and again neither French nor Latin offers a convincing model for it.

It is possible that these constructions depend on Irish syntax, or are at any rate reinforced by it. In Irish, a qualifying genitive follows the head noun: so, for example, *Tír Eoghain* 'Eoghan's Country', anglicised *Tyrone*. In Middle English, as in Old Norse, the qualifier normally precedes the head. The Anglo-Normans introduced the shire into

---

[14] *OED* notes that *county* in the sense of 'shire' is hardly to be found before the 15th century (s.v., sense 2). *MED* records *counte* so used in the French text of Britton, ca. 1290, but the Middle English citations proper are all from ca. 1400 onwards (s.v. *counte* n. 3, sense 2(a)). It would be of interest to establish the earlier usage of F *counté* in texts from Ireland.

Ireland, but they did not use the *-shire* suffix inherited with the administration of Anglo-Saxon England. Anglo-Norman usage, both in Latin and French, accorded with Irish practice in putting the head-noun — *comitatus* or *counté* — first in the phrase. The county in question was specified by a territorial name already established, and thus of Irish or Norse-Irish origin. So long as these names were used in Irish as well as in the colonial languages, the order of {head + qualifier} was continually reinforced; and since the Irish genitive is inflexional, the absence of a connecting particle is in the natural order of things.

The county-names are in effect compounds; in so far as the Irish county-names are anglicised, it is suggested, a syntactic principle has been transferred fron one language to another. Such transfer is well seen in three of the province-names of Ireland, where the facts are not in doubt. *Leinster*, *Munster*, and *Ulster* are Old Norse formations based on Irish *tír*; the qualifying element is an Irish proper name, but it precedes the head-noun and is linked to it by the Old Norse genitive suffix *-s*.[15] 'Inversion compounds' in which Germanic elements follow the Irish order are well-known from northern English place-names, monuments to Norse-Gaelic settlers from Western Scotland, Ireland and Man. So, for example, *Briggethorfin* and *Kirkoswald* (Cumberland), *Seat Sandal* and *Wathsutton* (Westmorland).

barne (5) vb. 'burn'.

rauusse (5) vb. inf. 'ravage, plunder, lay waste'
MED ravishen (OF *raviss-*, extended from *ravir*). The word happens not to have been recorded hitherto in this spelling, but the form is unremarkable.

co(u)ntre (6, 10, 18, 21, 29, 31, 36)
The word is here used in a primarily social sense. In Middle English, besides its territorial meanings, *countre* could refer generally to the people of a country or region, and, in a technical sense, to a jury consisting of the inhabitants of a judicial district; these senses are well-established, and recorded from the later 13th century onwards (*OED* s.v. *country*, I.6 & I.7; *MED* s.v. *contre(e*, 6(a) & 6(b)). In 16th-century accounts, *country* is the regular term for an Irish lordship. Such a lordship, as Mr Nicholls reminds us, is not to be 'conceived of as a closed and defined territory but rather as a complex of rights, tributes and authority';[16] the terrritorial, social and legal aspects of the English word are thus fused in the Irish context. In much the same way, these senses inhere in the Irish

---

[15] A. Sommerfelt, 'The Norse influence on Irish and Scottish Gaelic', in Brian Ó Cuív (ed.), *The Impact of the Scandinavian Invasions on the Celtic-speaking Peoples c. 800 – 1100 A.D.* (Dublin, 1962; repr. 1975), 73 – 7 (see p. 75).
[16] Kenneth Nicholls, *Gaelic and Gaelicised Ireland in the Middle Ages*, Gill History of Ireland 4 (Dublin, 1972), 22.

word *oireacht* (anglicised *iragh̃t* et var.), of which the primary meaning is 'assembly'.[17] Note how, in the present Statutes, the country may be politically agentive: 'þᵉ countre shold graunte þᵉ lord his Subsedy' (24 – 5). So also in the Tipperary complaint of 1542: 'the same is grauntid by the consent of all the cuntrey for helpe to suche buyldyng . . . as be for a comon welthe'.

In Latin texts, the term for such a polity is usually *patria*.[18] In the French of the Irish statute rolls, temp. Henry VI, the notion is rendered *pais*: 'li dit Oherdiskoll en tout son pais' (p. 192), 'al pais del dit Oneell' (p. 562).

The Irish *country* is identified typically by the name of its lord or chief captain, as in the French examples. A letter to the earl of Ormond, undated but assignable to 1487, provides an early instance of the first-person usage in Hiberno-English [HE]: 'writtyn at Byrtyston in my contray . . . Per vestrum specialem amicum dominum Iohannem Okerwayll sue nacionis capitaneum' (PRO SC 1/52/37; cf. *Cal. Ormond Deeds* iv, pp. 315 – 6).

As will appear from the following description in the *State of Ireland*, written ca. 1515, the boundaries of such a lordship were inevitably shifting:

> . . . understande that ther byn more then 60 countryes, called Regyons, in Ireland, inhabytyd with the Kinges Irishe enymyes; some region as bygge as a shyre, some more, some lesse, unto a lytyll; some as bygge as halffe a shyre, and some a lytyll lesse; where reygneith more then 60 Chyef Capytaynes, wherof some callyth themselffes Kynges, some Kynges Peyres, in ther langage, some Prynceis, some Dukes, some Archedukes, that lyveyth onely by the swerde, and obeyeth to no other temperall person, but onely to himself that is stronge: and every of the said Capytaynes makeyth warre and peace for hymself, and holdeith by swerde, and hathe imperiall jurysdyction within his rome, and obeyeth to noo other person, Englyshe ne Iryshe, except only to suche persones, as maye subdue hym by the swerde . . .
>
> Also, the sonne of eny of the said capytaines shalle not succede to his fader, withoute he be the strongeist of all his nation; for ther shalbe none chief captayn in eny of the said regions by lawfull succession, but by fort mayne and election; and he, that hathe strongyst armye and hardeyst swerde among them, hath best right and tytill; and by reason therof, ther be but fewe of the said regions that be in pease with themselff . . .[19]

The writer then lists 'the chyef Iryshe countreys' with the names of their chief captains; and continues (p. 6)

---

[17] Nicholls, *Gaelic and Gaelicised Ireland*, pp. 22 – 23.
[18] Nicholls, *Gaelic and Gaelicised Ireland*, p. 23.
[19] *State Papers* ii. 1 and 5.

> Also, ther is more then 30 greate captaines of thEnglyshe noble folke, that folowyth the same Iryshe ordre, and kepeith the same rule, and every of them makeith warre and pease for hymself, without any lycence of the King, or of any other temperall person, saive to hym that is strongeyst, and of suche that maye subdue them by the swerde.

Among them are Sir Piers Butler, and all the captains of the Butlers of the county of Kilkenny, and of the 'county' of Fethard in south-east Tipperary. The burdens that such an order placed upon the country are set out at length by the gentleman inheritors and freeholders of the County Tipperary in their complaint to the crown of 1542: they conclude that 'your said complay*nauntes* may not contynue after the sorte but fayne to leve all their frehold*es* waste'. There was ample precedent for desertion.

From the interchange of *country* and *county* in this and other texts, it may be supposed that the words are synonymous. That is not the case, though they can refer to the same thing. An Irish *country* cannot be called a *county*, for it was never constituted as a shire. A shire fully subject to the royal administration is not a *country* in the Irish sense. Tipperary was administered as a shire, but it was a recognised liberty, the dominion of a lord: it was the County Tipperary, but no less was it Ormond's country.

On the Irish idiom '(the) Country Tipperary', see under *counte* above.

lave (7) sb. 'law'.

recettours & mayntenours (8)

The phrase is recorded by *OED* (s.v. *resetter*) from ca. 1380 onwards. *Resetter* is a harbourer of thieves or criminals. A maintainer can be merely an abetter or supporter, but the word has also a special legal sense: 'one who interferes, usually with threat of violence, to prevent the due process of law from damaging his client's interests'.

Ientyll man (9) sb. 'gentleman'

'Properly, one who is entitled to bear arms, though not ranking among the nobility': so *OED*, s.v., 1, with examples from the late 13th century onwards. Spenser's comment on Irish usage (cited by *OED* ibid.) may be apposite here: 'Yf he can derive himselfe from the head of a septe . . . then he holdeth himselfe a gentellman'.[20]

---

[20] Edmund Spenser, *A View of the Present State of Ireland* (1596; entered on the Stationers' Register 1598). Ed. W. L. Renwick, modern spelling (Oxford, 1970). For a discussion of the term in late mediaeval English, and of the associated livery and maintenance, see R. L. Storey, ' "Bastard feudalism" revisited', *Bulletin of the Manorial Society* 3 (1983), 7 – 15.

ravaynnour (9) sb. '(plunderer), one who lives by exactions'?
The reading is clear, as Curtis notes (p. 99). His view that 'one might
expect *retainer*' is not altogether apposite, and 'raisers of revenue' is just a
guess. McNeill's identification of the word as *ravener* is correct, though
the precise meaning is unclear. *Ravinour* et var. is recorded by *MED* from
1384 onwards, meaning 'extortioner, plunderer, abductor' like its Old
French etymon (*ravineor* et var.). Contextually, however, *ravaynnour*
cannot well be so read. His presence, like the gentleman's, is taken for
granted, and legislation for public order can hardly approve the presence
of such people as are denoted by the Old French and Middle English
usages. The *ravaynnour* is merely prohibited from 'spending' the country,
that is, demanding food subsidies from the tenantry in return for
protection (see note on *spen*, below). The prohibition is not absolute: a
ravaynnour may be given the lord's permission to make such demands.
He is clearly a man of some authority: if he can offer protection, he must
be able to organise armed retainers. He cannot, if the lord is to license him
for maintaining public order, be an outlaw or casual villain.

The pejorative senses inherent in ME *ravinour* need not attach to the
Mediaeval Hiberno-English [MHE] word here: the *ravaynnour* is
someone who takes property from people, but is not stigmatised for so
doing — he is part of the approved order, something between a
gentleman and 'other folk'. His *ravening* — extortion — is probably no
more than the taking of subsidies from the tenantry and servile classes
that was traditional in the native, non-monetary society. To a society
whose nobility rests mainly on unfree labour, as in the feudal system, or
on rents and taxation in a monetary economy, the Irish nobles'
appropriation of goods at source may well look like plundering,
regardless of the degree of such exactions. *Ravaynnour*, as applied to
the Irish equivalent of *gentleman* or a little less, was doubtless
pejorative at first.[21] Perhaps it still echoed disapproval, but in this text it
is most probably neutral: the Statutes are the work of a legislator who
sought to control the Irish order within his lordship, but was certainly
not hostile to it — as witness his grant made at about this date to Donnell
Mac Clancy, for his services as a counsellor in Brehon law.[22]
spen (10, 18) vb. '(spend), exact food subsidies from'

[21] In some 16th-century HE writings it is undoubtedly so. *Ravyners* are clearly
'plunderers' in Lord Butler's letter of 1537 (*State Papers* ii. 477); cf. Robert
Cowley's letter of 1539, 'beeing honest men, and not ravenoures' (iii. 148). The
earl of Ormond wrote in 1538 that 'the late Omorys sonnys . . . being also the
chief and most notable raveners and malefactors, in comitting all maner offences
. . . ben nowe the Lorde Deputies chief darlinges' (iii, 78); it would be
interesting to know whether the lord deputy called them 'raveners' as well.
[22] Nicholls, *Gaelic and Gaelicised Ireland*, p. 48.

This is clearly the same word as *spend* in 'Defend me and spend me', reported by Payne (1590) and Spenser (1596). With such a meaning *spend* is recorded only in this expression; *OED* notes that it is peculiarly Irish (s.v.[1], I.1.d). Under *spene* v.(1.b), however, an earlier and independent example is cited: the earl of Ormond, in a letter of 1538, complains that Sir John Seyntlo's 'servauntes and his kerne dothe spene my tenauntes and fermoris in the barrony of Dunnbrathie, and other wheres in the countie of Weyxforde' (*State Papers* iii.48). The present Statutes show that *spen(d)* was so used at least a century before.

Formally, the correspondence of *spen(e)* and *spend* is unproblematic. Development of proto-MHE *spend-* to *spen(-)* is predictable, given the characteristic reduction of MHE *nd* to *n(n)*; this sound-change is largely an accommodation to Middle Irish phonology, in which the sequence /n/ + /d/ could occur only in sandhi. Nevertheless, *spen(e)* could as well be of Middle English origin: from the early Middle English past forms of *spenden* was formed a new inf. *spene*, on the analogy of such verbs as *wenen* 'expect' (so *OED*, s.v. *spend* v.[1]). Both types, *spen* and *spend*, are found in MHE.

Semantically, the word presents certain difficulties: the peculiarly Irish meaning has yet to be accounted for. The possibility that resemblance to ME *spen(d)-* is fortuitous, and that the HE word is adopted from Irish, is reasonably discounted. Goidelic *sp-* words, so far as their etymologies can be established, are themselves adoptions from other languages,[23] and there is no very plausible candidate as an etymon. Rather, an extension of meaning attaching to the Middle English word is likely.

Spend construed with an indirect object, 'spend on someone else's behalf', is a possible basis for the Irish usage: 'she spends me forty pounds a year' (Jonson). But *OED* records it only from Jonson and Pepys (s.v.[1], I.1.e), and the sense of burdensome obligation, of exaction and resignation, is hardly present in this construction. The senses 'consume' and 'exhaust' are the closest links: *OED* records them from 1297 onwards (s.v.[1], I.5.); cf. also OE *forspendan* 'spend utterly, consume', translating Lat. *consumere* (Bosworth-Toller, s.v.). Applied to human objects, *spend* is recorded in this sense once only by *OED* (I.1.5 *transf.*), interestingly from an Irish source: Ussher wrote of a plot to get rid of enemies by having Cambyses 'spend them there and never send them home again'. In 'Defend me and spend me', the speaker himself is implicitly the object of consumption. The basis for this transfer of meaning lies probably in the form of the exactions: traditionally, they

[23] T. F. O'Rahilly, 'Etymological notes — II', *Scottish Gaelic Studies* 2 (1927), 13 – 29 (see pp. 24 – 29).

were foodrents. The lord consumed what the tenant payed for his protection, and so could be said to consume the tenant himself.

Used explicitly of a lord's consumption of food-rents is OIr. *caithid* (*RIA Dict.* s.v., 55/68); more generally, it means 'consumes, spends, uses', and also (55/56 – 64) 'exhausts'. Alignment with *spend* probably accounts for the semantic extension of the MHE word. *Caithid* can also mean 'treat (somebody with something)' (55/78), a possible basis for construction of *spend* with a personal object. The corresponding verbal noun, *caithem*, appears to have had a somewhat wider range of meaning, from 'use, enjoyment' to 'pillaging, laying waste', and it is this form which appears in the Irish idiom answering to 'spend and defend'. In the Annals of the Four Masters, s.a. 1395, Philip Maguire, lord of Fermanagh, is described as *fear caithme 7 cohsanta a chriche* 'man of spending and defending of his territory'; the Annals were compiled in the years 1632 – 6, but the idiom may well be original. An example from the later 15th century appears in the Book of Lismore, and is the only citation in *RIA Dict.* (s.v. *caithem*, 54/2). A verbal noun is similarly recorded in HE: Spenser reports that 'Irish landlords . . . have a common spending upon their tenants' (cf. *OED* s.v., 2.b.).

The peculiarly (M)HE meaning of *spend* may derive solely from the Irish collocation *caithem 7 cosnam*, though it is unclear from *RIA Dict.* how far the Irish was a set phrase. In the (?M)HE rendering, the rhyme with *defend* is an obvious reinforcement for *spend* as opposed to some other word; it may be that an Irish alliterative pair found natural echo in MHE rhyme. Even so, *spend* was open to other contamination: Ir. *domeil* is likewise 'spends, uses up', but additionally 'eats' and 'makes use of' (*RIA Dict.*, s.v.).

coydhyhe (13, 30) sb. 'cuddy', i.e. a night's hospitality
In Modern English writings pertaining to Ireland, the word appears usually as *cuddy*, and is so recorded by *OED*. The etymon is Ir. *cuid* 'share' + *oidhche* 'night' gen. sg., virtually a compound save that *cuid* bears the inflexion. The Middle Irish pronunciation must have approximated to [kuᵈd′iːh′ə] or [kuᵈd′iːx′ə]: in MHE as in Middle English, written *oy* (*oi*) corresponds both to [ɔɪ] and [ʊɪ].[24] The identification of the MHE form with the Middle Irish is not in doubt, but the phonology is less straightforward than appears. Since these matters affect the view taken of certain sound-changes in Old Irish and its antecedents, they will be treated separately elsewhere.

The 'night share' was an exaction, the overnight hospitality that a lord, with his retinue, was entitled to claim from his tenantry. It

---

[24] Cf. E. J. Dobson, *English Pronunciation 1500 – 1700* (2 vols, Oxford, 2nd edn, 1968), §§ 252 – 260.

included food, lodging, and entertainment, and could be claimed either by direct billeting, or as a levy of goods to the same value; commutation to money payments became increasingly common in early modern Ireland. The prerogative was of great antiquity even by the date of these Statutes. Its origins lie in the *cóe* ('coshering visit, guesting') described in *Críth Gablach*, a legal tract compiled probably at the beginning of the 8th century, but which may incorporate much older materials.[25]

OED's first record of the word in English is from the statutes of Ireland for 28 Henry VI (1450),[26] where it appears as a pl. *cuddies*. The statute roll itself, however, has long been lost. The editions of Tottle[27] and Bolton[28] modernise the Middle English entries on the roll, and by the time of Berry's edition (*Statute Rolls . . .*, 1910) it was necessary to fall back on the post-mediaeval transcript in Trinity College, Dublin, MS E.1.41. The fact of the word's occurrence in the roll is not in doubt, but *cuddies* cannot be trusted as a 15th-century form. *OED* has no other mediaeval citations, and the word is not recorded by *MED*. In Scots sources it is known from 1505 onwards: so *DOST*, s.v. *cuddeich*. The present Statutes accordingly provide the only record of the word in a 15th-century hand.

OED's later citations are from Elizabethan writers: Hooker's version of Giraldus Cambrensis in Holinshed (1586, in which *cuddies* are listed with *coine and liuerie* and *cosheries*), and Spenser's *View of the Present State of Ireland* (1596, *cuddy* var. *cuddeehih*). From the *State Papers,* however, the 16th-century record can be much enlarged. In documents dated from 1515 to 1537, the index to vol. iii lists eight occurrences, all of them in the pl.: 1515 *codyes* (p. 30), 1524 *coyddeys, cod(d)eis, codeys* (pp. 111 – 3), 1533 *cuddees* (p. 162), 1534 *cuddeis* (p. 210, ordinances for the government of Ireland, printed in England), 1535 *coydeis* (p. 259), 1537 *cuddeis* (p. 495). All of these are in texts of HE origin, except for the ordinances (1534).

for(h)ogre (13, 30) sb.: an exaction of some kind, but the meaning is unclear.

The word is not otherwise known in English. Curtis (p. 99) thought it 'would seem to mean *foragers* or *purveyors*', but that is merely a guess. A connexion with *forage* cannot be ruled out on morphological grounds

[25] D. A. Binchy, *Críth Gablach*, Mediaeval and Modern Irish Series xi (Dublin, 1941), 81 and pp. xiii – xiv.
[26] *Statute Rolls of the Parliament of Ireland, reign of King Henry the Sixth*, ed. H. F. Berry (Dublin, 1910; Irish Record Office Series of Early Statutes, ii).
[27] R. Tottle, . . . *Statutes from the tenthe yere of king Henrie the sixt, to the xiiii. yere of . . . Queen Elyzabeth* (1572; *Short Title Catalogue* 14129).
[28] Sir R. Bolton, *The Statvtes of Ireland . . .* [3 Edward II to 11 James VI & I] (1621; *Short Title Catalogue* 14130).

entirely, though the correspondence presents difficulties enough; rather, the context does not support interpretation of *for(h)ogre* as a nomen agentis. Moreover, there is an Irish word that is formally identical, and given the association with *coydyhye*, it is inherently likely that an Irish word is in question. The problem is what, in this context, the word means. MIr. *forfócra* /forho:grə/ (cf. Mod.Ir. *forfhógra*), sb., is in essence 'prediction, forewarning, proclamation', whence the special senses 'summons', 'ordinance', 'declaring war', 'proscription', 'out-lawry', and so on. None of these fits *for(h)ogre* in the Statutes. Mr Nicholls (pers. comm.) thinks that it refers to the legislation by proclamation common in Irish lordships at this time: either economic legislation, the practice of proclaiming monopolies or rights of pre-emption in the lord; or, a proclamation for the cessing of troops on the country.

Certainly a transferred sense is required, not 'proclamation', but a particular that can be proclaimed. *For(h)ogre* is something that can be asked by a chieftain from a freeholder, in addition to cuddy or as an alternative to it (13). In (30), therefore, 'haue Coydhyhe' is not a particular of which 'sett forogre' is the general, nor is setting *for(h)ogre* a necessary preliminary to claiming cuddy. Asking — exacting — *for(h)ogre* is not in itself forbidden, but is a right reserved by the earl of Ormond; he may grant it to others, under privelege of his seal. It is possible, therefore, that *for(h)ogre* appears, perhaps by another name, in the 16th-century appeals to the traditional order. As with *vrlawus* (14), the word is identified but its meaning is unclear: a wider-ranging analysis of texts and collocations is needed.

freholer(e) (14, 30 – 1) sb. 'freeholder'.

mut(e) (14, 19) 'unless, except'

Curtis printed '[with]ouyt' and 'ouyt except' (p. 97), supposing *ouyt to be 'some form of *oute*'; he thought it stood for WITHOUT, which would yield the required senses (p. 99).[29] Empey printed *out(e)*, unremarked (p. 186). The manuscript, however, is clear, and the proper readings are not in doubt. Such forms have not been noted hitherto. Likewise, their congener *mot(e)* has all but escaped notice;[30] it is rare, and in Middle English unknown, but sufficiently established in other MHE sources. Morphologically, *mut(e)* and *mot(e)* could be taken for deviant forms of the word BUT; semantically, there is no difficulty in supposing such an

---

[29] *Wythe ouyt* 'unless, except' is found in NLI D 1766 (so MS), *Cal. Ormond Deeds* iii, no. 203. The document is referred to below, in the article on *connyw* (35).

[30] Cf. A. McIntosh, 'Some words in the *Northern Homily Collection*', *Neuphilologische Mitteilungen* 73 (1972), 196–208 (see p. 201); Benskin and McIntosh, 'Mediæval English manuscript', p. 129.

origin. The known occurrences are as follows:

Dublin City Hall, Corporation Archives, Dublin Assembly Roll I. Text of mm. 8r – d, dated 1455. *Mot* 'unless' once, beside *bot gyf þ*ᵗ once. For other BUT, *bot* once. Local document, dialect of Dublin.

Cambridge, Magdalene College MS 18 (*olim* F.4.18): *Prick of Conscience* in one hand. Page 83 line 8 *mot* 'only', and so *mote* p. 84 line 19. For other BUT, *bot* is regular, *but* rare. Copyist's dialect probably of the Dublin Pale.

Dublin, Trinity College MS 156 (*olim* D.4.8): *Prick of Conscience*. Main hand of MS, f. 52v, 12 lines up, *mot* 'except'. For other BUT, *bot* is regular, *but* rare. Copyist's dialect of Dublin, and so probably that of the exemplar.

London, Wellcome Historical Medical Library MS 406 (*olim* Loscombe MS): medica, etc. Main hand of MS, f. 13v *mot* 'except' once; cf. f. 17v, with *bot* in error for *mot* 'must' ('Þe londe bot wel y-dyngit be'). For other BUT: *bote*, *bot*, *but*, each thrice. Copyist's dialect probably of the Dublin Pale, and so that of the exemplar.

San Marino, California, Henry E. Huntington Library MS HM 129: *Northern Homily Collection*. Main hand of MS, *mot* 'except, unless' ff. 98r, 133r, 144v, 170r, 189r, 230v, and twice more between f. 194v and end of MS (ff. not noted in analysis). For other BUT, *bot* is regular, *but* rare and confined to the earlier part of the text. Copyist's dialect probably of the Dublin Pale, and so partially that of the exemplar.

Additionally, *mot* is attested in the 19th-century dialect of baronies Forth and Bargy in County Wexford. This dialect, with Fingallian, is the only well-documented survival of the mediaeval colonial language into modern times; elsewhere, the norm was replacement by Gaelic, or disruption by the New English of the 16th- and 17th-century plantations. Poole's Forth and Bargy texts[31] include *mot* twice for co-ordinating 'but', once for 'except'; in the glossary, an independent compilation, *mot* is entered simply as 'but' (p. 57). *EDD* has no other record of such a word, nor is it to be found in the *Survey of English Dialects*[32] (item VII.2.6).

On this evidence, conjunctional and prepositional *mut(e)* and *mot(e)* are purely Hiberno-English developments.

Except for BUT, there is no word of Old English origin to which these forms can be plausibly related. OE *mōtan*, in concessive usage, seems

[31] Ed. W. Barnes, *A Glossary . . . of the Old Dialect of the English Colony in the Baronies of Forth and Bargy, County of Wexford, Ireland* (1867).
[32] *Survey of English Dialects*, ed. H. Orton et al. (Leeds, 13 vols, 1962 – 68).

not impossible; but it strains ingenuity, and neither Old English nor Middle English practice affords a reasonable basis for it. ON *móti* 'against, on the opposite side', would yield M(H)E *mot(e)*, and in the latter sense is not far removed from 'except, unless'; but there is no trace of such a borrowing in those dialects of English most heavily influenced by Norse, and the MHE dialects in any case derive mainly from outwith Scandinavian England. There seems to be nothing in Middle Dutch or Middle Low German that would explain the MHE forms, and neither French nor Latin affords any clue as to their origin.

The forms appear to be restricted, save in the modern dialect, to the senses 'except, unless, only'. In MHE as in Middle English, *but* and *bot* are used regularly with those meanings. Even in the texts where *mot(e)* appears, the normal way of expressing 'unless' (etc.) is with *bot* (often as *bot* + IF); *mot(e)*, if indeed it be related to *bot*, is always a rare by-form. That there is some relation between them is implied by the vocalism and the geographical distribution of variants. In the five texts where *mot(e)* is found, *but* is never the dominant BUT-form; and in four of the five, it is either rare or absent. *Mot(e)* goes with *bot*, not with *but*. In the Statutes of the White Earl, there are no BUT-forms other than *mut(e)*, and it is thus far uncertain whether *mut(e)* goes with *bot* or *but*. The evidence of other writings, however, tells strongly against *bot* in this dialect: 15th-century sources from Tipperary, and indeed from the southern counties in general, have *but(t)* almost without exception.[33] So *mut(e)*, it may be inferred, goes with *but(t)*.

A simple derivation of *mut(e)* from *but(e)*, and of *mot(e)* from *bot(e)*, could perhaps be justified on the basis of Irish phonology. In Middle English, the replacement of /b-/ by /m-/ is unknown, but in Irish these consonants interchange according to syntactic rule. Archaic endings in

[33] The main sources as as follows. Dublin, National Library of Ireland: D 1435 ('Gracius & gay'), D 1517 (usages of Tipperary), D 1751 (Wexford petition, ca. 1455). Kilkenny Corporation, *Liber Primus*. Lambeth Palace Library: MS 598 (*Conquest of Ireland*), MS 633 (*Secreta Secretorum*), both Waterford. London, British Library, MS Harley 3765 (Register of St Saviour's Chantry, Waterford). London, Public Record Office: E 30/1563 (indenture, Youghal, Co. Cork, 1494), E 101/248/19 (do., 1495), SC 1/51/138 (letter of James Butler, Kiltenen (Tipperary), 1499). Oxford, Bodleian Library, MS Rawlinson B 490 (*Conquest of Ireland & Secreta Secretorum*, Waterford). Waterford Corporation, *Liber Antiquissimus Civitatis Waterford*. Late, but still dialectal, are National Library of Ireland D 25591 (notarial document, Cork 1523), D 25891 (do., ca. 1500). For further information on these items, see the Index of Sources to the *Linguistic Atlas of Late Mediaeval English* (by Angus McIntosh, M. L. Samuels and Michael Benskin, with the assistance of Margaret Laing and Keith Williamson [4 vols, Aberdeen, 1986]).

/-m/ and /-n/ affected the initial consonant of a following word in phonetically various ways, collectively called 'nasalisation' or 'eclipsis'. The voiceless stops /p-, t-, k-/ became voiced, and so also /f-/ became /v-/; the voiced stops /b-, d-, g-/ became nasal continuants, /m-, n-, ŋ-/.[34] By the time of the earliest writings in Old Irish, the final syllables that brought about these mutations had largely been lost, and what had begun as a phonetic assimilation in sandhi was already a morpho-syntactic complex.

In a bilingual community, it is not impossible that such interchange was transferred from Middle Irish to MHE: *mut(e)* and *mot(e)* could be the result of phonological interference and nothing more. Even in dialects of Modern Irish, there are sporadic instances of unhistorical /m-/ for /b-/, apparently independent of syntactic conditioning. From the dialect of Ring, Co. Waterford, Breatnach reports variation of the initial of a word as 'a result of analogy, due largely to the influence of the initial mutations'; among his examples, *main-tiarna* 'lady' from *bain-tighearna*.[35] Ó Cuív reports similar variation from West Muskerry in Co. Cork: in some cases, the unhistorical form has ousted the older usage, in others — as *mannrach* 'sheepfold' beside *bannrach* — they co-exist.[36]

Processes internal to MHE could likewise be posited. The replacement, it could be argued, is stress-conditioned. BUT is commonly unstressed: the /b-/ may then be lenis with little plosion, its distinctive qualities primarily 'bilabial', 'voiced' and 'non-fricative'. In this it need hardly differ from unstressed /m-/, in which nasality may scarcely be audible: the distinctive qualities could be the same as for lenis /b-/, which would then be open to reinterpretation as /m-/. Such a process could reinforce, or be reinforced by, the Irish eclipsis of /b-/ to /m-/.

Sound-change alone, however, is unlikely to be the whole explanation, for /b/ > /m/ is not known in any other MHE word. That is not to say that the unique example is no example: a sound-change has to begin somewhere, even if it is eventually diffused through the whole of the eligible lexicon. Nevertheless, the geographical spread of *mut(e)* and *mot(e)*, in the absence of any other /b/ > /m/, implies lexical besides phonological conditioning.

If the word in question were a noun, then in these circumstances Irish origins would naturally be sought. Conjunctions and prepositions,

---

[34] See further Rudolf Thurneysen, *A Grammar of Old Irish*. Revised and enlarged edition, translated from the German by D. A. Binchy and Osborn Bergin (Dublin, 1946; repr. 1970), §§ 236–9.
[35] Risteard B. Breatnach, *The Irish of Ring Co. Waterford: A Phonetic Study* (Dublin, 1947), § 556.
[36] Brian Ó Cuív, *The Irish of West Muskerry, Co. Cork: A Phonetic Study* (Dublin, 1944; repr. 1975), §409.

however, are part of the grammatical system, and in the conventional view such elements are not readily transferred from one language to another. Even so, it is not hard to find examples in English. Prepositional *til* for TO is admittedly found in Old Northumbrian, and relative *at* may be a reduced form of native *þæt*; but their Middle English distributions are solidly Scandinavian, and for the most part their origins lie in Old Norse. Undoubtedly of Old Norse origin is the infinite marker *at*. A document of 1439 from Corney in south Cumberland, has *emyll* for BETWEEN (ON *í millum*, cf. Norw. & Da. *imellem*), beside remodelled *etwyx* from the native *betwix*.[37] Modern standard usage includes, among others, *except* (Middle English from Latin *exceptus* ppl.) and *save* 'excluding' (Middle English from *safe* adj., Fr. *sauf*); adopted directly as a preposition is *versus* (Middle English, via legal Latin), and *re* (for *in re* 'in the matter of') is widely used in place of *about* or *concerning*. There is a close structural congruity between Old English and Old Norse, and a much looser affinity between Old English and Old French; but in so far as the structures of Latin and Middle English converge, they do so largely as a result of people's thinking in the one language while speaking or writing in the other — the transfer is reciprocal, as Mediaeval Latin syntax clearly shows. Structurally, Middle Irish and Middle English are very unlike, but there are still points of contact. Moreover, they co-existed for a very long time, and as English adoptions from Latin indicate, the exercise of a dual competence may effect structural as well as merely lexical transfer — witness Elizabethan prose, for example.

The main difficulty with supposing MHE *mut(e)* and *mot(e)* to be loanwords is the lack of a wholly straightforward etymon. The only candidate presented by the dictionaries is Mod. Ir. *moite*, in the set phrase *cé is moite de/do* 'except, with the exception of'.[38] The other elements are transparent: *cé* conj. 'although', *is* copula, *de/do* prep. 'from/to'. Hence *moite* is the distinctive element, combination apart, that establishes the sense 'except'. It is known also as *muite*, in the forms *césmuite* and *díomuite* ('apart from, besides'); these are absent from the dictionaries, but discussed by Breatnach.[39]

Breatnach assigns these constructions to the base *taobh a(s) muigh do* ('outside (of)'), whence *taobh is-muigh do*. On this account, the

---

[37] Carlisle: Cumbria Record Office, D/Penn/28/20, Bretby bundle, indenture dated 23 January 17 Henry VI.

[38] So P. S. Dinneen, *Foclóir Gaedhilge agus Béarla. An Irish-English Dictionary* (Dublin, 1927; repr. 1970) and Tomás de Bhaldraithe, *English-Irish Dictionary* (Dublin, 1959), s.vv. *moite* and *except*[2]; Niall Ó Dónaill, *Foclóir Gaeilge-Béarla* (Dublin, 1977), s.v. *cé*; RIA Dict. has no record of it.

[39] R. A. Breatnach, 'Nótaí gearra. I', *Celtica* 2 (1954), 341–345 (see pp. 341–342).

otherwise unexplained *muite* and *moite* are fusions of a noun with a
following preposition: *muigh* is the dat. sg. of *magh* sb. (The primary
sense of *magh* is 'plain, field'. For idiomatic usage, see Dinneen's
Dictionary, s.v.; and s.v. *taobh* sb. 'side, direction' for the collocations
— note esp. *taobh amuigh de sin* 'not counting that'.) The historically
regular dat. sg. is *maigh*; but the variant *muig(h)* is known from Old
Irish onwards, which development presupposes *moig(h)*.[40] Development of *ui* from *oi* is otherwise attested in various of the modern
dialects, and early Modern Irish examples are to be found; early Mod. Ir.
oi may also be developed from MIr. *ai*.[41] Thus far, the Irish variants
cohere sufficiently with the vocalism of MHE *mut(e)* and *mot(e)*; in view
of the MHE geographical distributions, it would be of interest to know
whether *moigh*, as opposed to *muigh*, were regular in the now-extinct
Irish of the Dublin Pale.[42]

It is unlikely that MHE *mot(e)* and *mut(e)* are simple adoptions of Ir.
moite, if indeed the connexion be rightly stated. The likelihood of
partial identification with BUT has already been shown; it may be added
that even if *moite* were absorbed into MHE independently of BUT at first,
the Forth and Bargy usage shows that the two were identified — in that
dialect, *mot* is used for co-ordinating BUT ('*and* plus surprise'), a sense
not attaching to Ir. *moite*.

keheryn ty(e) (17, 19, 40) 'kern(e)ty'
This represents late MIr. *ceithearn tighe* /k'ehern t'i:/ 'household
troops'. (*Tighe* is the gen. sg. of *teach* 'house'. On *ceithearn* 'kern', see
below.) *Kern(e)ty* in whatever guise is absent from the great dictionaries,
though its use by present-day Irish historians, if nothing else, qualifies it
as an English word. The present Statutes may be its earliest MHE record,
though as *kerynty* it appears also in the co-aeval usages of Tipperary
(NLI D 1517). A scrutiny of the Latin documents among the Ormond
deeds may well yield other 15th-century examples, but I have not found
it in any other MHE texts of the period.

The functions of the kernety are well-illustrated by two 16th-century
texts. An indenture of 1542, dated at Limerick, between the earl of

---

[40] Thurneysen, *Grammar*, § 80.a.
[41] T. F. O'Rahilly, *Irish Dialects Past and Present* (Dublin, 1972; a reprint, with
minor emendations, of the 1st edn [1932], 196 – 198; Ó Cuív, *Irish of West
Muskerry*, § 304, cf. § 306 n. 3; Breatnach, *Irish of Ring*, § 452, cf. § 458.
[42] Dinneen *et al.* mark *cé is moite de* as Connacht usage, but Breatnach notes
that *taobh is-muigh do* is found in the dialect of Ring, Co. Waterford ('Nótaí
gearra. I', 342, n. 6). Quiggin records *diomuite* [d"ïmwi:t'ə] from Donegal (E. C.
Quiggin, *A Dialect of Donegal: Being the Speech of Meenawannia in the Parish
of Glenties* [Cambridge, 1906], § 105). The range of the constructions relevant
to the MHE forms is greater than appears in the dictionaries.

Ormond and the sons of Donatus O'Kennedy of Kilhwonyn, refers to 'the officers, judges and *kernety* whom the earl shall temporarily appoint or send for the rule and governance of the said cantred of Ormond, and for all other things from time to time needing to be done'.[43] The Tipperary complaint, of the same year, refers to the legitimate 'retynue or kernetye', which

> were neue*r* grauntid . . . but oonly to therles of Ormounde for the mini*s*tration of Iustice and executing of suche *p*rocess*e* as shulde be by the Seneschall and other thofficers of the libe*r*tie adwarded from tyme to tyme.

The freeholders granted this retinue of their own free will, and exclusively to the earl,

> and he to haue the same but so longe as nede shulde require or the like shulde be vsid in the Counties of lyme*r*yk kylkenny Catherlaghe kyldare or Methe Aswell for the defence of yo*u*r Ma*i*es*t*ies said subiec*t*es against the forsaid Iniuries and wron*g*es and repressing of the Irishe Disobeysaunt*es* adyoyning to the said shire as for his assistence in Doing his Dutie to yo*u*r highnes in mini*s*tration of Iustice and se*r*uyng of *p*rocesse w'in the said Libe*r*tie and thapprehension of malefact*o*urs. whiche may not be doon without some force and assistence to mayntene the same . . .

In addition to the forms cited, the following have been noted. *keranthy* in the composition of 1517 between the earl of Ormond and the lord of Cahir (NLI D 2029, *Cal. Ormond Deeds* iv, no. 40; so in Empey's text, p. 187). *ke(he)ryntye* in the indenture between Piers, earl of Ormond, and the lord of Kiltenan, 1523 (so Curtis in *Cal. Ormond Deeds* iv, no. 86, p. 77). *kernite* in an indenture of 1544, between the earl of Ormond and the Butlers of Lisnatubbrid and Temple Etney (so Curtis, ibid., no. 327, pp. 268 – 9). The presentments of the juries in the survey of 1537 would doubtless extend the record: cf. *State Papers* ii, p. 511 (note).

Kern(e). Ir. *ceithearn* is a collective noun, meaning 'band, troop', and was applied particularly to light-armed militia, foot-soldiers without helmet or body armour. In English guise, the word is more familiar as *kern(e)*, which came to signify a member of such soldiery as well as the band to which he belonged; it is uncertain whether Ir. *ceithearn* was so

---

[43] Curtis, *Cal. Ormond Deeds* iv, no. 269. The Latin text there printed reads 'Et in executione statutorum et ordinatorum in iuvamen et auxilium officiorum tribunorum et kernety quos Comes pro regimine et gubernatione dicte cantrete de Ormond, et ad omnia alia agenda de tempore in tempus deputaverit vel miserit . . .'; Curtis' English rendering is somewhat free.

used.[44]From the singulative usage there developed a distributive pl. *kernes* (var. *keernes, kernys*), first recorded in the French of the Irish statute rolls (*MED* s.v., citations from 1316); a Latin rendering *kaernias* appears in a similar roll of 1297, but the ordinary Latin word was *turbarius*. The kern is frequently contrasted with the galloglas in 16th-century and later accounts: the galloglas (MIr. *gall-óglach* 'foreigner-warrior') was the mailed mercenary of Hebridean, Norse-Gaelic origin, whose accustomed weapon was the battle axe. (On the etymology, see pp. 64 – 7 below.) Mr Nicholls considers that the kern, rather than being a particular sort of infantry, should be regarded as the ordinary freeman at arms, whose means precluded owning a horse.[45]

Kern(e) is well-established in English writings from both Scotland and Ireland, duly recorded by *OED*, *MED* and *DOST*. *Ceithearn* was also anglicised from an older Irish pronunciation /k'eθ'ern/, at a time when the consonant represented by MIr. *th* was still a dental fricative: MHE *keþerin* appears in the poem on Pers of Bermingham, composed in late 1308 or after,[46] but such forms are otherwise attested only in Middle Scots (see *OED* s.v. *cateran*; *DOST* s.v. *catherane, katherane*[47]). The spelling of the present text, *keheryn*, reflects the ordinary Middle Irish development of /θ/ to /h/, apparently complete in all dialects by ca. 1400.[48] In Modern Irish, intervocalic /h/ is generally preserved, except in northern dialects;[49] but in Middle English, as in Old English and Modern English, /h/ occurs only as the initial of a stressed syllable. *Kern(e)* is

---

[44] Cf. *RIA Dict.* s.v. *ceithern*, 107/43 – 6. From *ceithe(a)rn* is formed an Ir. singulative *ceithernach*, 'member or leader of a *ceithern*, a kern; a bandit' (ibid., s.v.), MIr. /k'eθ'ernax/ whence /k'eh'ernax/. The word is anglicised as *kerna(u)gh*, recorded in *OED* first from the *State Papers* (1535, ii.242); additional forms, from the same collection, are *kernagh* (1537, ii.450), *kernoghes* gen. pl. (1543, iii.466). The word seems not to occur in MScots, though *OED* has *kearnachs* from Stewart's *Highlanders* (1822). *Kernagh* is not in *MED*, but the Irish statute rolls of temp. Henry VI include *kernagh* (1428, p. 16, from the French of the original roll), and *kernaghys* (1437/8, p. 92, from the transcript in the Dublin *Liber Albus*).

[45] Nicholls, *Gaelic and Gaelicised Ireland*, pp. 85 – 86.

[46] British Library MS Harley 913, written ca. 1330. Ed. Heuser, *Kildare-Gedichte*, pp. 158 – 164.

[47] MScots *cateran* et var., with medial *t* not *th*, are referred by *OED* and *DOST* to Mediaeval Latin intermediaries: the /t/ cannot well be derived from mediaeval Goidelic. Such forms have not been noted from Irish sources, and a reference in the *State of Ireland*, ca. 1515, implies that they were regarded as alien: 'the wylde Iryshe, with all ther galloglagheis, and Iryshe Scottes, called keteryns' (p. 25).

[48] T. F. O'Rahilly, 'Notes on Middle-Irish pronunciation', *Hermathena* 20 (1926), 152 – 195.

[49] O'Rahilly, *Irish Dialects*, pp. 174 – 5, 208.

assimilated to the English pattern: medial /h/ is lost, and the syllables it divided are fused. The adoption of the word into MHE cannot have been a once-for-all affair, as the chronology of the forms makes clear: *Kern(-)* appears in the records long before *keheryn* — *MED*'s earliest citation is from 1297 — but etymologically *keheryn* is clearly the prior form. It is not in the dictionaries so far: to the present examples may be added *keheryn* from an indenture between the earl of Ormond and the lord of Kiltenan, 1523 (so Curtis, *Cal. Ormond Deeds* iv, no. 86), and *kahernes* from a letter in Hiberno-English spelling dated 1521 (Sir John Stile to Wolsey, *State Papers* ii, p. 81). It may be wondered whether the use of *keheryn* rather than *kern* points to speech-habits more heavily conditioned by the use of Irish. Whereas a bilingual might habitually reproduce the Irish form, a monoglot English speaker might assimilate it on first hearing to his native syllable structure.

The final syllable of *keheryn* (and *keperin*) contains an epenthetic vowel not marked in traditional Irish spelling. Svarabhakti is characteristic of Modern Irish, though between /r/ and /n/ confined to the southern dialects.[50] I have no MHE examples of it with /rn/ of Germanic or Romance origin, but spellings like *harym* 'harm', *ferym* 'farm', *terym*, 'term', are not uncommon. For the vowels of unaccented syllables in MHE, *i* and *y* are by far the commonest spellings, and need not reflect the particular quality of the Irish vowel, which in the modern dialects is generally [ə].

MHE *keryn* and congeners derive either from metathesised *ceithrenn* /k'ehr'en'/, or from forms with svarabhakti (by loss of intervocalic /h/).

walke (17, 33) vb. '(walk), patrol'

This is clearly *walk* in the sense of *OED* v.[1] II.11 'go on foot in procession, to go in a regular circuit or to and fro over a prescribed track in the course of official duty'. Examples are given from 1594 onwards, including one from Spenser's *Present State of Ireland* (1596): 'The sheriff of the shire, whose peculiar office it is to walke continuallye up and downe his baly-wick . . . to snatch up all those runnagates . . . The sheriff may doe therin what he can, and yet the marshall may walke his course besides' — the second instance illustrating the cognate accusative, as in line 13 of the Statutes. This may be an unusually early example of the usage, but until the relevant part of *MED* appears, the matter remains doubtful. Note that in line 33, *walke* is apparently contrasted with *go*, and 'proceed on foot' is unlikely to be intended.

vrlawus (19) sb. '?forced loan, requisition, fine; ?rising-out'

The word has not otherwise been recorded in English, and is absent

---

[50] O'Rahilly, *Irish Dialects*, pp. 199 – 200; cf. Ó Cuív, *Irish of West Muskerry*, § 321, and Breatnach, *Irish of Ring*, § 516.

from the dictionaries. McNeill, cited by Curtis (p. 99), referred it to Ir. *urlámhas* or *forlámhas* 'authority, power'. For Middle Irish, see now *RIA Dict.*, s.v. *forlamus* 'supremacy, sway, domination' (the lenition of *m* — *mh* — is not marked by the spelling); the prefixes *ur-* and *for-* interchange (cf. Dinneen, s.v. *uir-*). Formally, *vrlawus* could represent MIr. *urlámhus* /urla:wus/ unaltered in pronunciation: MIr. *mh*, whether palatal or non-palatal, is normally rendered by MHE *w* in the southern dialects.

Contextually, however, the reading 'authority' is not persuasive. The preceding clauses in the same statute prohibit kernety from walking the country and spending the people, and the mere fact of these prohibitions makes clear that kernety are not invested with an independent authority. To follow this by prohibiting kernety from setting up authority is pointless: if *vrlawus* means 'authority', it must be some special authority for a particular and further end. The dictionaries give no indication that MIr. *urlámhus* was so used.[51] Moreover, a progression from the particular (*spen*) to the general ('set up authority') is out of place in a legal formulation: the natural continuity is either a qualification of *spen*, or treatment of some related and similarly restricted category.

Accordingly, *vrlawus* may be better traced to OIr. *airlámas*, 'custody, possession: *sequestratio*' (*RIA Dict.*, s.v.). The base, *airlám*, means likewise 'custody, possession'; it occurs also in the set legal phrase *airlám choitchend*, 'handing over of a pledge to a third (neutral) party or authority'. The Old Irish suffix *-as* (regularly *-us* in Middle Irish) is nominal and abstract, denoting the quality of being the thing specified, and OIr. *air-* appears commonly as *ur-* in Middle Irish.[52] MIr. *urlámhus*, therefore, could well represent OIr. *airlám* + *-as*. Mod.Ir. *urlámhas* combines both sets of senses, 'authority, power' and 'possession, custody, sequestation' (Dinneen, *Dictionary*, s.v.), and as much may be supposed for late MIr. *urlámhus*.

The expression *rere vrlawus* still admits various interpretations. The verb is Mod.E. *rear*, probably in the sense 'levy, raise, gather, collect

[51] Mr Nicholls (pers. comm.) suggests that the Irish word is by this date a technical term, though its meaning is unclear. *Urlámhas* was an authority that could be delegated, as appears from the *Annals of Connacht* 1310.6 and the *Annals of Ulster* ii, 462: Turlough O Connor, king of Connacht, gave the *urlámhas* of Uí Maine to Teig O Kelly, which seemingly established O Kelly as a lord. (References from Professor Donnchadh Ó Corráin, via Mr Nicholls.) Obviously this cannot be the same authority as that exercised by the kernety, who are merely instruments of the lord's will; Mr Nicholls suggests that the authority to keep order and punish wrongdoers may be intended.
[52] Thurneysen, *Grammar*, §§ 261 and 823.

(fines, rents, etc.)' as *rear* v.[1] III.14.a in *OED*. On one reading, the statute provides that no kernety except the lord's kernety are to patrol the country; that no kernety except the lord's are to spend the people; and that requisitioning of supplies, outwith what is understood by 'spending', is likewise forbidden to any kernety save the lord's. Against this, it can be objected that the exactions covered by *spending* are not well-defined, or at any rate are not known to be, and that a residual category 'other requisitioning' is therefore ill-founded. The objection is cogent, but we simply do not know enough about the participants' expectations in order to judge. On another reading, the statute relates to the collection of fines, well within the 'ministration of justice' described in the later accounts of kernety's proper employment.[53]

Whatever the precise meaning, it should cohere with the 16th-century rehearsals of kernety's legitimate and traditional powers. The present statute prohibits certain actions to kernety in general, and reserves them to the earl of Ormond's own, and it is to this order that the Tipperary freeholders of 1542 appealed.

sys-honys, sysen (20, 21) sb. '(court) session(s)'

The *OED* record (s.v. *session* sb.) is surprisingly patchy. As 'sessions of the peace', the word is attested from 1386 on, but in the more general judicial sense there is only one mediaeval example (senses 4.a,b). As 'a sitting together of a number of persons (esp. of a court . . .) for conference or the transaction of business' (sense 2), the word is cited from the rolls of parliament, 1444, but the next example is dated 1564. In explicitly parliamentary usage (sense 3.b), the earliest source is from 1577, but the present Statutes invite just that comparison by the wording of lines 23 – 4. However the MHE instances are classified, they appear to provide useful additional information on mediaeval usage.

The forms, though not among *OED*'s collection, are unremarkable in a MHE text. Raising of /ɛ/ to /i/ is indicated frequently by spellings with *i*

---

[53] Conceivably, *vrlawus* corresponds to the OIr. adj. *airlam*, with nominal *-as*, so '(persons in the condition of being) ready, willing to do something' (cf. *RIA Dict.*, s.v.). *Rere vrlawus* would then be 'summon (military) forces', perhaps 'proclaim the rising-out': this general summons of able-bodied men to serve at the lord's command was both a feudal and Gaelic institution (see further, D. B. Quinn and K. W. Nicholls, 'Ireland in 1534'; being chapter 1 (pp. 1 – 38) of *A New History of Ireland* iii [*Early Modern Ireland 1534 – 1691*], ed. T. W. Moody, F. X. Martin, and F. J. Byrne [Oxford, 1976], p. 31). Proclaiming it could well have fallen within the policing activities of kernety, and is not very different from the arrangement recommended by John Alen, master of the rolls in Ireland, in 1537: 'It is also necessary to have in every paryshe 2 connestables, whiche shall rere oute, and bring all the hable men of the same unto the said capytaynes, to be orderid by them for the defence of the countre . . .' (*State Papers* ii, p. 482). Cf. *OED rear* v.[1] III.14.b, 'raise troops' (ca. 1400 – 50).

and *y*, though it seems to be sporadic, both regionally and lexically. Comparable spellings are found in Hiberno-Latin.

hole (24) vb. 'hold'.

horssyn (35) sb. pl. 'horses'

For this word, pl. *-yn* is not uncommon in MHE, even in late texts. Similar forms are found in Middle English (see *MED* s.v. *hors*), apparently generalised from the late Old English dat. pl. *-an*. The pl. is irregular in various words relating to livestock; analogy with *ox/oxen* may have reinforced the weak suffix here.

knawys (35) sb. pl. 'boys, attendants, servants'

The MHE spelling with *w* for historical /v/ is characteristic. Horses and boys are regularly listed in accounts of billeting (see, e.g., the résumé in *State Papers* ii, pp. 510 – 12).

connyw (35) sb., 'coynye, billeting'

The institution as known in early modern Ireland is described by John Dymmok (1600): 'a placinge of men and boyes upon the cuntrye, vsed by a prerogatyve of the Brehon law, whereby they are permitted to take meate, drinke, aqua vitae and money of their hostes, without paye-makinge therefore'.[54] The adoption of coynye in the *terre engleis* became a serious abuse, the subject of variously ineffective legislation.[55] Its pervasiveness may be judged from an ordinance of 1534, 'that no gentylman (saufe only marchers) dwellynge within the Englyshe pale, goinge with the Kinges Deputie through the same, take no coyne ne lyverie with in the sayde Inglishe pale, duringe that tyme; but to be upon their owne costes, comynge and goinge' (*State Papers* ii, p. 208).

OED gives Ir. *coinnemh* [koin^yeṽ] as the etymon for *coynye* (s.v.), but erroneously:[56] rather, the English forms represent Ir. *coinnmheadh* in the pronunciations *coinní* or *cuinní*, which are the regular Munster developments. *OED*'s first citation is from 1449; *MED* has *coyngez* pl. from a French text of ca. 1407 (s.v. *coigne*), with normal F *gn/ng* for the palatalised nasal (here, Ir. /n'/).

Phonemically, *coinnmheadh* had short /o/ in the first syllable, but with an allophonic [i]-glide to palatal /n'/ following. Such glide vowels vary in their prominence.[57] *Coinnmheadh* is anglicised regularly with *oi* or *oy* for Ir. /o/, which vowel is therefore identified with early Mod.E. /ɔɪ/ or /ʊɪ/; Spenser records that some people have supposed the word to

---

[54] Cited by T. F. O'Rahilly, 'Varia II', *Celtica* 1 (1950), 328 – 386 (see 370); cf. *OED* s.v.

[55] For some account, see Empey and Simms, 'Ordinances of the White Earl', esp. pp. 178 – 83.

[56] Cf. O'Rahilly, 'Varia II', p. 370.

[57] Cf. Breatnach, *Irish of Ring*, §§ 274 – 293.

be the English *coin*.[58] Forms like *connyw*, with simple *o* in the first syllable, have not hitherto been noted from (M)HE sources. (They are, however, regular in Middle Scots: see *DOST* s.v. *conveth*.) To *connyw* can be added *connue*, from NLI D 1766 (*Cal. Ormond Deeds* iii, no. 203), an indenture dated 1457, of uncertain local origin within the Butler lordship (?Co. Kilkenny): 'no man to Charge them w^t enny man*er* of Charges of the Countree of ȝewyng & ȝyldyng connue . . .'

Professor Gillies (pers. com.) suggests that the proximate source of *connyw* is *coinneamh*, simplified and metathesised from *coinnmheadh*;[59] this is the type assumed by *OED* as the etymon for *coynye*. Ir. *mh* was vocalised by this date, and is identified regularly with MHE *w*; but *-nyw* perhaps represents an identification of morphemes rather than of phonemes, for it is sometimes the spelling of 'new' in the southerly MHE dialects.[60]

awarle (36) prep. 'overall'
Curtis (p. 99) notes that the form is 'curious' and that 'possibly it is for *ower all*'. This is clearly what the context requires, and efforts to explain the form otherwise have led nowhere. *Awarle* is recorded only from the Statutes, and it may have been a purely local development. The following history is possible.

MHE *oweral(l)* was the base, with characteristic /w/ from proto-MHE /v/; simplex *ower* is amply attested. *Ower-* was then reduced to *owr-*: compare the reduction of *over* to *o'er* in dialects which otherwise preserve medial /v/, and *our-al* among *MED*'s variants (s.v. *over-al*). Disyllabic *owral* was stressed on the second syllable. That may have been the original accentuation, though *EDD*'s account of such compounds suggests not (s.v. *over*, prep.). Rather, accommodation to the stress pattern of southern Irish is likely. In Old Irish, the first syllable was strongly accented, save in certain compounds. This pattern is preserved by the dialects of the Northern Half, but in the south, the accent was shifted to the second syllable whenever that syllable was long; the shift belongs to the period ca. 1200 – 1550. That it affected the MHE dialects of the south appears from Stanyhurst's description of

[58] *View of the Present State of Ireland*, p. 34 of 1970 edn.
[59] Cf. O'Rahilly, 'Varia II', p. 370.
[60] *nyw(e)* 'new': Kilkenny Corporation, *Liber Primus*, entries of temp. Henry VII – VIII; British Libr. Harley 3765, Register of St Saviour's Chantry, Waterford, f. 11r, 1466; London, PRO SC 1/51/153, letter of Thomas Comyn, Limerick, 1508 or after; Waterford Corporation, *Liber Secundus* f. 204r – v, 8 – 12 Henry VIII. Cf. *tryw(e)* 'true': London, PRO E 101/248/19, indenture dated at Youghal, Co. Cork, 1495; PRO SC 1/52/70, letter of James Butler, in the hand of a Kiltenan (Tipperary) scribe, 1499.

Wexford English (1577), confirmed by 19th-century reports.[61] *Owral*, with a long vowel in the second syllable, conformed to southern Irish speech habits only if *-al* bore the accent. From *owrál* to *owárl* is then a plausible enough metathesis, though it cannot be paralleled in MHE so far as I know; but metathesis is a sporadic and unpredictable phenomenon.[62] The replacement of *o-* by *a-* is then analogical: prefixed *a-* is well established in MHE generally (*a-bout*, *a-bove*, *a-fore*, *a-mong*, *a-pon*) but *o-* is uncommon, and in the southern dialects hardly to be found. The final *-e* is unhistorical, and a normal feature of MHE spelling.

It is not impossible, however, that *a-* in *awarle* is original from the MHE point of view. *MED* records *aure* 'over' as north-west Midland, with citations from the Fairfax *Cursor Mundi* (Lancaster) and the Towneley Plays (*awre*). Theobald Botiller, founder of the Ormond line, held lands in Amounderness, that is, Lancashire between the Ribble and the Cocker; it is likely that the tenantry of his Irish lordships was drawn partly from that area. There are one or two elements in the MHE of Co. Tipperary, not found in southern MHE generally, that could well be of north-west Midland origin. *Awarle* is perhaps of their number.

galloglass. *OED*'s earliest attestation of the word is as a distributive pl. *galloglasseis* from a text of ca. 1515, *State of Ireland, and Plan for it's Reformation*. Probably a decade earlier is its appearance in a letter to the absentee earl of Ormond from Edmond Goldyng, a man of old settler stock. The letter is dated at Drogheda; the year is torn away, but the contents indicate ca. 1500 – 1506.[63] Goldyng describes the decay of the land about him, and the continual encroachment of Irishry on the English Pale. 'And .y. Mylord', he continues, 'y ham an Englishe Man', anxious of a future when 'shal cu*m* ahorse Man and Agalleglaighe in my stede' (PRO SC 1/58/66, cited from MS). The interest of this occurrence lies not in the antedating of *OED*'s citation, for that is trivial, but in the morphology.

The Middle Irish word is *gall-óglach*, amply attested in a variety of sources from the thirteenth century onwards. The nom. and acc. pl. is usually *gall-óglacha* (fem. *ā* declension), sometimes *gall-óglóich* (masc. *o* declension). *OED* notes that 'the etymologically correct form *galloglagh* appears later than the erroneous *galloglass*, which was prob.

---

[61] See further O'Rahilly, *Irish Dialects*, pp. 83 – 98, of which the foregoing is a summary; and Bliss, *Spoken English in Ireland*, pp. 194 – 198.

[62] Metathesis of /r/, associated with the southern accent shift, is reported by Breatnach (*Irish of Ring*, § 560), though the examples involve /r/ in the unstressed syllable: the sequence C/r/V > CV/r/. Similar examples are noted by Ó Cuív (*Irish of West Muskerry*, §§ 418 – 21).

[63] So D. B. Quinn, in *Cal. Ormond Deeds* iv, where the text is printed on pp. 356 – 358.

the result of the pl. *gallogla(gh)s*; in some early instances *galloglas* seems to be used as a pl.; but *galloglasses* is found already in our earliest quot.' It is unclear how far the *galloglagh*-variants listed at the head of the article are merely inferred from attestations of the *galloglaghes*-type: the only certain illustration is from Martin Martin's *Description of the Western Islands of Scotland* (1703). Otherwise the account is somewhat confused by failure to distinguish between the singulative, the collective pl., and the distributive pl.

The *State Papers* provide numerous examples of the word in documents mainly of Irish origin, from the period ca. 1515 – 1546. The following notes depend on a scanning guided mainly by the index; these volumes, which the *OED* contributor seems not to have read very closely, await a more detailed investigation elsewhere. All citations, unless otherwise stated, are from documents which, on the evidence of their morphology and spelling, are by Hiberno-English hands.

(1) *galloglagh*. In Robert Cowley's letter of 1537 appears *galloglagh*, from the context clearly singulative: 'there is noo Yryshman of war, horsman, kernagh, ne galloglagh . . .' (ii.450). This, with Goldyng's *galleglaighe*, is simply Ir. *gall-óglach* in anglicised spelling: the spoken equivalents need not have differed.[64]

(2) *galloglaghes* is a pl., either collective or distributive. Apparently distributive is an example from the *State of Ireland*, missed by *OED*: 'the wylde Iryshe, with all ther galloglagheis, and Iryshe Scottes, called keteryns' (ii.25). Cowley's letter of 1537 provides perhaps better illustration: 'Galloglaghes are noon other but as a kynde of sowchyn-ners' (ii.448). Collective usage appears in the *Report on Ireland* addressed to Henry VIII (1534): '10 scor spearys, callid gallagloghis; which 10 score sparris amountith to 20 score men' (ii.185). Seven instances of the type were noted, four from Cowley (ii.448). The usage in this text is clearly *galloglagh* sgv., *galloglaghes* coll. and distr. pl., which bears out *OED*'s derivation of *galloglass*. The coll. pl. could be reinterpreted as a sgv., whence a new pl., overtly distr., is formed by adding *-es*; this in turn reinforces the sgv. use of *gallogla(ghe)s*, and

---

[64] Goldyng's *-aigh* is not evidence for a palatalised final consonant. Rather, *i* is associated with vowel length, as in *boithe* 'both' from the same text; other writers of the same period and from Goldyng's area use *i* sporadically in this way. The final vowel of MIr. *óglach* is short, though in the anglicised form it could have been lengthened by absorbtion of /x/. On the other hand, it is possible that Goldyng's *-aigh* interprets distinctive vowel quality in an unstressed syllable as length: whereas the dialects of Connacht and Munster have /-əx/ for *-ach*, those of Ulster and North Meath preserve the original /-ɑx/ (O'Rahilly, *Irish Dialects*, p. 109).

galloglagh disappears. Certainly *galloglasses* presupposes *galloglass* as a sgv.

As a pl. marker, *-es* cannot be of Irish origin, but morphologically it may be more complicated than appears. It could represent the abstract nominal suffix OIr. *-as*, MIr. *-us*: to OIr. *óclach* corresponds *óclachas*, 'the condition of being an *óclach*'. For this noun, *RIA Dict.* records, *inter alia*, the senses 'quality or functions of a warrior' and 'service, vassalage' (s.v.); *gall-óclachus* is cited from the *Annals of the Four Masters* (s.v. *gall*), in the sense 'leadership of galloglasses'. It is possible that confusion of the coll. pl. with the sgv. was hastened by these forms.

(3) *galloglas*. Fourteen examples noted, from twelve texts though perhaps only nine hands. No sgv. uses appear; most are coll. pl. So '18 baners of galoglas, which bee comonly in every baner 80 men' (1520, ii.46), 'all galoglasse and kerne' (1546, iii.584). It is questionable how reliably coll. and distr. pls. can be distinguished from one another.[65] Arguably, a preceding numeral settles the matter; but 'twoo hundreth galloglasse' (1544, iii.502) could as well be construed 'two hundred *of* galloglass', like 'two hundred infantry' — 'two hundred infantries', if indeed it can be used at all, is not the same as 'two hundred infantrymen'. The ending *-asse* is not obviously pl.; *-es* is so, but the sgv. *gallogle* implied by '2 battail of gallogles' (1538, iii.54) is unrecorded. In 'well warded with gunners, galowglas, and horsemen' (1536, ii.351) the flanking nouns imply a distr., but it may be coll. A letter from Cowley, dated 1539, has '800 galoglas, and so many kerne' (iii.146); this form is grammatically equivalent to *galloglaghes* of his 1537 letter, but the hands may not be the same, and it is so far uncertain whether these forms were co-variants in the same idiolect.

(4) *galloglasses*, in virtue of its morphology, is distr. pl. almost by definition. Even so, the individual members of the plurality need be no more clearly focussed in '500 galloglasseis' (1515, ii.5) and 'two batell of gallowglassheis' (1537), ii.490) than in the equivalent constructions with *galloglas*: semantically, they could as well be coll. pls. as distr. or compositional. In some cases, no doubt, the distr. or comp. aspect was indeed at issue; and once the *-glas* type was regularly sgv. as well as coll. pl., the *-glasses* type was the only explicit rendering. The ambivalence inherent in ordinary usage is neatly pointed by a Latin indenture between the lord deputy and Odonell: 'cum . . . [centum et viginti] . . . Scoticis, alias galoglas' (1541, iii.318) restates an overt pl. as a grammatical sg., for *galogla* is unrecorded.

---

[65] Cf. H. W. Fowler, *A Dictionary of Modern English Usage* (Oxford, 2nd edn, 1965), s.v. number 6.

The *-glas(s)heis* spelling seems not to have been noted hitherto. The occurrences are as follows: Justice Luttrells Booke 1537 (ii.503, 506, and twice on 507; beside *-glasseis* ii.502, 503, and 506); J. Alen to Sentleger 1537 (ii.490, beside *galloglasse* (coll.) ibid.) Here, medial *s(s)h* may reflect the sporadic [ʃ] for [s] characteristic in 16th-century and later Hiberno-English;[66] but in view of the absence of any other *s(s)h* for historical *s(s)* in these texts, origins in Ir. palatalised /x'/, from *gall-óglaóich* (see above, p. 64), are rather to be sought. Professor Gillies (pers. com.) notes that Goidelic /x'/ is sporadically identified as English /ʃ/ all along the Gaelic-English interface; in *gall-óglaóich*, the palatal quality of *-ch* is the more prominent by contrast with the preceding velarised group.

Postscript.
An earlier instance of 'galloglass(-)' than any cited above emerges in checking the proofs of this article: my linguistic analysis of John O'Carroll's letter, PRO SC 1/52/37 (see p. 45 above), notes the form *Gyllaglasses*. Evidently the word qualifies for inclusion in the intended supplement to *MED*.

---

[66] For discussion see Bliss, *Spoken English in Ireland*, pp. 233 – 8.

ADAM'S DILEMMA: A NOTE ON THE EARLY NAMING OF KINDS AT THE CAPE

Jean Branford

And out of the ground the Lord God formed every beast of the field, and every fowl of the air; and brought them unto Adam to see what he would call them: and whatsoever Adam called every living creature that was the name thereof

Genesis II, 19.

Naming has always been a problematical exercise and full of pitfalls. One has witnessed the deliberations of parents, trying to compromise between their own tastes and family expediency, which often result in disastrous sets of initials like B.R.A., W.C. or J.A.W., which can cause lifelong embarrassment. Taxonomists, on the other hand, unlike, parents, have simply to identify family, genus and species without a care for Aunt Maud's feelings, add perhaps an *-ensis* tag to locate the creature, and their deed is done. If the popular name of the animal should become in time in vernacular parlance *kommetjiegatkat* ('a cat with a basin-shaped vent') when they called it *Atilax paludinosus* (marsh mongoose) and its relation, with which it tends to be classed together, *Mayonax pulverulentus* (the grey Cape mongoose), that is no problem of theirs.

One can imagine a mythical Adam, with the Lord God watching over his shoulder, confronted by his queue of candidates for names recoiling as the forbears of the Gadarene swine waddled into sight, with distaste and an expressive 'Cha![1] Chazer!'[2] and the beast was named. 'Next please . . .'

When the Dutch first set foot on the Southern tip of Africa to establish a victualling station and colony for the Dutch East India Company, they were faced like Adam with a brave new world of flora and fauna. Unlike Adam, however, they were not culture-free with a clean slate to start off

---

[1] 'Ga' /xa/ a South African expression of extreme disgust.
[2] Hebrew: pig /'xazə/

with, for long experience, both in Europe and the East, had been at work in many of them. Some of what they saw was partially familiar, some of it totally unfamiliar and some, clearly, completely bewildering.

Even the little brown people found there didn't have a proper name. Earlier travellers and passers-by at the Cape of Storms had called them Hottentots, Hadmadods, Hotantots, Hottentods, Hatten-totes, Hodman-dods — all manner of strange names thought by later scholarship[3] to be onomatopoeic attempts to reflect repeated phrases in the songs they sometimes sang, since the name they used for themselves was found two centuries later to be *Khoi-Khoin* 'men of men'.

As Van Riebeeck later learned, the 'Ottentoos', as he called them, consisted of many different peoples with unpronounceable names like Charingourinas, Chibonars, Chainoquas and Gorachauquas, all of whom were a severe strain on his spelling. In his *Daghregister*[4] or journal he named them, greatly simplifying the issue, Kaepmans (Cape people); Vismans (fishing people); Watermans (water, 'boat'? people); Saldanhers or Saldaniers (people from further north near Saldanha Bay); Strand-lopers (beach nomads); and with slightly more edge, Tabacqdieven (tobacco thieves) and Daggamakers (cultivators presumably of dagga, *Cannabis sativa*). A settlement of one of these peoples or clans he described as a *leg(g)er* — the forerunner of the term *laager* known world-wide today — usually in its figurative sense of a politically protective environment.

He had heard tell through other travellers of 'Herry die Ottento die Engelss spreeckt' (Harry the Hottentot who speaks English) and mentioned him in his journal on 7.4.1652, the day after he had landed at the Cape. As his only go-between with the many local tribes — for cattle-trading was a primary essential — 'Herry' (as they were apparently convinced he was named) proved to be a most tiresome and equivocal character. So much so indeed that Van Riebeeck wrote wistfully (24.11.1652) of the desirability of dropping Herry and all his family on ''t Robben Eiland',[5] seven months having sufficed to exhaust his patience. He was to write in some exasperation several years later of Herry (13.5.1656) 'een slime gast . . . van dagh to dagh noch al slimmer ende erghlistiger worden' ('a wily fellow, from day to day becoming wilier and worse').

Naturally at that stage the main preoccupations of the colonists were those of day-to-day survival and ensuring future supplies. The latter they

---

[3] *The word 'Hottentot'*: articles extracted from the *Transactions of the Philological Society*, London, 1886.

[4] Jan Anthonisz van Riebeeck, *Daghregister* (1652 – 1662), Van Riebeeck Society, I (1952), II (1955), III (1957).

[5] Robben (Seals) Island.

would be called upon to provide for victualling 'Jan Compagnie's' ships, from cattle trading 'assisted' by Herry and from raising crops from the precious seeds — wheat, barley, rye and vegetables — which they had brought with them. But crops were going to take time in this soil and climate, and were not going to keep them or their slaves fed. Even more precious were the 'wingerd stokke' (vine cuttings) which were lovingly cultivated. One of the most joyful of the entries in Van Riebeeck's *Daghregister* is that of 2.2.1659 'Heeden is Gode loff van de Kaepse druyven d'eerste mael wijn geparst' ('Today, God be praised, wine was pressed for the first time from the Cape grapes').

Naturally enough, the first things to which they gave names were those on which they subsisted.

For primary survival they fell to fishing with a will, catching *harders* or *herders* (mullet) and *steenbrassems* (stone bream), and occasionally something similar to 'haringh', the true herring sacred to the Dutch, for salting, drying and for immediate consumption.

Their names were very much hit and miss, chosen for some imagined likeness to the familiar European species. One party for example caught what they described as *see-snoeckjens*, the *see* being added as the *snoeck* of Holland is the freshwater pike, which has just such terrifying teeth and snapping jaws as the *snoek* of the Cape. *Snoek* remains to this day the name of this typically South African fish. Another party, however, encountered a freshwater fish they called *barmer*, possibly a barbel, which they described as being 'graetachtich gelijck de Hollandse snoek' ('bony like the pike of Holland'). The spiny marine crustacean (French *langouste*) sometimes called 'Cape rock lobster' had something in common with the lobster of Europe (French *homard*, Dutch *kreeft*), and was accordingly called *kreeft*. The term *kreef* is still fully in use, though the even less accurate *crayfish* (from French *écrevisse*, the freshwater crayfish) is more often used in English. Another fish named for the same good reason, similarly, was *kabeljauw* (cod), the name we still use, often abbreviated to *kob* or *cob*. It is a Sciaeanid fish of a totally different order and family from that of the Northern hemisphere cod (Gadidae family) which has no true Southern hemisphere relative, except the Merlucciidae we call erroneously *stockfish*. Dutch *stockvisch*, a basic staple, was salted dried cod, similar to the *bacalao* or *morue* of the Mediterranean countries, which they brought in quantity with them.

Fish they fortunately had in abundance, and the shoaling of the *harders* and the *marsbanker* (mackerel) kept hunger at bay, but the slaves had to be fed too, and no edible opportunity could be overlooked. So, a less attractive thought, the colonists went after the black cormorants which they called simply *duyckers* (divers, a name later to be given as well to small and very agile antelopes), which they salted down, and whose eggs they likewise gathered to vary their diet.

The small brown rock hyrax which frequented the Cape, and which swarmed over a not too distant island, reminded them of the *das* or badger of Europe, if a little undersized, and the *dasje*, 'little badger', was hunted also, for preserving and for the ever-ready pot. These were considered a delicacy even at a later period[6] and boats were sent to Dassen Eilandt, as they called it, to bring them back in hundreds. Today we still call them *dassies*, usually in happy ignorance of the fact that most of us have never been nearer a real *das* than *The Wind in the Willows*.

Van Riebeeck on the whole was enthusiastic about the quality of the fish at the Cape and described them on several occasions as being as 'sweet and delicate as those of the Fatherland' — even if some other fish furnished his 'schoonste pekel-haringh' (24.2.1654).

One not mentioned by him, I think, was called the *springer* by many later settlers and travellers. The name 'springer', now dropped from the latest taxonomies, was given from the early days to various species from the 'skipjack' or 'tenpounder' *Elops machnatus* — inaccurately known as 'Cape Salmon', as, alas, South Africa has no salmon — to the humble estuarine mullet known even today by its Dutch name *harder*. Lady Anne Barnard wrote of the 'springer' (probably of the *harder*) 'Admirable! It is a fish that would make the fortune of anyone that could convey it by spawn to England';[7] while Captain Robert Percival, with possibly a more capricious digestion, wrote '. . . the springer, a flat fish of a heavy, fat luscious quality, particularly well adapted for the palate of a Dutchman'.[8] It was the same Captain Percival who was to write a comprehensive and probably better justified description of the poor quality of Cape beef, noting particularly its stringiness and lack of fat.

The earliest colonists, possibly shown by the Strandlopers or by Herry himself, found certain edible and even palatable wild vegetables, including *suiringh* (sorrel) roots and bulbs. Later travellers described some of these, when roasted, as tasting like chestnuts, but the Dutch called them *uintjes* (little bulbs) probably from *ajuin(tje)* onion, though many of these *uintjes* were species of *Moraea* and not, it is thought, of the Allium family to which onions, leeks and garlic belong. Another, which they called *anijswortel* (anise root), was probably the enlarged root of the wild fennel *Foeniculum vulgare* (now often called *vinkel*

---

[6] T. Phillips, *Scenes and Occurrences in Albany and Cafferland* (1827) '. . . das or coney. This little creature seems to be of a species between the rabbit and the guineapig and is esteemed good eating . . . the flesh is white, but from its paws resembling those of a cat it is not inviting'.

[7] *Letters and Journals* (1797 – 1801).

[8] *Account of the Cape of Good Hope* (1804).

with an initial /f/ sound), which grows wild over much of the Cape and produces a delicious seed far more fragrant than carraway or aniseed, used locally in cookery by Indians, by whom it is known as *sauf* or *saunf*.

As far as the rest of the animal and vegetable kingdoms went, Van Riebeeck and his people — not forgetting Adam — had to make a start, and in many cases the names they bestowed on denizens of either tended to be just as 'approximative' as those given to their various articles of diet. If there was any resemblance or fancied resemblance to a European or even Far Eastern species — bearing in mind that many came from the Dutch East Indies — the name of that species tended to be adopted without question.

Not long after his arrival (18.9.1652) Van Riebeeck wrote of 'rechte boomen', 'real trees', which they found on Table Mountain 'bynae als essen ende boekenhout' ('almost like ash and beech'). Today we use *essenhout* and *boekenhout*, as well as *kershout* (cherry), *wit-* or *rooi-els* (white or red alder) of our trees, without considering that none of these is indigenous to Africa.

The woodcutters of the Company, who founded a timber station near Knysna, used descriptive names: *geelhout* (yellowwood), *stinkhout* (smelly wood), *swarthout* (black wood), and so on. One type of yellowwood however became known (and still is) by the picturesque name of *Kalander*, a corruption of 'Outeniekwalander' (one from Outeniqualand). 'Outenikwa' is said to mean 'honey-bees', the Khoi name of the Outeniqua mountains behind the forests. So much was the *geelhout* abused by reckless cutting, that as early as 12.10.1658 a 'placaat' (edict) for the protection of this timber was issued.

The Malay word *kajaten* (*kaju*, timber, teak) in the form *kiaat* exists today for a teak-like local wood, and in Van Riebeeck's journal (9.9.1656) there is even a reference to *groen ebbenhout* (green ebony, which he hopes will be sturdy and durable), also surely a case of mistaken identity with the ebony of the East.

The Eastern element was a very real one, and one of the longest-living 'misnomers' has been *tijger* (Afrikaans *tier*) which one still occasionally hears used today of a leopard, and which certainly lives on in plant- and place-names such as *tierhout* (wood), *tierbekvygie* (var. of *Mesembryanthemum*), *Tiervlei* (lake), and *Tierhoek* (corner). The fact that the big patterned cats they found at the Cape had spots rather than stripes bothered them not at all, although their depredations among their hard-won livestock did, quite intensely.

On one of their expeditions into the mountains they found a dead animal, probably a baboon, which they were hungry enough to eat. Van Riebeeck described it as a 'bosmanneken' (24.4.1654), an almost exact reversed translation of the Malay *ōrang* (man) *ūtan* (forest).[9]

One of the strangest and most unaccountably inappropriate names chosen in the early days is *meerkat*. It is used all over South Africa (*meerkat* or *meercat*) for various suricate mammals. Frederick Boyle[10] later described them: '. . . meercat . . . Of these animals there are several kinds, only to be classed together by their habit of living in holes upon the veldt and standing on hind legs to survey the prospect in a very droll manner'.

Meerkat, however, according to *Van Dale's Groot Woordenboek der Nederlandse Taal*, is an *ape* (Cercopithecus) found in its natural state in North Africa and Gibraltar.[11] By what wild flight of imagination could the Dutch seafarers' term for a Barbary ape have been dreamed of for numerous inquisitive varieties of mongoose, or by what anomaly can it have survived to become a household word, — for which there is no substitute — at the other end of the African Continent?

Of the numerous varieties of buck and antelope Van Riebeeck wrote, as of the trees, with European names; *herten*, *hinden*, *ree(tjies)* (harts, hinds, and little roes) (18.9.1652), names which have not survived. But others did: *reebock* (roebuck) which he did use, and we use still in English and Afrikaans in the forms *rhebok*, *reebok*, and *ribbok*, and *steenbok* (ibex). Other early uses of European names are *eland* (elk) and *gems* (chamois), now *gemsbok*, which are in use today for two of the largest species of antelope. Neither has an English name.

One which seems to have truly undergone a sea change is *zeekoe* (sea-cow), a Dutch word for 'manatee' or walrus, which became used later in South Africa for the *hippopotamus* or 'river horse'. Well inland the term *seekoegat* is found in several places for a hippopotamus 'wallow'. Van Riebeeck described one specimen as 'een seer groote monstreuse zeekoe' ('a very great monstrous sea cow'; 26.10.1652) which was disporting itself in the bay, in this case probably a walrus. This is made likelier by a reference a month or so later (14.11.1652) to finding *zeekoe tanden* (teeth) possibly walrus tusks, on the beach. The other 'marine' puzzle is a southern right whale which he found beached on 2.3.1654, 'with reasonably thick blubber and much baleen' (whalebone),[12] and dubbed a *Noordkaper walvis* a 'north Cape whale' for no very clear reason.

A pleasing name just possibly attributable to Van Riebeeck or his people and which we find used in 1786[13] is *ystervark* (iron pig), which is

---

[9] The orangutan is not found in South Africa.
[10] *To the Cape for Diamonds* (1873).
[11] Translated.
[12] Translated.
[13] A. Sparrman, *Travels*, I, trans. G. Forster.

'porcupine'. It is also a Dutch word for a hedgehog, usually called *egel*, and one can only imagine the horrified Dutchman among the rattling quills deciding that it was a larger and more dangerous variety of the round prickly ball of ''t Vaderlandt'.

Another rather horrendous prehistoric-looking creature is the monitor lizard (*Varanus* spp.) which was called *leguaan*, apparently from the French *l'iguane*, *the iguana*, though there are almost certainly those who used the term *kaaiman* (from Spanish *cayman*, alligator) and this name survives even today in place names. George Thompson wrote about this apparent confusion as early as 1827[14] '. . . a tremendous ravine called the Kaayman's-gat (Crocodile's hole). This name it has probably received from being frequented by the leguaan, a species of amphibious lizard, growing to the length sometimes of six feet, but quite innoxious' — a necessary assurance, perhaps, since a *leguaan* (Afrikaans *likkewaan*) does look like a junior dragon.

Like real dragons, South Africa has no wolves, but to the first colonists whose hard-won and haggled-for herds were plagued not only by 'tijgers' but also by various hyenas, *wolf* was an entirely satisfactory term for these menacing creatures. Van Riebeeck even noted on 27.1.1653 that a wolf had that day seized its prey by the body within sight of a herdsman — a fair indication of their boldness. The name has not survived in English on its own, but is still found in compounds like *strandwolf* (beach wolf), *streepwolf* (striped wolf), and *aardwolf* (earth wolf, the maned jackal).

On 5.2.1656 Van Riebeeck bitterly complained that all the people were kept awake — 'out of sleep' as he put it — by the 'multitude of seacows, lions, tigers and other wild animals'.[15] Indeed predators were so great a problem that not long afterwards he issued a 'placaat' (edict) offering rewards 'for a lion caught or shot, 6, for a "tijger" or "wolff" 4 and a "lupert" 3 "ra van 8en" '[16] plus a goodly ration of Spanish wine and tobacco as an extra inducement (17.6.1656). It is from this placaat that the expression '*Lion and Tiger* money arose, and the custom of offering monetary rewards for killing vermin. It is curious that *lupert* should be listed on the placaat, and should be worthy of a smaller reward than a 'tijger'. In this connection, however, it is worth noting that on 11.11.1657 Van Riebeeck records that they caught a *boscat* (bush cat)[17] which he describes as being 'wel so groot als een redelijcke lupert' ('about as big as a reasonable (sized) leopard').

[14] *Travels and Adventures in Southern Africa*, I (1827).
[15] Translated.
[16] Translated. Presumably 'pieces of eight'.
[17] Glossed by the Editors of the *Daghregister* in 1952 as *Felis serval*.

There is no native pheasant either, but Van Riebeek wrote on 29.7.1653 listing the 'wilt' (game) he had seen: *harten, hinden, reetjies, steenbocken, elanden, bergeenden* (mountain ducks), *patrijsen* (patridges), *phaisanten* (pheasants) . . . *dassen* (hyraxes) ende *hasen* (hares). Another curious, unexplained entry records his seeing on 21.3.1658 'seer schone groot paerden in 't wilt' ('very beautiful big horses in the wild state'). 'Pheasant' (Afrikaans *fisant*) is still used today for various francolins and was regularly used by the early travellers. One Englishman, 'N. Polson' (a Captain Nicholson), remarked '. . . a bird styled a pheasant, though about as like a pheasant of England as a Dutch boer is to a Bond Street beau'.[18]

Another name probably also originally from the Dutch of the East Indies for a high stepping 'beau' of a bird was *pauw* (Afrikaans *pou*), peacock, which was applied to various species of bustard (Otidae family) including some of the smaller ones also called *korhaan*. These were found highly palatable by those lucky enough to shoot them, including Rider Haggard who mentions them in *King Solomon's Mines* (1895). George Thompson too wrote of 'the pouw', which is a sort of large bustard and very delicate eating, and 'the koraan, a smaller sort of bustard much prized by epicures'.[19]

Something not prized by epicures, including the already mentioned Captain Percival, was the Cape beef, which early earned itself the name of 'trek ox', being as tough and tasteless as a thin and worn-out draught animal. C. Norris Newman commented upon the Boers getting 'a profusion of good beef . . . not like the trek-ox "Tommy Atkins" had to put up with'.[20] The Christmas Day Menu of 1899 during the siege of Ladysmith listed with wry English humour:

Entrees Nil. *Roti* Rosbif a l'Anglais (Trek ox).[21]

Horrid as it doubtless was, the beef was a far cry from the fishy *duyckers* (cormorants) and other strange comestibles (not forgetting the *bosmanneken*) which formed much of the diet of the first colonists, seeking sustenance of whatever kind they could. At quite an early stage, too (25.9.1652), Van Riebeeck noted down that their 'stockvis' was 'op' (stockfish was finished). This was, according to *Van Dale's Groot Woordenboek der Nederlandse Taal*, 'op stokken hard gedroogde visch', 'fish dried as hard as a board/stick etc.', and described as 'a sort of cod', 'eene soorte kabeljauwen (*gadus merluccius*)'.

These two names are of fish now regarded as belonging to different

---

[18] *A Subaltern's Sick Leave*, Bengal Military Orphan Press, Calcutta (1837).
[19] *Travels*, I.
[20] *With the Boers in the Transvaal* (1882).
[21] *The Ladysmith Lyre* (1899).

orders (Gadiformes and Perciformes) let alone different families, Gadidae and Sparidae. By a later linguistic twist, however, the commonest edible marine fish caught in Cape waters, *Merluccius capensis* and its deep water relation *M. paradoxus* were always called *stockfish* (perhaps meaning 'ordinary' or 'in regular supply'), but certainly the name had nothing to do with Van Riebeeck's staple, hard dried salt cod. In recent years the fish processing industry has adopted the term *hake*, as presumably more euphonious, and which appears on the English side of the packets. The Afrikaans side has *stokvis*.

When the colonists' crops for which virgin soil had had to be 'broken in', wheat, barley and rye, came up they had plenty of competition from 'rispe ende wormen' (caterpillars and worms) which were later recorded (27.11.1657) as having done 'veei quaet' (much harm). *Rusper* is still in use for destructive larvae of various kinds, whether they attack grazing veld or fruit trees.

Although they are not, I think, mentioned, there can be little doubt that the farming Free Burghers had trouble in plenty with small cheeky seed eaters, *musjes* (sparrows) from which our common term *mossie* has taken over from 'sparrow' in both English and Afrikaans.

James Ewart remarked of barley, wheat and rice at the Cape 'it has a great enemy in a small bird called the fink [cognate with finch] which perch upon it in flocks of several thousands. There are also great numbers of sprews and other larger birds'.[22] *Fink* (Africaans *vink*, weaver bird) and *spreeu* (starling) are still two of the commoner bird names in general use in English. Other seed eaters were more literally known as *koornvogels* (*koringvoels* 'corn birds) or *koornvreters*. These were described by William Burchell in his entry of 8 August 1811 '. . . a troublesome bird to farmers and deserving of the name they have given it of koornvreter (corn eater). It has very much the manners of the common sparrow of Europe'.[23]

By some strange linguistic lacuna the word *oranje*, so significant in Holland has been lost to the Afrikaans language (*lemoen* is an orange and a *suurlemoen* is a lemon), though Van Riebeeck did plant oranges for his prospective scurvy-ridden clients. He records on 18.7.1661 planting '1162 jonge orangie-, lemoen- ende pompelmoesboomen, 10 pisangh, 2 olijffen . . .' ('1162 young orange, lemon and grapefruit/shaddock trees (pompelmoesboomen), 10 bananas, 2 olives . . .'). Among the earlier seeds recorded as being planted (17.12.1652) were those of *water-limoenen* and *meloenen*, the first showing the metathesis still heard today in the name of a favourite traditional conserve, *waatlemoen*

---

[22] *Journal 1811 – 1814.*
[23] *Travels in Southern Africa*, I (1822).

konfyt, made of watermelon rind, which also contributes to the lasting confusion of *lemoen*.

The term *pompelmoes* is said to be from the Malay *pumpalmas* (shaddock), a term brought from the East Indies, from which the French word *pamplemousse* (grapefruit *or* shaddock) is derived. In South Africa *pomelo* (pomelo), which Dutch speakers in the far East heard used for the true shaddock, is the term used usually for a grapefruit proper.

To Van Riebeeck's own men, deprived as they were of much in the way of fresh food, what he described as 'wilde vijgen hier op de aerde wassende' ('wild figs growing here on the ground'; 9.1.1653) proved a tremendous temptation. What is still called a *sour fig* or *suurvy* is the fruit or seed pod of the large Mesembryanthemum *Carpobrotus edulis* (of which the Khoi name *ghokum* has also survived). It is eaten, sometimes candied, in many parts especially where it grows on the coastal sand dunes. It is totally unrelated to any fig but is slightly — very slightly — similar to a fig in shape.[24] Van Riebeeck was appalled by his men's lack of moderation in gorging (*gesnoeyt*) these '*wilde vijgen*'. He soon had large numbers of them suffering from diarrhoea which he called 'de loop' (which can only be translated as 'the trots').

As a ship's surgeon himself he regarded this as particularly reprehensible, and wrote mournfully ''t Is eene verdrietige saecke, dat t' gemeene volck soo roekeloos over haer eygen gesontheyt sijn ende geen maet weten te houden voordat met de neus in de coy raecken' ('It is a lamentable business that the common people should be so careless of their own health and know no sense of moderation before taking nose first to their beds').

The names of the three Eastern spices, *boreh* (Malay, turmeric, now widely called *borrie*), *saffraan* (Dutch form of *saffron*), and *rissie* (Malay, chilli) have been incorporated into various South African names. *Saffraan* was adopted for a yellow timbered tree (*Cassine crocea*) and *rissie*, especially among Afrikaans speakers, for the chilli family. A *soetrissie* (sweet) is a capsicum more frequently called a green pepper (or sweet pepper if ripe) in English, but curiously enough 'butter chilli' by South African Indians. The chilli proper is called *skerprissie* (sharp), occasionally *rooirissie* for the ingredient used for cayenne pepper. *Borrie* is the common household term for turmeric (except in Indian

---

[24] Burchell *Travels*, I, described them as 'Hottentot figs' 'spreading over the ground in large patches . . . It produces . . . in all seasons of the year a fruit of the size of a small fig, of a very pleasant acid taste when perfectly ripe . . . Its name was given by the first colonists on account of the form bearing some little resemblance to a fig and because it is every where eaten by the Hottentots.' (This fact is commented upon by Van Riebeeck who used the term 'inwoonders' (inhabitants).)

households where it is known as *arad* or *haldi/hardi*) and is clearly cognate with the Hindi *purree* for yellow colouring matter.[25] *Borrie* is used in a favourite traditional Cape rice dish with raisins, and linguistically in numerous compounds describing anything bright yellow: *borrievink* (the yellow weaver bird), *borriepatat* (the yellow-fleshed sweet potato or yam *Ipomoea batatas*), *borriekweper* (quince), and *borriehout* (timber).

The form *bringal*, for the aubergine or egg plant (Portuguese *berinjela*), is that used in the East[25] and is the household word in South Africa, possibly from the influence of the Indian population, though few other Indian vegetables are available except chillis and green ginger unless there are large communities to grow and use them.

The Dutch landed on the smallest and yet the most prolifically endowed of the world's floristic kingdoms, which has an unparalleled diversity of 8550 plants species classifiable as 'Capensis'. Naturally the first colonists were heavily pre-occupied with the problem of subsistence, and later defence, including the building of the first fort at the Cape. Botany therefore was clearly not for them a subject of any importance as it was for the naturalists who came later, especially in the eighteenth century. For them the identification of species was a serious matter. With their arrival the style and tenor of naming changed, for they were dedicated professionals with the treasures of nature of a new continent to plunder and to make known to the outside world. They were writing for a Europe avid for knowledge of the dark continent and what it held. For the naturalists, accuracy, and for their readers, the exotic, were of great importance, and it is probably to the latter need that we owe the preservation of the Khoisan *gnu* and *kwagga* (Qua ha) beside the *wildebeest* (wild ox) and *wildepard* (wild horse) of the Dutch colonists. Many beautiful indigenous names — for example, *oribi*, *impala*, *inyala*, *lechwe*, *kudu*, and *ipiti* among the antelope; *titihoya*, *sakabula*, *indwe*, and *mahem* among the birds — might well have been lost were it not for them.

And indeed certain strange Khoi plant names like *buchu* (*Agathosma* and *Diosma* spp.), *kukumakranka* (Gethyllis spp.), *!naras* (*Acanthicyos horrida*), and *dagga* (*Cannabis sativa*) are still without English equivalents today (if one discounts the multiple arcane terms for marijuana).

Much of the vernacular naming is of the run of the mill variety: by colour — *rooibessie* (red berry), *bloubok* (blue buck), *grysbok* (grey buck), *vaalbos* (tawny (leaved) bush); by habitat — *bosbok* (bushbuck),

---

[25] G. Subba Rao, *Indian Words in English* (Oxford, 1954), dates *purree* in English 1852, and *brinjal* 1611 as Portuguese alt. Sanskrit.

rietbok (reedbuck), *waterskaap* ('water sheep', kudu); by appearance —
dikkop (thick head), *dikheksysie* (broad beaked siskin), *swartwitpens*
('black and white belly', the sable antelope or Harris buck); by habit —
rainbird (several spp.), *springbok* (jumping buck), *klipspringer* (rock
jumper), *blaasop* ('inflate', used of a frog, a fish and an insect), *duiker*
(diver, cormorant or an antelope called by some early travellers 'diving
goat'); by some other quality such as weight, shape or hardness —
ysterhout (iron wood), *hardekool* (lead wood), *kreupelboom* ('crippled
tree', from its twisted branches); and, predictably, the birds by imitation
of their calls — *tingtinkie* (warblers, Sylviidae fam.), *piet-my-vrou*,
diederik (Cuculidae fam.), *Jan Frederik* (Cape robin, *Cossypha* spp.),
bokmakierie (Laniidae fam.), and the raucous *hadedah* (an ibis of the
Threskiornithidae fam.).

Most of these names are predictable, useful, and usually fairly
uninspiring, and the taxonomy to which they are mere tags was
undertaken in a systematic and careful manner, matching Northern and
Southern hemisphere species where possible, and generally making the
first efforts towards a tidy classification of the flora and fauna of South
Africa — a task still under way and subject to frequent change.

While I acknowledge that we do owe to the eighteenth and nineteenth
century naturalists the preservation of many original indigenous names
of plants, birds and beasts, their arrival on the scene put an end to the
naming, like that of the First Man by inspired guess, which has so much
enriched our daily vocabulary.

LEGISLATIVE LEXICOGRAPHY

Robert D. Eagleson

Lawyers do not see themselves as lexicographers, nevertheless the law is the scene of constant lexicographical activity. So many legal documents contain definitions or interpretation sections, that one without its list of defined terms appears almost incomplete.

Definitions sections can serve useful functions, especially in statutes. They can confine a word to only part of its range of meanings, a particularly valuable role given the polysemous character of most words, for example *oil* means any liquid hydrocarbon. Alternatively they can specify in what part of a document particular meanings are being used, for example:

'employee' means —
(a) in relation to Part II — a public employee;
(b) in relation to the remainder of this Act — a person appointed to the Public Service (including a Chief Executive Officer).
— Government Management and Employment Act 1985 (U.K.).

The objective here is to obtain clarity, not to introduce new meanings or to break away from the ordinary usage of the community. If the usage is only partially established, for example *in vitro fertilisation*, *disflation*, *joint float*, the inclusion of the item may help to promote understanding, especially where a neologism is only just finding its way into dictionaries.

The definitions section can also be used to add precision where the ordinary meaning of a word is vague or loose, for example:

'serious offence' means an indictable offence, or an offence punishable by imprisonment for 2 years or more
— Recodifying Criminal Law (Law Reform Commission of Canada Report 30: p. 10)

or to remove uncertainty, as in:

> *spouse* includes de facto spouse
> *damage* includes destruction.

From time to time legislative drafters turn the convention of the definitions section to their own advantage. It lets them invent a term or extend the use of an established one to make a document shorter and preferably more readable as well as by allowing a concept to be expressed in a single word or compound, for example:

> *odd lot* means a parcel of shares that is less than a marketable parcel
> — Companies (Acquisition of shares) (Victoria) Code: plain English version.

Documents could become even more cumbersome than they are without this facility.

Despite the valuable benefits to be had through definitions sections for precision, understanding and readability, the craft of lexicography is not practised as well as it could be by legal writers. The current thrust for plain English in legislation and in legal documents generally is bringing to light many inadequacies in definitions and exposing how practice fails to consider seriously the needs of readers. Too often interpretation sections give the appearance of being compiled for the convenience of the drafters rather than the readers and only end up complicating the task of comprehending documents instead of smoothing the way.

The force of this criticism is glaringly revealed by the definition of *unmarried person* in the Social Securities Act 1947 (Commonwealth):

> 'unmarried person' means a person who is not married.

Admittedly this has to be read in the context of the definition of married person which is presented earlier:

> 'married person' includes a de facto spouse but does not include —
> (a) a legally married person (not being a de facto spouse) who is living separately and apart from the spouse of the person on a permanent basis; or
> (b) a person who, for any special reason in any particular case, the Director-General determines in writing should not be treated as a married person.

This may be very neat, but only from the drafters' point of view. Are readers to be expected to remember that *unmarried person* has an unusual sense whenever they come across it in the 177 pages of the Act, especially when the term is not identified in the text in any special way to show that it is a defined term? The drafters needed to take a different approach altogether and one which attended more sympathetically to the way in which general readers used the term.

It would have been better for instance, if they had introduced some such category as 'eligible married person' or even coined a special term: this would have signalled a qualification to *married* and left *unmarried* undisturbed.

Perhaps even more remarkable is the definition found in Section 5 of the Fair Trading Act 1985 (Victoria):

'goods' includes —
(a) ships, aircraft and other vehicles;
(b) animals, including fish;
(c) minerals, trees and crops, whether on, under or attached to land or not; and
(d) gas and electricity.

This is certainly providing the drafter with a shorthand form but it can only be perplexing for readers. Frustratingly the drafter had a solution which did not involve ignoring the common meaning of *goods*, for it would have been valid to say that the Act applies to (a), (b), (c) and (d) in the same way as it applies to goods. This solution would have been immediately intelligible and more helpful for readers.

With these definitions of *unmarried person* and *goods* it is possible to detect some gain at least for drafters. Elsewhere the departure from the general meaning of a word seems aimless if not downright perverse. The Corrections Bill which was tabled in the Victorian Parliament in 1986 presented a strange sense of *formal*:

46. (1) A person who wishes to enter or remain in a prison as a visitor must, if asked, submit to a formal search.
    (2) In this section '**formal search**' means a search to detect the presence of drugs weapons or metal articles carried out by an electronic or mechanical device.
    (3) If, when asked, a person does not submit to a formal search, a prison officer may prohibit the person from entering the prison or if the person is in the prison order the person to leave the prison immediately.

Not only does this definition wrench the word away from its accepted meanings, but the whole endeavour is a needless imposition on readers and a waste of time for the drafter. Subsection (1) could have appeared as:

> (1)　If asked, a visitor to a prison must submit to a search by an electronic or mechanical device for drugs, weapons, or metal articles.

Subsection (2) could have been abandoned and Subsection (3) modified to:

> If the visitor does not submit to the search, . . .

The whole enterprise of introducing the concept of 'formal search' is unnecessary.

The defining exercise degenerates into a meaningless activity when *day* becomes 'four o'clock':

> 'Appointed day' means four o'clock in the afternoon of the day before the proclaimed day.
> — Accident Compensation Act 1985 (Victoria).

In other Victorian Acts *day* manages to preserve its generally accepted sense:

> 'Appointed day' is the day proclaimed as the appointed day for the purpose of Section 24 of the Principal Act.
> — Construction Industry Long Service Leave (Amendment) Act
> 1985 (Victoria).

The drafter has seemingly clung onto *day* because it was the traditional term to use. There can be no other justification for this break from commonsense.[1]

Legal drafters display violent swings in behaviour. When they are not being obscure as with *appointed day*, they descend into the obvious:

[1] Dickerson, R. *The Fundamentals of Legal Drafting* (Boston, 1965), 101, reports an American Act which declared:
'September 16, 1940 means June 27, 1950.'
This must have been even more puzzling for readers.

'unsolicited goods' means goods sent to a person without any request made by or on behalf of that person
— Fair Trading Act 1985 (Victoria).

Fortunately most readers would not think of consulting the interpretation section when they come across *unsolicited goods* in the body of the Act, but if they did they could be perplexed by this definition. Readers try hard to cooperate with writers; they look for sense in statements. Confronted with a definition like this they could be misled into wasting time trying to discover some hidden meaning because they would not image that a writer would be so tritely obvious.

These needless definitions uncover an even more serious fault in the practice of defining in legislation. The endeavour is haphazard and unsystematic. There often seems little rhyme or reason behind the selection of terms. In the Credit Act 1984 (Victoria), for instance, *mortgage*, *mortgagee* and *mortgagor* are all defined, but *execute* (a document) and *consideration* miss out. *Chairperson* is constantly defined even though the Acts are referring to only one board or commission and there can be no possibility of misunderstanding. Meanwhile ordinary words with special legal senses, such as *action*, *instrument* and *information*, are neglected. Yet general readers need help with these words if they are going to come to a full understanding of a legal text. *Action*, for example, can be dangerously ambiguous in 'this is a criminal action'. It is not being argued that definitions sections should offer a complete coverage of every term used in a legal document, but the present undirected and arbitrary selection is most unsatisfactory. It bespeaks an uncertain perception of the function and potential of definitions.

This lack of thoroughness in recognising words which need attention if general readers are to be helped is matched by an abdication of responsibility. Definitions sections are generally introduced with the words 'unless the contrary intention appears' or equivalent disclaimer. This qualification is added in case drafters have overlooked the use of a word in a different sense somewhere in the text. The practice, however, does not help readers but only causes uncertainty: they are left each time to decide whether a word has the meaning indicated in a given definition or whether it is operating in one of its other meanings. While the qualification might have had some justification in the past — and even this is doubtful in most cases — it is completely unwarranted in these days of word processors and computer-generated concordances. Concordances make it possible to check speedily whether a word is being used in more than one sense and to substitute an alternative for it in some contexts so that it can be restricted to one meaning.

Legislative drafters appear to delight in definitions. They seem to be constantly creating opportunities to introduce them. The De Facto Relationships Act 1984 (NSW) offers a good illustration in Section 15:

(1) A court shall not make an order under this Part unless it is satisfied —
(a) . . .
(b) that —
   (i) both parties were resident within New South Wales for a substantial period of their de facto relationship; or
   (ii) substantial contributions of the kind referred to in Section 20 (1)(a) or (b) have been made in New South Wales by the applicant.

Substantial period is too vague a term and so the drafter apparently comes to the rescue of readers by inserting a definition in subsection (2):

(2) For the purposes of sub-section (1)(b)(i), the parties to an application shall be taken to have been resident within New South Wales for a substantial period of their de facto relationship if they have lived together in the State for a period equivalent to at least one-third of the duration of their relationship.

But this is a longwinded solution to the problem in which readers are left in suspense while they cope with paragraph (b)(ii) before they receive any enlightenment. The drafter would have served readers far better by abandoning the concept of 'substantial period' and its definition, and inserting the important information in paragraph (b)(i) as:

(b) That —
   (i) both parties lived together in NSW for at least one-third of their relationship.

Commercial lawyers seem to have the same predilection for these one-off definitions which involve readers in taking two steps before they reach the full information. A draft insurance policy approached a clause in this way:

We may refuse a claim, or cancel a policy, or do both if:
. . .
(c) you carry out building work on the building or at the site, unless you tell us in writing beforehand and we agree to cover you.

Note: By 'building work' we mean work that involves the alteration or removal of all or part of any wall, foundation, roof or structural component of the building or the building of a new structure (including a swimming pool) at the site.

Again, this divided material could be combined into:

(c) you alter or remove all or part of any wall, foundation, roof or structural component of the building, or build a new structure (including a swimming pool) at the site.

There was no need for the convoluted presentation of the material through a definition. Perhaps general lawyers have been influenced by all the statutes they have to read!

All these deficiencies in definitions in legal documents demonstrate the need for lawyers to study lexicography more systematically. It is clearly not satisfactory for them to be left to simply pick up the art over time: it rarely happens. Because definitions play a prominent role in their writing they need to be brought in touch with lexicographers and the knowledge and skills they have acquired as they have concentrated on compiling dictionaries.

Lawyers could get even more help from lexicographers than this. Lexicographers might be put to establishing authoritatively that *acknowledge* is the same as *confess*, and *fit* equals *proper*, that *cease* means no more than *desist*, that *give*, *devise* and *bequeath* amount to the same. This might at least eliminate from legal documents the time-honoured doublets and triplets which so frequently overburden them and deaden the senses of readers. Admittedly this information is already available in dictionaries and Melinkoff[2] has incisively exposed the worthlessness of so many conventional doublets and triplets, but the force of his information has not penetrated the consciousness of the legal profession. There is almost a need for a special task force of lexicographers to rescue lawyers from prolixity, to make them aware of what lexicographers have known for so long so that lawyers will feel safe in abandoning *null*, *force*, and *have* if they also intend to use *void*, *effect* and *hold*.

Lawyers are also unlike lexicographers in not keeping their documents up-to-date. Where dictionaries mark words for obsolescence or archaism, legal documents persist with the old. As a result tenancy agreements continue to refer to 'demised' rather than 'rented' premises

[2] D. Melinkoff, *The Language of the Law* (Boston, 1965).

and other contracts talk of being 'seised' of a property rather than 'owning' one. That some of these outmoded terms have been the subject of intense litigation should no longer be taken as a reason for persisting with them when they are meaningless to general readers. Instead lawyers should be devising methods to cope with change and to allow them to introduce plain English equivalents. Ironically the much beloved definitions section could provide a solution here. It could, for example, offer entries along the lines of:

> *rented* means demised
> or
> *rented* has the same legal force as demised.

If indexes were also associated with legal documents as a general rule, then these could provide users with a tool for tracking down current substitutes through a series of cross-references. Consequently an index to an Act might contain an entry:

> presents   see DOCUMENT

In this way a lawyer used to an older term would have a means of finding information without too much trouble, while the member of the community affected by the document would be able to understand immediately by having its ideas expressed in current words. Guidance on what these current or plain English equivalents might be could conveniently be received from lexicographers.

The skills of lexicographers might also be called upon to help legal drafters arrive at a suitable generic term. All too frequently they resort to lists of closely related terms in the hope of covering all eventualities. Instead they only create uncertainty as this attempt in the Mental Health Act 1985 (Victoria) illustrated:

> 112 (3) (c) assaults, obstructs, hinders, threatens, intimidates or attempts to obstruct or intimidate a community visitor.

This use of five words does not produce tranquillity in readers; instead it raises questions about other potential terms. What of *thwart*, *curb*, *impede*, *block*, *delay*, *frighten*? Are they covered or has the drafter overlooked them? Does *hinder* fill the same semantic space between *obstruct* and *threaten*? It is a case where a generic word, for example, *interfere with*, would have been more satisfying than a string of words. By splitting hairs between *threaten* and *intimidate*, the drafter is only encouraging readers to look for gaps between all the words, especially when he or she has not continued the full set after *attempts*. In effect this practice of drafters is self-defeating because it induces readers and judges into assigning limited senses to each of the words in a list, so that a provision which contains them does not become all-inclusive as the drafters intended. In the end it would seem safer to rely on the commonsense of the community and judges to cope with a generic word.

Even with mechanical matters legal drafters have not shown themselves to be particularly imaginative or considerate of readers. While they may decide to use a word in a particular way in an Act and enter it in the definitions sections, they make no attempt to identify it in any special way in the body of the Act. This means that readers have in effect to memorise the definitions section or continually refer to it. Neither of these operations is convenient, particularly in long Acts which may run to over 150 pages and which may contain 100 or more defined words. The task is made even more impractical by the fact that Acts are rarely read from beginning to end but are rather consulted a section or two at a time. There is thus not the opportunity to build up a real familiarity with the contents of the definitions section. The solution is simple: identify the defined words by some distinctive typographical device, such as italics or small caps, then readers would be warned to consult the definitions section. It is thoughtless to leave readers without a warning signal, especially when the words could be comprehensible in some other sense. Amazingly this simple aid is rarely practised.

Again while definitions sections are generally located towards the beginning of an Act so that readers who read it right through are given at least early warning that some words are being used with specified meanings, not all definitions are placed in the definitions section. Some may be inserted as well at the beginning of Parts and Divisions. This means that readers might have to look in 2 or 3 places before they find the relevant definition. In the meantime they are beginning to forget the context and so may have to start all over again.

Even worse is the practice of putting a definition at the end of a section, especially one with many long subsections. As consulting the definitions section brings no help, readers have to toil on in the dark, until they stumble at last upon the resolution of the mystery. This is just no way to handle critical information.

There is good reason that many of the current lexicographical activities in legal writing should continue. What is urgently needed is the development of sounder practices. Lawyers clearly need to know more of lexicography and to be brought into closer contact with lexicographers. The isolation of the two professions should not continue. It is a cause of satisfaction that our general dictionaries are improving in quality and to this Bob Burchfield has made a significant and lively contribution. It is disturbing that these advances are not being witnessed in a special area which impinges directly on the rights and obligations of the community. Here is an area of endeavour in need of systematic professional attention.

'INTERDISCIPLINARY': THE FIRST HALF-CENTURY

Roberta Frank

> What a splendid book one could put together by narrating the life and adventures of a word. The events for which a word was used have undoubtedly left various imprints on it; depending on place it has awakened different notions; but does it not become grander still when considered in its trinity of soul, body, and movement?
>
> Honoré de Balzac, *Louis Lambert*[1]

'Interdisciplinary' was probably born in New York City in the mid 1920s, most likely at the corner of 42nd and Madison. The word seems to have begun life in the corridors and meeting rooms of the Social Science Research Council as a kind of bureaucratic shorthand for what the Council saw as its chief function, the promotion of research that involved two or more of its seven constituent societies.[2] 'Interdisciplinary' started out with a reasonably bounded set of senses. Then, subjected to indecent abuse in the 50s and 60s, it acquired a precocious middle-age spread. Now not only is the word everywhere but no one can pin down what people have in mind when they utter it.

Whoever coined 'interdisciplinary' never claimed paternity, the way Jeremy Bentham apologized for creating a new compound: 'The word *international*, it must be acknowledged, is a new one; though, it is hoped, sufficiently analogous and intelligible.'[3] Professor Robert Sessions Woodworth (1869 – 1962), the distinguished Columbia University psychologist and the first person I have caught using 'interdisciplinary'

---

[1] *OEuvres complètes de M. de Balzac. La Comédie humaine*, vol. 16.2 (Paris, 1846), 111.

[2] Founded in 1923, the Council was, according to Charles E. Merriam, its first President, ordinarily to 'deal only with such problems as involve two or more disciplines'. ('Report for the Year 1925 Made to the American Political Science Association by Charles E. Merriam, Chairman', *American Political Science Review* 20 [1926], 186.)

[3] *An Introduction to the Principles of Morals and Legislation* (London, 1780 [1789]), xvii, 25.

in public, neither apologizes nor treats the word as a neologism. On Monday evening, August 30, 1926, in Hanover, New Hampshire, where members of SSRC had gathered to escape the heat of New York City and to devise 'A Constructive Program for the SSRC', he spoke about the range of research appropriate for the Council: 'There is a certain limitation in the fact that we are an assembly of several disciplines, and in our official statements again it is expressed that we shall attempt to foster research which brings in more than one discipline.'[4] He continued a few sentences later: 'There would be no other body, unless we assume the function ourselves, charged with the duty of considering where the best chances were for coordinated or interdisciplinary work.' Professor Woodworth, at the time a member of the founding SSRC Committee on Problems and Policy and soon to be President of the Council (1931 – 32), had just served as Chairman of the division of anthropology and psychology of the National Research Council in Washington (1924 – 25). He clearly had an interest in and sensitivity to the language used by planners in both Councils: at a 1931 Brookings Institution conference on cooperative research, when his colleagues got tangled up in the differences between cooperation, collaboration, and coordination, Woodworth was able to report that the word 'co-ordination' had been favored at the NRC a decade earlier 'as a refuge from some worse word which I don't seem to remember'.[5]

That 'worse word' was not 'interdisciplinary', which, if it existed, has left no trace, as far as I can determine, in the *Reports*, *Minutes*, and Archives of the NRC or the National Academy of Sciences. The scientists came close of course. George Ellery Hale, in 1916 the first President of the NRC, had proposed as early as 1912 that the Academy should foster interest in 'subjects lying between the old-established divisions of science'[6] and insisted in 1914 on 'the inter-relationship of the sciences'.[7] In the 20s and 30s, the most popular terms at the NRC were 'new fields', 'overlapping projects', 'interrelated research', and — winners by a mile — 'borderlands' and 'borderline research'.[8]

---

[4] *SSRC Hanover Conference*, vol. II (Dartmouth College, August 23 – September 2, 1926), 445.
[5] Brookings Institution, *Co-operative Research* (Washington, D.C., 1931), 67.
[6] G. E. Hale to C. D. Walcott, May 17, 1912. Cited by Rexmond C. Cochrane, *The National Academy of Sciences: The First Hundred Years, 1863 – 1963* (Washington, D.C., 1978), 327.
[7] 'National Academies and the Progress of Research II. The First Half-Century of the National Academy of Sciences', *Science* 39 (February 6, 1914); cited Cochrane, p. 196.
[8] Cochrane, p. 322.

Outside SSRC committee rooms, 'interdisciplinary' seems not to have been current among social scientists in the 20s or 30s, even though the years between the founding of the New School for Social Research (1919) and the Yale Institute of Human Relations (1929) produced a mountain of documents calling for the integration of the social sciences and the related arts of industry, government, and public welfare. Rising stars like Margaret Mead called not for interdisciplinary activity but for 'co-operation for cross-fertilization in the social sciences', while established luminaries like Harold Laski lamented the 'endless committees to co-ordinate or correlate or integrate'.[9] 'Interdisciplinary' seems not to have made it into the fifteen-volume *Encyclopaedia of the Social Sciences* (1930 – 35), plans for which were laid in 1923. 'Cooperative research' is the usual term in a half-dozen books published between 1925 – 30 that present the whole field of social science as a unit. They stress the 'interrelation', 'mutual interdependence', 'interpenetration', 'intercommunication', 'cross-relationships', 'interfiliations', and, of course, 'interaction' of the various disciplines, along with the need to explore 'twilight zones' and 'border areas', to fill out 'unoccupied spaces', and to encourage the 'active cultivation of borderlands between the several disciplines'. But 'interdisciplinary' never once raises its head.[10]

Meanwhile, back at the Social Science Research Council, the word was beginning to flex its muscles. At the 1930 Hanover conference, the Council adopted a statement of purpose, quoted in the *Annual Report* for 1929 – 30: 'It is probable that the Council's interest will continue to run strongly in the direction of these inter-discipline activities.' The same report also warned with disquieting ambiguity that 'Concern with co-operative research' or 'inter-discipline problems' should not be

[9] *American Journal of Sociology* 37 (1931), 274; 'Foundations, Universities, and Research', *Harper's Magazine* 157 (1928), 295 – 303.

[10] E.g., Harry Elmer Barnes et al., ed., *The History and Prospects of the Social Sciences* (New York, 1925); Edward Cary Hayes, ed., *Recent Developments in the Social Sciences* (Philadelphia, 1927); William F. Ogburn and Alexander A. Goldenweiser, ed., *The Social Sciences and their Interrelations* (Boston, 1927); Frederick A. Ogg, *Research in the Humanities and Social Sciences* (New York, 1928); Wilson P. Gee, ed., *The Fundamental Objectives and Methods of Research in the Social Sciences* (New York, 1929); Howard W. Odum and Katherine Jocher, *An Introduction to Social Research* (New York, 1929); Leonard D. White, ed., *The New Social Science* (Chicago, 1930); W. E. Spahr and R. J. Swenson, *Methods and Status of Scientific Research with Particular Application to the Social Sciences* (New York, 1930).

allowed to hamper the first-rate mind . . .'[11] By 1933, in an SSRC fellowship notice appearing in the *American Journal of Sociology*, 'interdisciplinary' had regained its *-ary* and broadened its reference to include 'education' as well as 'problems': 'The fellowships were designed to afford opportunity for research training, preferably interdisciplinary in nature.'[12] The first citation for 'interdisciplinary' in *Webster's Ninth New Collegiate Dictionary* and *A Supplement to the Oxford English Dictionary* is from the December 1937 issue of the *Journal of Educational Sociology*, in a subsequent notice concerning SSRC postdoctoral fellowships: 'The primary purpose of these fellowships is to broaden the research training and equipment of promising young social scientists. . . . Programs of study submitted should provide either for study of an interdisciplinary nature, for advanced training within the applicants' fields of specialization, or for field work or other experimental training intended to supplement more formal academic preparation for research.'[13] By August 1937, when the University of Chicago sociologist Louis Wirth submitted his mimeographed report on Council policies, 'interdisciplinary' is branded as an in-house vogue word: 'It may also be said the Council has allowed itself to some extent to become obsessed at times by catch phrases and slogans which were not sufficiently critically examined. Thus there is some justification for saying that much of the talk in connection with Council policy, especially in the early years, about cooperation and interdisciplinary research turned out to be a delusion.'[14] On Friday, December 1, 1939, in the University of Chicago's Social Science Research Building, at a session entitled 'The Social Sciences: One or Many', Robert T. Crane representing the SSRC spoke in a similar fashion about the old days: 'The Social

[11] Social Science Research Council, Sixth Annual Report, 1929–1930, p. 18. First communicated to me in a letter, David L. Sills, Executive Associate, SSRC, October 7, 1985, and cited by him in 'A Note on the Origin of "Interdisciplinary" ', *Items* 40 (March 1986), 18. (At the 1931 Brookings conference on cooperative research, Robert S. Lynd, the Permanent Secretary of SSRC, twice spoke of 'cross-discipline cooperation' [*Cooperative Research*, p. 12].) I am grateful to Dr. Sills for his interest in my original enquiry (letter R. Frank to D. Sills, July 10, 1985) and for his kindness in sharing with me material from SSRC archives.

[12] *American Journal of Sociology* 39 (July 1933), 106; also 40 (July 1934), 108. SSRC notices before 1933 lack 'interdisciplinary' and seem more pointed: 'The major objective of these fellowships continues to be the development of more adequately trained research investigators . . .' (*AJS* 38 [July 1932], 118).

[13] 2, 251. The same announcement appeared in the *American Journal of Sociology* 41 (September 1935), 239 and 42 (July 1936), 104.

[14] Social Science Research Council, 'Report on the History, Activities and Policies of the Social Science Research Council. Prepared for the Committee on Review of Council Policy', p. 145. Cited Sills, 'A Note', p. 18.

Science Research Council has talked less in recent than in earlier years about integration of the sciences, about cross-fertilization, and about a multi-disciplinary or interdisciplinary approach to problems.'[15] Mark May, representing the Institute of Human Relations at Yale, recalled how 'the Social Science Research Council, seeing the great need of integration, attempted to stress interdisciplinary forms of research as well as interdisciplinary training under its fellowship program. . . . I distinctly remember attending meetings of the Council at which time the phrase "cross-fertilization" was translated into "cross-sterilization" with the obvious intent of discrediting interdisciplinary activities'.[16]

The American Council of Learned Societies, founded in 1919, did without the word for two decades. In the spring of 1940, however, the Council sponsored a conference in Washington, D. C., on 'The Interdisciplinary Aspects of Negro Studies'.[17] The relative novelty at ACLS of such phrases as 'interdisciplinary cooperation' (5), 'interdisciplinary cross-fertilization' (15), 'inter-disciplinary character' (101), and 'inter-disciplinary nature' (108) may be reflected in the copy editor's oscillation between hyphenated and non-hyphenated forms. In the 1964 ACLS *Report of the Commission on the Humanities*, only three societies and the index boast of 'interdisciplinary relationships'. But any residual shyness disappears in the 1985 ACLS *Report to the Congress of the United States on the State of the Humanities*, in which all twenty-eight constituent societies openly acknowledge their interdisciplinary intentions and their desire to transcend disciplinary perimeters, melt boundaries, fill gaps, and escape narrow confines. The Bibliographical Society of America, for example, expresses its willingness to enter into 'interdisciplinary partnerships' (159) and to receive funding for 'interdisciplinary programs' (146) and 'interdisciplinary conferences' (160). The Medieval Academy of America mentions its interdisciplinary inclinations six times in about as many pages; while the American Society for Eighteenth-Century Studies, a bit ahead with twelve, observes suggestively 'that the United States of America is itself one of the great interdisciplinary achievements of the eighteenth century' (115).

By mid-century 'interdisciplinary' was common coin in the social sciences. As early as 1951, an editorial in the journal *Human Organization*, commenting on an essay in that issue entitled 'Pitfalls in the Organization of Interdisciplinary Research', complained that 'present fashion makes the stressing of the interdisciplinary aspects of any

---

[15] Louis Wirth, ed., *Eleven Twenty-Six: A Decade of Social Science Research* (Chicago, 1940), 122.
[16] *Eleven Twenty-Six*, p. 133.
[17] See ACLS Bulletin 32, September 1941.

project almost mandatory'.[18] Numerous how-to-do-it manuals and articles, by and for social scientists, began appearing, culminating in Margaret B. Luszki's *Interdisciplinary Team Research: Methods and Problems* (Washington: National Training Laboratories, 1958).[19] By the late 50s, the idea even seemed old-hat: 'Ten years ago interdisciplinary research was very much in vogue.'[20] The adjective reached political science circles in France by 1959 ('ce que l'on nomme dans le jargon usuel le travail "interdisciplinaire" ')[21]; the noun arrived a decade later, just in time to appear on Marianne's banner at the barricades of May 1968 ('pluridisciplinarité et interdisciplinarité: deux termes barbares, même s'ils sont d'actualité').[22]

In the course of the 60s 'interdisciplinary' changed from a series of widely scattered occurrences into a kind of weather. An international conference held in Nice in 1969, under the auspices of the Organization for Economic Co-operation and Development, produced the first of many guides that in the 70s taught us to taste the subtle differences between interdisciplinary, metadisciplinary, extradisciplinary, multidisciplinary, pluridisciplinary, crossdisciplinary, transdisciplinary, nondisciplinary, adisciplinary, and polydisciplinary, and to discriminate knowingly between the seven brands of interdisciplinarity (teleological, normative, purposive, subject-oriented, problem-oriented, field-theory, and General Systems theory).[23] In the 1970s interior designers were

[18]   10 (Winter 1951), 3.
[19]   E.g., Dorothy S. Thomas, 'Experiences in Interdisciplinary Research', *American Sociological Review* 17 (1952), 663 – 69; R. Richard Wohl, 'Some Observations on the Social Organization of Interdisciplinary Social Science Research', *Social Forces* 23 (1955), 374 – 90. The production of such guides continued through the 60s: see *Interdisciplinary Relationships in the Social Sciences,* ed. Muzafer Sherif and Carolyn W. Sherif (Chicago, 1969).
[20]   Elizabeth Bott, *Family and Social Network: Roles, Norms, and External Relationships in Ordinary Urban Families* (London, 1957), ii, 35. Yet the concept seemed new again to authors in the 60s: 'The writing of this book . . . represents fundamentally an exercise in what is now called "interdisciplinary research" ' (Ben B. Seligman, *Most Notorious Victory* [New York, 1966], p. xi).
[21]   Pierre Gilbert, *Dictionnaire des mots nouveaux* (Paris, 1971), 277. Also Organization for Economic Co-operation and Development, *Interdisciplinary Cooperation in Technical and Economic Agricultural Research* (Paris, 1961).
[22]   *Le Figaro*, 8 September 1970.
[23]   *Interdisciplinarity: Problems of Teaching and Research in Universities* (Paris: OECD/Centre for Educational Research and Innovation, 1972). See also Harry Finestone and Michael F. Shugrue, ed., *Prospects for the 70s: English Departments and Multidisciplinary Study* (New York, 1973); Helmut Holzhey, ed., *Interdisziplinär: Interdisziplinäre Arbeit und Wissenschaftstheorie* (Basel, 1974); Geoffrey Squires, *Interdisciplinarity* (London, 1975); Joseph J. Kockelmans, ed., *Interdisciplinarity and Higher Education* (College Park, 1979).

among the more fervent interdisciplinarians. The August 1975 issue of the *Designer* teaches subscribers that 'There is a wide gap between multi-disciplinary teams and inter-disciplinary teams. Multi-disciplinary applies when various disciplines provide their views with minimal cooperative interaction. Interdisciplinarity requires coordination among disciplines and synthesis of material through a higher-level organizing concept'.[24] Educators defined 'interdisciplinary' with their usual flair: 'Interdisciplinary research (or activity) requires day-to-day interaction between persons from different disciplines . . . and the interchange *in interactive mode* of samples, ideas, and results. Naturally, this is facilitated greatly by physical propinquity.'[25]

Humanists slowly discovered that their careers, too, could be fostered by the use of 'interdisciplinary': 'I believe that English must become interdisciplinary, but with caution and no illusions. In the 1970s English must become interdisciplinary, multidisciplinary, crossdisciplinary. . . . We must become interdisciplinary, first of all, for self-preservation.'[26] 'Interdisciplinary' made its first appearance in *Speculum*, the journal of the Medieval Academy of America, in 1951, as part of an ACLS fellowship notice (757), the same year that an SSRC study appeared showing that social scientists were supported four or five times as generously as humanists.[27] The word does not reappear in *Speculum* until 1967, when Johns Hopkins University boasts of an interdisciplinary program (774), followed in 1968 by Ohio State University (764). In the same year, the new annual *Viator* announces its interest in 'interdisciplinary and intercultural research' (765); in 1970 the University of Connecticut is in possession of an 'interdisciplinary program' (189), University College, Dublin, of an 'inter-disciplinary approach' (346), and the field of British studies of a 'triannual interdisciplinary newsletter' (189). In 1971 the Medieval Academy published a brochure entitled *Interdisciplinary Medieval Programs and the Training of Students: A Discussion*. In 1972 it sponsored a panel discussion on marriage in the Middle Ages 'employing the interdisciplinary method'

---

[24] Definition by Sherry R. Arnstein of the Academy for Contemporary Problems. Cited by Edwin Newman, *A Civil Tongue* (New York, 1975), 157.
[25] Rustum Roy, 'Interdisciplinary Science on Campus: The Elusive Dream', in Kockelmans, *Interdisciplinarity*, p. 170.
[26] Alan M. Hollingsworth, 'Beyond Literacy', *ADE Bulletin*, no. 36 (March 1973), 7. See Elizabeth Bayerl, *Interdisciplinary Studies in the Humanities: A Directory* (Metuchen, N.J., 1977), whose 1091 pages suggest overkill more than self-preservation.
[27] Elbridge Sibley, *Support for Independent Scholarship and Research* (New York: SSRC, 1951); see also Abraham Flexner, *Funds and Foundations: Their Policies, Past and Present* (New York, 1952).

(582).[28] The next year the word appears in a *Speculum* article ('Abelardian research will become more and more interdisciplinary' [485]). By 1982 'interdisciplinary' has made it into the Memoirs of Fellows of the Academy, a clear sign of respectability: the deceased is praised for his 'very early realization of the concept of interdisciplinary medieval studies' (701), his creation of an 'interdisciplinary group' and 'an interdisciplinary Centre' (709). Contributors to a 1982 book-length survey *Medieval Studies in North America: Past, Present, and Future* use 'interdisciplinary' frequently and fervently.[29] There is so little consciousness of mimicking the antics of those who were first at the federal feast that one essay concludes: 'Outside the humanities there is widespread resistance to the notion of interdisciplinarity . . .' (209). It is not surprising that the authors would rather belong to an expanding interdiscipline like Medieval Studies than to an established discipline like Medieval Studies. 'Interdisciplinary' sometimes turns into a disembodied smile, a floating demi-lune coming to rest on whatever we already value.

Its silhouette, however, has definitely thickened with the years. No lean, plain word to begin with, 'interdisciplinary' was soon larded with thick greasy syllables front and back. Nouns include interdiscipline, interdisciplinarian, interdisciplinarianship, interdisciplinism, and interdisciplinarity (with a plural *-ies*, as in 'previous potential interdisciplinarities').[30] An adverb is attested ('persons who are active interdisciplinarily').[31] Since there is a verb 'to pluridiscipline' ('applied fields have always tended to be crossdisciplinary and its [*sic*] practitioners pluridisciplined'),[32] the corresponding 'to interdiscipline' may be just around the corner. I could find no citation for 'interdisciplinated', as in 'chocolated laxatives'. As the word got fatter, it was contained by acronyms such as IDE (Interdisciplinary Enquiry, 1965), IDR (Interdisciplinary Research, 1980), IDU (Interdisciplinary Units, 1979), IGPH (Interdisciplinary Graduate Program in the Humanities, 1970), ISC

---

[28] The discussion took place at the annual meeting of the Medieval Academy in Los Angeles, 15 April 1972, and was published in *Viator* 4 (1973), 413 – 501.
[29] Ed. Francis G. Gentry and Christopher Kleinhenz (Kalamazoo, Mich.: Medieval Institute Publications).
[30] Wolfram W. Swoboda, 'Disciplines and Interdisciplinarity: A Historical Perspective', in Kockelmans, *Interdisciplinarity*, p. 82. The files of the Oxford Dictionaries contain citations for *interdiscipline, interdisciplinarity, interdisciplinism,* and *interdisciplinarian; interdisciplinarianship* (along with the other nouns) is included in Merriam-Webster's files. This information was kindly supplied by Freda J. Thornton, Assistant Editor, *Shorter Oxford English Dictionary,* and Frederick C. Mish, Editorial Director, Merriam-Webster Inc.
[31] Robert L. Scott, 'Personal and Institutional Problems Encountered in Being Interdisciplinary', in Kockelmans, p. 324.
[32] *Ibid.*, p. 325.

(Interdisciplinary Studies Context, 1971), IRRPOS (Interdisciplinary Research Relevant to the Problems of Our Society, 1970), and the most recent entry, a journal title designed to indicate graphically that interdisciplinarity is central to the editors' purpose: AVISTA (Association Villard de Honnecourt for the Interdisciplinary Study of Medieval Technology, Science, and Art, 1986).[33] In 1977 'interdisciplinary' made *The Dictionary of Diseased English*.[34]

The stretching out of syllables (as in 'pseudo-interdisciplinarity')[35] went hand-in-hand with an extension of meaning. Different and even conflicting concepts now hang onto the word, vaguely increasing its meaningfulness without limiting it to any specific sense. 'Interdisciplinary' always promises good. Fellowship applicants use the word to hint at the innovative, problem-solving, socially committed nature of their research (= worthy of support). When used by the granting agency, 'to develop interdisciplinary interests' sounds so natural, so inevitable, like 'willingness to grow'; but it can still mean 'to retool', the basic Depression sense: 'The fellowships broaden the scholar's competence in an interdisciplinary way, or give that scholar the opportunity to retrain for a nonacademic career.'[36] Some fellowships sound like more fun: the Rockefeller Foundation promises that 'fellowships are offered as residencies in order to foster interdisciplinary work . . .', the Kellogg National Fellowships, that 'fellows will carry out a nondegree, interdisciplinary, self-directed activity to expand their personal horizons'.[37] It turns out that 'real life is interdisciplinary', that 'finally, life is interdisciplinary', that 'contemporary issues are interdisciplinary', and that 'the interdisciplinarity of the major societal issues of the decade —

---

[33] (IDE) *Ideas* no. 1 and *Ideas* no. 2 (bulletins obtainable from U. of London, Goldsmiths' College Curriculum Laboratory, 6 Dixon Road, New Cross); (IDR) Neil Nelson, 'Issues in Funding and Evaluating Interdisciplinary Research', *Journal of Canadian Studies* 15/3 (Fall 1980), 25; (IDU) Roy in Kockelmans, *Interdisciplinarity*, pp. 171 – 2; (IGPH) in Kockelmans, *Interdisciplinarity*, p. viii; (ISC) Daniel Bernd, 'Prolegomenon to a Definition of Interdisciplinary Studies: The Experience at Governors State University', *ADE Bulletin*, 31 (November 1971), 8 – 14; (IRRPOS) *National Science Foundation Factbook*, ed. Alvin Renetzky et al. (Orange, N.J., 1970).
[34] Kenneth Hudson, *The Dictionary of Diseased English* (London, 1977), 125.
[35] G. W. Leckie, *Interdisciplinary Research in the University Setting* (Univ. of Manitoba: Centre for Settlement Studies, 1975), 4.
[36] Announcement of Boston University Professors Postdoctoral Fellowships in *Directory of Research Grants* (Phoenix, Ariz., 1986), no. 617.
[37] Announcements in *PMLA* 100/4 (September 1985), 642 and in *Directory of Research Grants*, no. 2075.

or century — calls for interdisciplinary solutions'.[38] We are taught that 'some disciplines seem to be more interdisciplinary than others', that 'if we are to have interdisciplinary achievement, we must have interdisciplinary language', that 'the new science isn't "interdisciplinary" in the old sense of the word', and that students profit from 'courses giving an interdisciplinary introduction to the disciplines judged by experienced scholars to be essential for the historical approach to medieval studies'.[39] A new quarterly aimed at generous, politically liberal alumni describes itself as 'an interdisciplinary journal . . . founded on the notion that highly sophisticated academic material could be rendered accessible to readers from all disciplines'.[40] Another side warns that 'the thematic of interdisciplinarity opens up a dangerous fissure in the continuity of bourgeois knowledge'.[41] 'Interdisciplinary' can be somewhat indiscriminate in its collocations: 'The program . . . is unstructured and interdisciplinary, yet directed and rigorous.'[42] Thanks to this openness, reviewers are no longer in the hateful position of having to specify whether a book is cultured, erudite, thorough, original, or conversely, superficial, facile, general, derivative: the one all-purpose adjective keeps readers alert and authors friendly.

Unlike its nearest rivals — borderlands, interdepartmental, cooperative, coordinated — 'interdisciplinary' has something to please everyone. Its base, *discipline*, is hoary and antiseptic; its prefix, *inter*, is hairy and friendly. Unlike fields, with their mud, cows, and corn, the Latinate *discipline* comes encased in stainless steel: it suggests something rigorous, aggressive, hazardous to master. *Inter* hints that knowledge is a warm, mutually developing, consultative thing. The prefix not only has the right feel but, like an unhinged magnet, draws to itself all other inters. And from the twenties on between-ness was where

---

[38] *Report of the Association of American Colleges* 1985; Neil Nelson, 'Issues in Funding and Evaluating Interdisciplinary Research', *Journal of Canadian Studies* 15/3 (Fall 1980), 25; Henry Winthrop, 'Interdisciplinary Studies: Variations in Meaning, Objectives, and Accomplishments', *ADE Bulletin*, no. 33 (May 1972), 29 (reprinted in *Prospects for the 70s*, p. 168); Nelson, 'Issues in Funding', 25.

[39] Carl R. Hausman, 'Disciplinarity or Interdisciplinarity?', in Kockelmans, *Interdisciplinarity*, p. 8; R. I. Page, *Anglo-Saxon Aptitudes* (Inaugural Lecture, Cambridge, 1985), 25; George Cook, 'Renewal 1987', *University of Toronto Alumni Magazine* 14 (1987), 8; *Pontifical Institute of Mediaeval Studies Syllabus 1979 – 80* (Toronto, 1979), 6.

[40] *Harvard Graduate Society Newsletter* (Summer 1986), 9.

[41] Arthur Krober, 'Migration from the Disciplines', *Journal of Canadian Studies* 15/3 (Fall 1980), 7.

[42] *Medieval Studies in North America*, p. 73.

the action was: from interpersonal, intergroup, interreligious, interethnic, interracial, interregional and international relations to intertextuality, things coming together in the state known as inter encapsulated the greatest problems facing society in the twentieth century.[43] 'Interdisciplinary' combined the notion that nothing is static or fixed, that discovery comes from breaking some conventional limit or barrier, with the desire to see things whole. It is perhaps not totally coincidental that the earliest citation I could find for 'interdisciplinary' comes from the same year in which Jan C. Smuts coined 'holistic', referring to 'the tendency in nature to produce wholes from the ordered grouping of unit structures'.[44] The 1920s had launched a number of new terms for reciprocal interaction within a total system. By 1928, Harold Laski was complaining that 'in our own day it has become fashionable for the observer to apply to the social process the latest discoveries of psychology'.[45] And the fashion has lasted. 'Interdisciplinary', now entering its seventh decade, shows little sign of fading away. Indeed, it is hard to imagine getting through the rest of the century without it.

[43] Peggy Rosenthal, *Words and Values: Some Leading Words* (New York and Oxford, 1984). Also David Lodge, 'Where It's At: California Language', in *The State of the Language*, ed. Leonard Michaels and Christopher Ricks (Berkeley and Los Angeles, 1980), 503 – 513; published in a slightly different form in *Encounter* magazine under the title 'Where It's At: The Poetry of Psychobabble'.

[44] *A Supplement to the Oxford English Dictionary*, s.v., citing *Holism and Evolution* (London, 1926), p. 99.

[45] 'Foundations, Universities, and Research', p. 295.

A NOTE ON SIXTEENTH-CENTURY PURISM[1]

Douglas Gray

Histories of the English language almost invariably include some remarks on the phenomenon of 'sixteenth-century purism' or 'Cambridge purism', but more often than not the treatment is so scrappy and disconnected that it must seem to the general reader to be a phenomenon that exists in a mysterious isolation. The purpose of this note is simply to suggest that though the question is a complicated one, this 'purism' makes more sense if it is seen in the intellectual context of its own time. A good deal of the disconnectedness in the treatment of this topic — and of other aspects of the discussions of the nature of the vernacular in the Renaissance — comes from a tendency to ignore contexts — not only the larger contexts of intellectual history but also sometimes the local context of the argument of a writer or a text. Passages or even phrases are wrenched from their surroundings without much consideration. Sometimes little distinction seems to be made between statements which show some kind of thoughtful attention to the problems of the language and remarks which seem to be simply repetitions of common topics, or which are really moves in arguments rather different from those that interest historians of the language. Thus, if we examine the imposing list that can be compiled of 'complaints about the inadequacy of the vernacular', some are simple reiterations of what had become by the early sixteenth century a *locus communis*, while others seem to be adapting it to a different rhetorical *topos*, the writer's modest apology for the inadequacy of his own eloquence. Moreover, it is easy to forget that the authors of these statements about the nature and destiny of the English language are themselves not historical philologists, but users of

[1] The train of thought in this note was suggested by the two articles of J. B. Trapp on 'The Conformity of Greek and the Vernacular' in R. R. Bolgar (ed.), *Classical Influences on European Culture, AD 500 – 1500* (London, 1971), pp. 239 – 44, and in *Words. Wai-te-ata Studies in English* 4 (1973), 8 – 21. All students of Renaissance theories of language look forward eagerly to the completion of the study of which these are a foretaste.

the language, writers and educators. A number perhaps belong to that large class of English speakers who, armed only with their prejudices, have throughout the ages pontificated about their language; by 'the English language' many probably mean something more like 'the language of the educated' or 'the language of poetry'. Literary and moral judgments are inextricably involved with their thoughts about language.

Besides the more general intellectual background to the question of 'purism', there is a particular linguistic context to be considered. A sort of half-explanation of the phenomenon sometimes offered is as a reaction against the expansion of the vocabulary in the Renaissance period. That many new words did enter the vocabulary then is undeniable, but this had happened before (notably with French loan-words), and was to happen again (notably with the industrial, scientific, and technological coinages of the nineteenth and the twentieth centuries). It seems reasonable therefore to seek the chief causes of this particular reaction in Renaissance cultural history. However, it is the case that varieties of 'purism' seem to emerge when speakers feel that their language is 'under threat' for one reason or another, or sometimes even when they are confronted with words 'unfamiliar' or foreign in sound or in appearance, which they find offensive.[2] Notoriously, languages differ in the degree of 'tolerance' that they offer in the acceptance of such words: in Modern English almost all the barriers are down. One cannot but wonder what a sixteenth-century opponent of 'strange' or 'affected' diction would have made of the variety of aural and visual patterns that we have come to tolerate — *czar*, *khaki*, *kimono*, *spaghetti*, *kiosk*, *Zeitgeist*, *beatnik*, *tattoo*, *bungalow*, *pyjamas* — not to mention those that still excite some resistance, like *interface* or *megabyte*. This is obviously a factor to be considered. On the other hand — as the record of sixteenth-century English reactions to 'ink-horn terms' and foreign loanwords so clearly shows — there may also be a strong personal (not to say idiosyncratic) element in such judgements: what one man thinks of as 'half-changed Latin' may seem to another a brilliant innovation.

Obviously the most significant intellectual 'context' is the intense discussion which went on — first in Italy, later in Northern Europe — about the *questione della lingua*, that central topic of Renaissance culture. The vernacular (which could then seem a poor thing in comparison with Latin, both because of the paucity of its literary achievements and because as a language it seemed unstable, without rules, not yet 'reduced to art') needed to be defended and improved:

[2] See U. Weinreich, *Languages in Contact* (New York, 1953), pp. 64–5, 99–103.

'there was no country in Europe during the sixteenth century where the attempt was not made to improve the vernacular to a point where it could compete, on equal terms, with Latin'.[3] Such attempts inevitably raised questions of 'augmentation' by lexical borrowing or other means. At the same time, the excitement generated by the humanist rediscovery of 'correct' classical Latin had given a special 'resonance' to some of the value-words often applied to language or to style (and which were bound to be used in any discussion of lexical 'augmentation'), words like 'pure' and 'purity', 'elegant' and 'elegance'[4] — or their wicked opposites, 'corrupt' and 'corruption', 'barbarous' and 'barbarity'. This 'rediscovery' was a restoration to a former purity, to a language that was good, old, and true. Since much humanist philology was not narrowly linguistic, but was a search for truth through the word,[5] it is not surprising that discussions of language sometimes have a very strong moral (and indeed Christian) substratum — witness the intensity with which Colet banishes from his St Paul's School 'all barbarye and corrupcioun, all Laten adulterate' which has 'distaynyde and poysonyde the olde Laten speche and the veray Romayne tonge', and insists that the boys should study 'goode auctours suche as have the veray Romayne eloquence joynyde withe wisdome, specially Cristen auctours that wrote there wisdome with clene and chast Latten. . .'

Behind the dispute over 'inkhorn terms' and borrowings lie some very ancient arguments, the most famous of which is Plato's *Cratylus*, a debate on the origin and nature of language, on the relation between words and meanings, and on the rival claim of nature (*physis*) and convention (*nomos*) — whether tacit convention or legislation. Cratylus holds that the relationship is based on a natural affinity between the form of a word and its meaning ('everything has a right name of its own, which comes by nature'). His opponent Hermogenes claims, on the other hand, that 'whatever name you give to a thing is its right name'. This is a conventionalist or 'contractualist' view — the vocabulary can change or be changed by 'convention', and once the change is accepted, the language will continue to be equally efficient. At the beginning of the dialogue, this is put in an extreme way by Hermogenes (almost amounting to Alice's 'words mean what I what them to mean'). Socrates

[3] Trapp, *Words*, p. 8.
[4] On eighteenth-century uses of 'elegance' for 'correctness', see P. Ingham, 'Dr Johnson's "Elegance" ', *RES* 19 (1968), 271 – 8. Like so many Augustan rhetorical and linguistic ideas this is a reflex of earlier humanist theory. Significantly, the word forms part of the title of that influential fifteenth-century treatise, Valla's *De Elegantiis linguae latinae*.
[5] On this see Cecil Grayson, *A Renaissance Controversy: Latin or Italian* (Oxford, 1960).

(who claims he has not formed any conclusion on the subject) takes him to task: if propositions can be true or false, so can names. The correctness of names is based on the intention of showing the nature of the things named. A name is a vocal imitation of that which is imitated, and — in its letters and its syllables — it is an imitation of the essential nature of the thing. Here Socrates is not far from the 'naturalist' position. The demonstration of the 'correctness' of names depends on the presence of onomatopoeia or sound symbolism, or the restoration of the original 'natural' forms by the use of etymology. Some pages are devoted to this and are filled with examples that are decidedly far-fetched. It may be that in some at least Socrates is making fun of etymologists, but the basic technique is taken seriously. Socrates admits that we cannot find out about the earliest forms of words — sometimes, he says (significantly), because the words are foreign (*barbarikos*). Cratylus now agrees with Socrates quite unreservedly that the 'correctness of a name is the quality of showing the nature of the thing named', whereupon Socrates turns his critical eye upon this, demonstrates to Cratylus some of the difficulties of an extreme position, and sends him off to think further about it.

Echoes of this debate can be heard throughout antiquity.[6] Aristotle holds to a 'conventionalist' view; the Stoics, on the other hand, with a characteristic emphasis on 'nature' as a guide to the good life, favour the idea that words have a natural origin, that the first sounds imitated the things which they name (and that through etymology one could recover these onomatopoeic 'original forms' or 'first sounds'). (After Christianity, it was fairly easy to fit into this discussion the Judaeo-Christian myth of the confusion of tongues at Babel,[7] before which 'the whole earth was of one language, and of one speech', and the idea that what was lost was not only the original unity (whether or not the first language was Hebrew), but also the original purity:

> In Eden, ere yet innocence of heart
> Had faded, poetry was not an art;
> Language, above all teaching, or, if taught,
> Only by gratitude and glowing thought,
> Elegant as simplicity, and warm
> As ecstasy, unmanacled by form . . .[8])

[6] See the discussions in R. H. Robins, *A Short History of Linguistics* (London, 1967), and R. Harris, *The Language-Makers* (London, 1980).
[7] See Arno Borst, *Der Turmbau von Babel. Geschichte der Meinungen über Ursprung und Vielfalt der Sprachen und Völker* (Stuttgart, 1957 – 63).
[8] William Cowper, *Table Talk*, 584 – 9. Such views lie behind the opinion of

Anti-primitivists like Diodorus Siculus or Cicero take an 'evolutionary' view, that language developed from confused and unformed sounds by social agreement or by reason. It must of course be stressed that such attitudes are opposed in a general way, and rarely accord exactly with those of Cratylus and Hermogenes. Their views may be held in extreme or less extreme forms; others may prefer an eclectic or 'middle of the way' position. There is too a further complication in that a 'conventionalist' position leads very easily (since in practice it is evident that there may be disagreement about which linguistic 'conventions' are to be accepted) to a 'prescriptive' or 'normative' view of language which can be as strict as that of Cratylus in its listing of solecisms, barbarisms, etc.[9]

Some of the wider ramifications of this debate in the rhetorical tradition of antiquity have been explored in an article by E. H. Gombrich.[10] Plato's attacks on the sophists as corrupters of youth — especially Gorgias, the founder of the elaborate 'Asiatic' style, which in Plato's eyes is ostentatious and depraved (Gombrich remarks [p. 26] how in this term 'ideas of patriotism . . . mixed with conservatism in matters of language, as they have often done since. The exotic, the newfangled word or phrase is a hallmark of affectation and of servility to fashion. The reformer of language, like the reformer of religion, raises the banner of purity, of a return to origins and a contempt of innovations'), found an echo in the Roman rhetoricians in the debate between 'Atticists' and 'Asianists', with each side again accusing the other of moral turpitude (the Asiatic rhetoric is 'intolerably ostentatious, shameless and dissolute . . . vulgar . . . and offensive'; it had reduced Hellas to the plight of the household ruled by a riotous mistress, spurning the free-born, virtuous wedded wife[11]). Those of the Attic school were regarded as 'concise and healthy' (*pressi et integri*), those of the Asiatic 'empty

---

Hildegard of Bingen that Adam, who before the Fall knew the song of angels and every kind of music, after it lost his musical voice, which was replaced by loud laughing and boorish jeering, or its equivalent in those noble savages of late antiquity, the Brahmins of the Alexander legends, who say that in their happy primitive existence they 'do not speak many words' and do not teach the art of eloquence because they have natural eloquence (G. Boas, *Essays on Primitivism and Related Ideas in the Middle Ages*, Baltimore, 1948, pp. 75, 142).

[9] Harris, p. 102.

[10] E. H. Gombrich, 'The Debate on Primitivism in Ancient Rhetoric', *JWCI* 29 (1966), 24 – 38.

[11] Dionysius of Halicarnassus, quoted by Gombrich, pp. 25 – 6.

and inflated' (*inflati . . . et inanes*).[12] Cicero's defence of his style, attacked as 'too soft to be manly' by the Atticists, involves a notion of progress; Cato may be a model for those who admire roughness and simplicity, but he is not polished, and a greater perfection is possible. With his practical view of oratory as a means of persuasion, he has an 'instrumental view of progress'. This he elaborates in *De Oratore*. He insists on decorum, and the need for restraint, but this for him has less to do with the avoiding of corruption than with craftsmanship. His awareness of the way in which taste changes — things which delight us when they first appear quickly become tiresome ('although it is also true that in the case of old pictures the actual roughness and old-fashioned style are an attraction') — leads to a kind of relativism ('later art . . . is not better than the earlier phase, it is only different'). As Gombrich says, 'with this transformation of history into a succession of modes the way was clearly open for the appreciation of archaic art and primitive styles'.

Quintilian adopts a moderate position (which was to be most influential in the Renaissance), opposed to both extremes. Ornament (VIII.iii, 66ff.) must be 'bold, manly, and chaste' (*virilis et fortis et sanctus*), shining in 'health and vigour' (*sanguine et viribus*) and 'free from effeminate smoothness' (*nec effeminatam levitatem . . . amet*). In every kind of style *cacozelia* or 'perverse affectation' (*mala adfectatio*) is a fault, and he speaks of its 'corrupting' effects (VIII.iii, 56ff.). But on the other hand, the orator cannot follow the practice of the first men, who knew nothing of that art: 'what art was ever born full-grown?' Yet he should not be over-fastidious in the choice of words. In the case of appropriate words, antiquity gives a dignity (*propriis dignitatem dat antiquitas*), for these, which not everyone would use, make the discourse more venerable and majestic (*sanctiorem et magis admirabilem faciunt orationem*).[13] Virgil is masterly in his use of them. Alongside a firm sense of progress in the art of oratory goes a sensitivity 'to the spell of these archaic modes', as in the famous remarks on Ennius, 'who deserves our reverence, but only as those groves whose age has made them sacred, but whose huge and ancient trunks inspire us with religious awe rather than with admiration for their beauty' [tr. Butler] (*non tantam habent speciem quantam religionem*) — 'there are other poets nearer to us, and for what we are discussing, more useful' (X.1, 88) — which are echoed by Ben Jonson in his remarks on Spenser.

[12] Quintilian, XII.x,13.
[13] Quintilian is pragmatic about new formations (VIII.iii,32ff.): some formed from the Greek 'are regarded as unduly harsh', but some become established (*perdurant*).

As Gombrich points out, in an 'expressionist' view of style — like Longinus's sublime, which is 'the ring of a noble soul' — it is easy for this *religio* to flourish as primitivism:

> Pride in progress is easily accompanied by guilt feelings. For have we not departed from the ways and manners of our fathers? Thus the physiognomic reaction to early styles becomes bound up with a moral nostalgia. We are no longer capable of the sublime because we lack the noble soul that alone can produce it. Paradoxically this physiognomic reaction can be reinforced by that image of progress which was the one known to the classical tradition — the image of growth and decay in the life-cycle of arts and skills. If the arts had their childhood before they reached maturity and declined towards an inevitable death their early phase could gather upon itself all the emotions that we usually project on to childhood and youth. Those were the days of innocence, spontaneity and naïve enjoyment, of uncorrupted chastity and guileless honesty. Imperceptibly, and thus all the more powerfully the two contradictory images could merge. The stern old ancestors were at the same time innocent youth. They were old because they were born so long ago, they were young because they lived in the childhood of the world.[14]

Perhaps, as he suggests, one of the attractions of primitive style is that it can unite both 'soft' primitivism (the dream of the golden age of peace and plenty) with 'hard' primitivism (the myth of the heroic age): 'when we are most worried about the softness and effeminacy of our civilisation it will be the strength and robustness of the past that will appeal to us most. When we are more aware of our moral failings it will be the innocence of the idyll that will captivate our imagination.'

These ancient arguments contain a number of ideas — both large (like the attraction of the lost Golden Age, or the association of language with civilisation and with morality) and small (such as the admiration of simplicity, brevity,[15] conciseness) — that are of obvious significance for Renaissance discussions of the nature and improvement of the vernaculars. Two in particular deserve special mention. If a man is sympathetic to the views of Cratylus, he will be disposed (though not obliged) to wish to reform the language from its corruption, to restore it to its original purity, and disposed to resist the unnecessary 'borrowing' of foreign words. If however he inclines to those of Hermogenes, clearly these sentiments will not be held so deeply; change is not only possible, but — depending on how generous his acceptance of 'convention' is — may be a positive advantage. 'Loanwords' and 'inkhorn terms' will be

---

[14] Gombrich, pp. 36 – 7.
[15] See E. R. Curtius, *European Literature in the Latin Middle Ages* (tr. Willard R. Trask, London, 1953), Excursus XIII 'Brevity as an ideal of Style'.

judged variously according to criteria of efficiency or regularity. Similarly, the insistence of Socrates on the importance of etymology — however far-fetched (a tradition gloriously continuing into the *Doctor in Linguas* of Minsheu and *The Diversions of Purley* of Horne Tooke, who will have everything from Anglo-Saxon rather than from that mere modern language Latin) — also has its *Nachleben* throughout antiquity, the Middle Ages and the Renaissance.[16] It may be used for grander purposes than those of humble philology — for (separately and in combination) philosophical argument (as in Lucretius's association of *umor* 'seed' and *amor*), for understanding the divine harmony that expresses itself through created things (as in the encyclopedia of Isidore of Seville, significantly named *Originum sive Etymologiarum Libri XX*), for effect in rhetoric and poetry, for awakening the comprehension of listeners in church (in England from Ælfric explaining the significance of the names Stephen or Rachel to Lancelot Andrewes, punning not only on the celebrated *Verbum infans* but elsewhere — 'What could they [the shepherds] wish, but *O quod erit Signum! Natus est*, ô that He were *Signatus*? O that we had a *signe* to find Him by!') or in schools (where the *sententia* that *education* means 'a drawing out' rather than 'a putting in' is still not quite dead). Clearly, etymology is likely to be a necessary interest to those of Cratylist sympathies.

But it is time to turn to Renaissance English 'purism' and to the central figure of Sir John Cheke (1514 – 1557), famous as a distinguished scholar (who, as Milton says, taught Cambridge and King Edward Greek — as Regius Professor from 1540 – 51) and as a firm Protestant as well as one who had views on the English vernacular. He is best known for his letter (written in the year of his death) to Hoby, the translator of Castiglione,[17] in which he states his views on English. If we look again at this famous passage in the light of the ancient discussions of language and style, we find ideas that are familiar and words that are filled with familiar connotations. Our own tongue 'shold be written cleane and pure, unmixt and unmangeled with borowing of other tunges'. Words and images with moral connotations of ancient honesty and 'uncorrupted chastity' are invoked in his excursus on 'loan-words' (to use the nineteenth-century term) and their possible bad effects: if our tongue goes on 'ever borowing and never payeng, she shall be fain to keep her house as bankrupt'. The old image of the 'mother tongue' as the virtuous mistress of the house is succeeded by another — that of honest plain

---

[16] See Curtius, Excursus XIV 'Etymology as a Category of Thought'.
[17] Whose book, *The Courtier*, contains a celebrated discussion of the question of language.

dress, genuinely one's own, as against affected foreign finery: 'for then doth our tung naturallie and praisablie utter her meaning, when she borouweth no counterfeitness of other tunges to attire her self withall, but useth plainlie her own . . .' 'She' should behave in the manner of a chaste, modest matron: 'if she want [i.e. lack] at ani tijm (as being unperfight she must)', let her borrow with 'bashfulnes' — preferably fashioning 'a woord of our own' according to 'the mould of our own tong' or using 'the old denisoned wordes' rather than boldly venturing 'unknowen words'. (It is often pointed out that Cheke is not such an extreme purist that he objects to *all* borrowings: he praises Hoby because in the few cases where he has had to use a 'strange word' 'it seemeth of grow out of the matter and not to be sought for'.) Throughout, there is an insistence on purity and integrity (notice the word *naturallie* with its implication of conformity to the 'mould' of the language, that which is old and true), which will afford a good (notice the word *praisablie*) model of style.

As we shall see, there is a certain consistency in his linguistic views. Without wishing to press the evidence too far, it may also be suggested that there is some consistency between his moral views and his (morally based?) linguistic views. Here, both the fact that he was a firm Protestant and that he was a professor of Greek may have some significance. In his *Hurt of Sedition* (1549), written against the insurrection of Ket the Tanner, he defends the reformed religion against the charge that it is 'new'. It is in fact the true, old and pure religion, now restored and brought into conformity with the teachings of Christ, the oldest and the truest of the 'doctors', and cleansed from later corruption:

> Ye will have the old still. Will ye have any older than that as Christ left, and His apostles taught, and the first church after Christ did use? . . . And do you prefer the bishops from Rome afore Christ, man's inventions afore God's law, the newer sort of worship before the older? Ye seek no religion, ye be deceived, ye seek traditions . . . If ye seek what the old doctors say, yet look what Christ the oldest of all saith . . .

It is hard not to associate this view with that which impelled him to translate the gospel using old words and eschewing those which might suggest the 'traditions' of the 'newer' religion. Similar ideas were 'in the air' at this time. The preface to the Great Bible (1539) notes that even before the Wycliffite version, the Bible had been translated into English: 'many hundred yeares before that, it was translated and redde in the Saxones tonge, whiche at that tyme was oure mothers tonge, wherof there remaineth yet divers copyes founde lately in olde abbeys, of suche antique maners of wrytynge and speakynge, that fewe men nowe ben able to reade and understande them . . .' and, in its eloquent Protestant

111

manifesto for the Bible in the vulgar tongue, contrasts the practical simplicity of the Scriptures with the 'Asiatic' finery of the gentiles:

> [in them] as well publicanes, fysshers, and shepherdes maye fynde theyr edificacion, as greate doctours theyr erudicion: for these bookes were not made to vayne glorye lyke as were the wrytynges of the gentyll philosophers and rethoricians to the entent the makers shoulde be had in admiration for theyr hye stiles and obscure maner and wrytynge whereof nothynge can be understande without a master or an expositoure . . .

It was not long before a few men did read and understand Saxon texts, and use them to argue that the reformed English church was 'not a new reformation of things begun' but 'rather a reduction of the church to the pristine state of olde conformitie, which once it had'.[18] The labours of Archbishop Parker and his secretary Joscelyn were soon to produce *A Testimonie of Antiquitie* (1565 – 6) in which Ælfric is made to support Anglican doctrine. Antiquarian interest dates from the days of Cheke's contemporaries Bale and Leland; the beginnings of the long study of Anglo-Saxon laws and institutions can be seen in Lambarde's *Archaionomia* (1568). With this came an interest in lexicography and language. By the seventeenth century Anglo-Saxon is being praised for being 'so pure English of the time' (Lisle, 1623 — who remarks that the authors of the Saxon Bibles, 'these monuments of reverend antiquity', do not (unlike some later translators) 'stuffe the text with such fustian, such inkehorne termes, as may seeme to favour their parts; or darken at least the true meaning of holy Scripture': 'Witnesse their *Parasceve of the Pasche*, their *Azimes*, . . . their *Supererogate*, their *Supersubstantiall bread*, and many the like'), and the Anglo-Saxons were endowed by late sixteenth and early seventeenth-century antiquarians with the primitive

---

[18] On early Anglo-Saxon studies, see Eleanor N. Adams, *Old English Scholarship in England 1566 – 1800* (Yale Studies in English 55, 1917), R. F. Jones, *The Triumph of the English Language* (Stanford, 1953), chapters vii – viii, C. T. Berkhout and M. McC. Gatch (eds.), *Anglo-Saxon Scholarship, The First Three Centuries* (Boston, 1982), R. Tuve, 'Ancients, Moderns, and Saxons' *ELH* 6 (1939), 165 – 190, E. G. Stanley, 'The Scholarly Recovery of the Significance of Anglo-Saxon Records in Prose and Verse: A New Bibliography' and 'The Bibliography of Old English: The Past', both reprinted in his *A Collection of Papers with Emphasis on Old English Literature* (Toronto, 1987).

virtues of strength, manliness, simplicity, and laconic brevity. Putten-ham says that most words in 'our naturall and primitive language of the Saxon English' are monosyllables; Camden speaks of the 'succinct brevitie' of their names, and praises their 'singular valour and wisdom'. Richard Verstegen (1605) laments the way in which English has become mixed with other languages (unlike Dryden later, he does not hold that 'from Chaucer the purity of the English tongue began'). At the end of the century Bishop Sprat makes his famous call for a return to 'primitive purity and shortness'. Cheke's 'Saxonism' is of an earlier and less theoretical kind, but it is — chronologically at least — not far from the genesis of this significant theological, antiquarian and philological tradition.

The importance of the rediscovery of Greek for the Renaissance *questione della lingua* has been shown by Professor J. B. Trapp.[19] In brief, the defence of the vernaculars against the classical languages cannot always be seen simply as a straightforward combat with Latin. By establishing the 'conformity' of Greek with a vernacular (by claiming early Greek settlement by colonists or merchants or by detecting in the two languages similarities of word, phrase or spirit — thus Sir Thomas Elyot in the preface to his translation of Isocrates (c. 1533) says 'the forme of speakyng, used of the Grekes, called . . . *Phrasis*, muche nere approcheth to that, whiche at this daie we use: than the order of the latine tonge: I meane in the sentences, not in the wordes . . .'), a writer could attempt to establish the independence of the vernacular by 'going behind' Latin, or suggest ways in which the younger language could be helped to manhood by linguistic or literary borrowing.[20] The use of Greek models could improve style by giving a rich, sententious brevity (a 'laconic'[21] style as against a diffuse Ciceronian one, for instance). Such arguments are often associated with linguistic chauvinism or purism. The most elaborate discussions of these matters took place in France (and there are some marked effects in the practice of the Hellenizing poets of the Pléiade), but they seem also to have been known in England. Tyndale remarks on the conformity of English with Greek and Hebrew in his preface to *The Obedience of a Christian Man* (1528), and Elyot seems clearly to have been interested in experimenting with the stylistic

---

[19] In the articles listed in note 1 above.
[20] Castiglione, for instance, uses it to argue against the idea of a single standard of literary Tuscan. See Trapp, *Words*, p. 12.
[21] The quotations in *OED* under *laconic, laconian, laconical, laconicism, laconism*, etc. make interesting reading in this respect.

possibilities of 'conformity' with Greek — he says of his Isocrates 'this little booke . . . I have translated out of Greeke . . . to thintent onely that I wolde assaie, if our Englisshe tunge mought receive the quicke and propre sentences pronounced by the Greekes'. As with 'Saxonism' the notion of 'conformity with Greek' seems to have been 'in the air'. Professor Trapp suggests that Cheke (and his pupil Ascham) had some knowledge of the idea of 'conformity'. There are hints of it in Cheke's Gospel translation and in his writings on Greek pronunciation, and possibly also in his teaching practice — cf. the story in Strype:[22] 'Dr Wylson . . . asserted, that he had better skill in our English speech, to judg of the phrases, and properties of words, and to divide sentences, than any else had, that he knew; and that he was thought by some judicious men, greatly to have improved the language by a practice he had, when he read his Greek lectures, to take the book, and only looking upon the Greek, to read it into English. Whereby he did not only give a clearer understanding of the author, but enabled his hearers the better to judg of the things, and to perfect their tongue and utterance, as was remembred before.'

With Thomas Smith, Cheke played an important role in the reformation of the pronunciation of Greek. His exchanges with his opponent Bishop Gardiner (who was opposed to him on theological as well as linguistic matters) in a series of letters[23] are sometimes reminiscent of the argument in the *Cratylus* and its aftermath in antiquity. Gardiner warns him (in Strype's words) 'that he would not be too much a Stoic in weighing of sounds [*ne sis in excutiendis sonis nimium Stoicus*]; and to remember, that as words, so also sounds, receive their authority from use and from reason [*arbitrium ab usu autoritatem non a ratione accipere*]. *Utere*, added he, *antiquis moribus, verbis vero praesentibus, et multo magis sonis*, i.e. use antient manners, but present words, and much more sounds', and expresses the fear that Cheke would 'turn Cambridge into Babylon by a woful Metamorphosis, or if anything be more confused than Babylon.' Cheke objects that 'letters and sound were changed and defiled in the last barbarous age, which it was better to cleanse and restore, than to imitate', speaking like a good humanist (and appealing to 'Erasmus and other learned men that had taken notice of these errors') and like a good Cratylist. Like Hermogenes, Gardiner argues that the change is not

---

[22] J. Strype, *Life of Cheke* (1705), p. 212.
[23] Written in 1542; printed in *De Pronunciatione linguae graecae* (Basel, 1555).

'contamination', 'but a mutation only', and that 'every change was not to be disproved'. He holds that it is 'convenient and decent to pronounce according to the custom and mode of the present age, a new way of pronouncing words being so surprizing, and the reducing it to the use of the antients, offensive to peoples ears' (using an English example, he claims that no-one would pronounce the word *kyss* as *kuss*, 'the old rude way' (*quae antiquioribus et rudibus sonabat u*) — his phraseology clearly appealing to the idea of linguistic progress — instead of the modern way with 'i' (*urbanitatis causa*).[24] Where Cheke urges that sounds should be reduced 'to their first and original truth', Gardiner says 'let all things have their age, and their youth, and as words do words, so let us allow sounds to succeed sounds' (*sit omnibus rebus suum senium, sua juventus, et ut verba verbis, sic etiam sonis sonos succedere permittamus*). Cheke also defends his reformed system on practical grounds — students learn the language more efficiently and quickly — and on aesthetic — 'there was now so much delight and sweetness now perceived in Homers or Sophocles verses, by reason of the variety of sounds, and modulation of the numbers, that no music, no lute could be more pleasant' — but the basic argument is that modern errors should be removed and ancient purity restored — 'it was not novelty, to discover this way of pronouncing Greek words according to the truth; since it was only intermitted and laid away for a time. Nor was this to innovate any things, to introduce that which was antient and profitable.'

It is not surprising that a man who held such views on Greek sounds seems to have held similar ones on English spelling,[25] of which, says Strype, 'he endeavoured the correcting and regulating': 'he would have none of the letter E put to the end of words, as needless and unexpressive of any sounds . . . unless where it is sounded, and then to be writ with a double E, as in *Necessitee*; 'where the letter A was sounded long, he would have it writ with a double A', etc. It looks here as if the principles are as much those of economy as of an attempt to restore original or primitive spellings — though something like that may lie behind it, when (Strype) he 'changed the spelling in some words to make them the better expressive of the sounds'.

[24] Interestingly, Cheke derives the form *kuss* from Greek *kusai* (pp. 84 – 5).
[25] See E. J. Dobson, *English Pronunciation 1500 – 1700* (Oxford, 2nd edn, 1968), I, pp. 38 – 46. That Cheke is inconsistent simply shows that for all his interest in language he was not a modern 'scientific' phonetician or spelling reformer.

115

His practice with the vocabulary of English in his translation of St Matthew's gospel (and the beginning of St Mark's)[26] also seems to follow a pattern, though not a rigid one. Strype says that 'he laboured to use only true English Saxon words', but in this 'over-laboured' translation he was 'forced to make use of several words of foreign derivation'. The truth is a little more complicated. There is a conscious attempt to produce a simple, old, and generally 'Saxon' complexion by the use of some 'old denisoned wordes' — by no means all of Anglo-Saxon origin: thus, instead of *crucified* he has *crossed* (a word not of Old English origin, but which is found in texts of the fourteenth and fifteenth centuries; the absence of examples after Cheke suggests that it was archaic or becoming archaic in his day); *wisards* for *magi* (perhaps more exact than Tyndale and Cranmer's *wise men*, and less 'learned' than the Wycliffite *astromyens*). *Tollers* in the phrase 'many tollers and sinners' is an old word for tax- or toll-gatherer, still in use in the sixteenth century; it is presumably preferred to *publicans* because it sounds 'native' — though *publican* was common enough in religious writing (e.g. in *The Parson's Tale*). *Lepernes* (8:1) is presumably meant to sound more 'Saxon' than (Tyndale's) *leprosye*; where Tyndale has *servant*, Cheke (Matt. 20:27) has *waiter on*. Sometimes he will extend the sense of an already existing native word. This seems to be the case with his *hunderder* for the not uncommon word *centurion* (perhaps adapted from the existing word *hundreder* = 'bailiff of a hundred'; possibly suggested by a note in Tyndale's translation of Matt. 8:5 'whom I call sometimes a centurion but for the most part a hunder-captain' [*OED*]), and may be the case with *freschman* = 'proselyte' (if either of the senses 'newcomer, novice' or 'first-year student' attested later in the sixteenth century were — as seems likely — current in Cheke's day). Perhaps the rather specialized 'proselyte', although it is Greek (and in the MS the Greek word is written in the margin of Matt. 23) was thought to be 'strange' and not understanded of the people. A similar possible case of extension is *tabler* = 'money-lender' (attested only in the sense of 'player at backgammon' in the sixteenth century), but perhaps this is

---

[26] Available only in the edition of J. Goodwin (London, 1843). This translation must be set against the background of theological discussion and argument generated by the various Reformation translations of the Scriptures. In 1542, when the question of a new translation was in the air, Bishop Gardiner (who had been allocated one of the Gospels) presented to Convocation a list of Latin words which he thought should be retained or translated with as little alteration as possible (see R. W. Dixon, *History of the Church of England* ii (London, 1881), pp. 285 – 9). It is an odd list (containing words or phrases like *sanctus spiritus, confessio, ecclesia, tetrarcha, mysterium, parabola, baptizare* — a number of which are of relevance to the student of Cheke), and it may reflect not only his conservative views but also his concern and feeling for Latin.

formed from *table* (i.e. one who keeps accounts in 'tablets'). Certainly, Cheke will sometimes fashion a word of his own from native elements according to the 'mould' of the tongue: thus *outpeopling* (= 'emptying the country of people', where the Wycliffite version has *transmygracioun*) or *moond* (= 'lunatic'). One or two of his notes may support the idea that a kind of 'Saxonism' is at work; in ch. 10 he notes that just as the Egyptians and the Greeks called every country except their own barbarous, and Romans called others *externos*, so 'the Germans and our old Saxons called the lijk welsch men' and 'we now cal them strangers and outborns, and outlandisch'. And when (ch. 16) he is discussing the word *ekklesia*,[27] he remarks that the word *church* comes from Greek *kuriakon* — we following the Greek 'calle this house, as the north doth yet moor truli sound it, the kurk, and we moor corruptli and frenchlike, the church' — an early example of the idea that because the Northern dialect is closer to old forms it is 'truer' and more pure (Puttenham later, though he would not have a courtly poet use the terms of the Northern men, says that 'no one can deny that theirs is the purer English Saxon at this day').

But Cheke is not as thoroughgoing a 'Saxonist' as William Barnes was later to be. He uses words such as *extremitie, divorce, repentence, pinnacle, hypocrites* (with an explanatory note), *sacrifice* (with a careful theological note — Tyndale had preferred *offering*) and many others. Alongside *il wordes* he sometimes has *blasphemies*; alongside *wasching, baptism*. He says 'hord not yourself greet hoords on the earth', but he also uses the word *treasure*. To us it seems surprising that he has *margarites* for *pearls* — but the fact that the Wycliffite version also has it (Matt. 7:6) may well show that this word, still in use in the sixteenth century, was thought to be as 'homely' as *pearl*; Cheke must also have been pleased by its conformity with its Greek original, which is written in the margin. Similarly, alongside *biwordes* (from Old English, and still in sixteenth-century use, but normally in the sense of 'proverbs' or 'proverbial sayings') he will use the Greek *parables*.

It seems that he is not only striving for a precise translation (or 'trutorn' as he likes to call it) of the Greek, but for a larger 'conformity'. One or two words are taken over, e.g. *Corbon* (Matt. 27:6, where Tyndale has *treasury* — the Rheims version of 1582 keeps 'the Corbana'), or more startlingly, the *acrids* that John the Baptist eats with his wild honey (3:4) — but it may be that *locusts* were not as familiar in

---

[27] This word was, of course, a tricky one for the translator (cf. the preceding note), and Cheke, though not following the clearly Protestant *congregation* of Tyndale, gives *church* a careful Protestant definition.

the earlier sixteenth century as they became later.[28] Elsewhere he seems to be trying to imitate the concision of Greek word-formation and syntax. Thus the earlier translations *hadden develis* or *were possessed with devils* are rejected for *develled* in imitation of the single Greek word. Similarly, he prefers *smalfaithed* to *of little faith*; and where Tyndale has (20:25) 'have dominacion over them . . . exercise power over them' he has 'overmaster them . . . overrule them'. In general, too, the example of Greek seems to have encouraged him (as it did some later English writers) to use the native English pattern of compounding to very good effect: cf. *the bloudground*, *the sculplace*, *outcalled*, etc. 'Conformity' with Greek and 'Saxonism' work together intimately and powerfully. At its best his translation is not 'laboured', but combines a native vigour ('the hoole citi was on a stirre') with clarity and 'purity',[29] and the 'quick and proper sentences' of the Greeks.

The influence of Cheke can be clearly seen in those who met him or studied under him at Cambridge — his pupil Ascham with his ideal of eloquence, a lucid and 'comely' style (in the description of which he uses moral epithets like 'pure' and 'chaste') and his insistence that there must be 'no devorse betwixt the tong and the hart';[30] Thomas Wilson, another firm Protestant, and another who insists on plainness ('an oratour must . . . utter his mind in plaine words, such as are usually received, and tell it orderly, without going about the bush') and who makes fun of 'straunge ynkehorne termes'; or Ralph Lever, with his attempts to find 'terms of art' in native English.[31] 'Purism' is not a clearly defined intellectual creed; there is much eclecticism, and it contains many strands; the moderation of Quintilian is probably more in evidence than the extremer theories of Cratylus, expressing itself in an admiration for language that is 'manly' and 'chaste', and a veneration for old words properly used.

The complex of ideas described by the word 'purism' not only makes sense in the context of Renaissance cultural history, but is of considerable importance for the English literature of this period. Fairly obviously it relies on — and emphasizes — the humanist view that

[28] Although the word appears in early translations (and in Cheke's own *Mark*, ch. 1), one or two of the glosses or explanations recorded in *OED* (svv. *locust* and *locusta*) may suggest this.

[29] Cf. the characteristically worded note in ch. 6: 'clene, unmixt, as clene wheet, cleen barli that hath no other thing mixt withal' (this is the Greek word *haplous* translated by Tyndale as 'single' — 'the light of the body is in thyne eye. Wherfore if thyne eye be syngle all thy body shalbe ful of light'; Cheke has 'cleen').

[30] See the excellent article of Thomas M. Greene, 'Roger Ascham: The Proper End of Shooting', *ELH* 36 (1969), 609 – 25.

[31] On Lever's practice, see R. F. Jones, pp. 124 – 9.

language has a central role in civilization. Less obviously perhaps, it influences stylistic theories and practices that are quite opposed to each other. Thus it may not be fanciful to relate it both to the practice of Spenser, who delighted more in 'dark conceits' and in the power of ancient words than Ascham or Wilson might have approved of (and, one suspects, in a more intense and Cratylist way than E.K., with his Ciceronian talk of decorum and of the 'ornament' afforded by 'auncient solemne wordes', would allow — in a way which may be closer to Ronsard's view of the original 'nayve' and divine poetry), and to the criticisms of Spenser's practice by Sidney and Jonson. This creative tension between augmentation and experiment on the one hand and criticism of what may appear excessive or over-ingenious augmentation and experiment on the other seems central to the great literary achievements of Renaissance England.

'DEVY' OR 'DENY'?

Richard Hamer

'Do way,' quoþ þat derf mon, 'my dere, þat speche,
For þat durst I not do, lest I deuayed were;
If I were werned, I were wrang, iwysse, ȝif I profered.'
'Ma fay,' quoþ þe mere wyf, 'ȝe may not be werned,
ȝe ar stif innoghe to constrayne wyth strenkþe, ȝif yow lykez,
ȝif any were so vilanous þat yow devaye wolde.'

Sir Gawain ll.1492 – 7

OED records no word *devy* or *devay*; *MED* records *devayen*, citing only
the above two examples from *Gawain*, both of which appear with *n* for
v in *OED* s.v. *deny* v. sense 6, as they do in the earliest editions of the
poem. The scribe, like many in this period, writes *u* and *n* indistinguishably, so at l.1493 either is possible; but at l.1497 the manuscript
clearly has *de vaye*, and the early editors substituted *denaye* to conform
with what they thought was preceding *denayed*, despite the requirement of the alliteration. Gollancz in his 1897 revision of Morris's edition
printed *devaye*, and in 1915 C. Brett discussed the derivation of this
word, which represents the not uncommon French *deveer/devier*,
meaning 'refuse, forbid', most probably from Latin **devetare*, formed
on *vetare*, 'forbid'.[1] The 1940 EETS edition[2] argues for *deuayed* at
l.1493, which has been accepted by subsequent editors and *MED*. The
Lady is teasing Gawain by repeating his rare word. As it happens, *deny*
occurs nowhere else in this manuscript. It is probable that if the scribe
had not chanced to write a *v* at l.1497 this would have been regarded
simply as a rare case of alliterative freedom by the poet, and the word
devay would not be thought to exist at all.

Since in many other cases *deny* (French *denier/deneier*) and *devy*
would be effectively identical in sense, to distinguish between them one

[1] C. Brett, *MLR* 10 (1915), 194 – 5.
[2] Ed. I. Gollancz, with introductory essays by M. Day and M. S. Serjeantson,
EETS 210.

would need a scribe who consistently differentiated *n* and *u*, or who happened to write *v* rather than *u* in the latter; the difficulty would have been the same for medieval copyists, so there may well be instances where they have substituted one for the other. Given its apparent rarity, *devy* is more likely to have been the loser, and, as originally happened with the *Gawain* examples, it may have suffered further from its unfamiliarity to modern editors.

In the *Gilte Legende*, translated in 1438 from Jean de Vignay's *Legende Dorée*, there are over twenty occurrences of *deny/deuy*. Most of the scribes of the eight surviving manuscripts often write *n* and *u* indistinguishably, though some differentiate them as a general rule. Since for this text there seem to have been at least two manuscripts between the original and the survivors, there would have been plenty of scope for substitution of *deny* for *deuy*, and as no instances are spelt with *v*, all are ambiguous about the intention of the translator. The word is used for *MED* senses 1 and 2 s.v. *denien*, 'to deny (a fact etc.)' and 'to refuse (permission etc.)'. *Gilte Legende* also has frequent *renien* (*MED*, s.v. *reneien*) for the former sense and *refusen* for the latter, and in these cases usually the translator has simply adopted the anglicised form of the French word used, *renoier* and *refuser* respectively; similarly most instances of *deny/deuy* correspond to *Legende Dorée deveer*, though in *Inventio Crucis* (Egerton 876 (E) f.99ra) *hadde denied* (to do sacrifice) translates *ot refusé*; in *Brice* (E f.269rb) *denied* twice translates *renoia*: *he denied it for shame* (that he had said Martin was mad), and *he denyed this strongely* (paternity); and in *Cecilia* (E ff.214vb and 276ra — *Cecilia* is repeated for some reason) *we that knowe the holy name of God mow not denie hym*, translating *nier*. It seems likely that in *Brice* and *Cecilia* the translator wrote *deny*; while in the other cases, which all have the senses 'refuse' or 'forbid', he was probably following his usual practice and anglicising *deveer* as *devy*, except in *Inventio Crucis*, where he apparently introduced it himself, indicating if so that he recognised it as more than a translator's equivalent. Typical examples are: *Nicholas* (E f.4rb) *he kneled downe and wold haue kyst his fete but he denied hym*; *Conversion of Paul* (E f.42ra) *there was in oure fader etyng of the fruit denyed*; *Ambrose* (E f.83a) *denyeng hym the entre*; *Mary Egyptian* (E f.78vb) *and ther I putte myselff xvij yere to lyue as a comune woman. I denyed neuer to none*.

That so many instances translate *deveer* is not conclusive, but it does suggest that the translator's word was *devy* in these cases, even though the various copyists seem to have thought they were writing *deny*. Yet there are places where scribes were apparently puzzled by the form before them, perhaps because it was the relatively rare *devy*. Thus for the forbidden fruit in *Conversion of Paul*, Douce 372 (D) and Harley

4775 (H2) (a very close copy of D) have *defyed*, and in the passage from *Nicholas* Gloucester Cathedral MS XII (G) has *deuoydid*, and H2 has *deuoid* (D is defective at this point). D, H2 and G are in a different branch of the stemma from E, and it may be that for unfamiliar *devy* spelt with *v* the not very suitable verb *deuoyden* was substituted in some common ancestor. These two instances seem more likely to be attempts at correction of *devy* than of *deny*.

Other examples of *devy* may be lurking among the *MED* citations for *denien* sense 2, though no doubt many of them are from manuscripts in which *n* and *u* are unambiguously distinct. The editors of the texts containing these citations express no doubts about the form of this word, and the only positive piece of evidence for *devy* so far found is in Lydgate's *Siege of Thebes*, 1.3785,[3] where the apparatus records a manuscript reading *deveyd* for *denyed* in *Our right which is vs denyed*, suggesting, to put it no higher, that at least the scribe of the Marquis of Bath's MS 257 believed in the existence of the word. There may be other spellings with *v* in manuscripts of some of these texts unknown to earlier editors; and of course instances may be irrecoverably concealed by the similarity of *n* and *u* in some hands.

[3] *Lydgate's Siege of Thebes Part I*, ed. A. Erdmann, EETS E.S. 108 (1911).

THE ETYMOLOGY OF 'CABIN' AND 'CABINET'

T. F. Hoad

The four volumes of the Burchfield *Supplement* to the *Oxford English Dictionary* are outstandingly successful in building on the main dictionary so as properly to reflect the lexical state of English up to the 1980s, and in keying in to the structure raised by Sir James Murray and his collaborators the new words and senses of the later nineteenth and the twentieth centuries. That structure has proved itself well able to support such further development, and the resultant whole is a very rich and intricate representation of the evolving lexical system of English from the Middle Ages onwards.

The task of extending the *OED* material up to the most recent times is not the only one with which the *Supplement* concerns itself. Attention has frequently been given to the revision of the treatment of earlier words and senses. The aim of covering the modern vocabulary is, however, the principal one, and it is entirely right that this should be so.

In what follows, I will discuss a pair of related words which entered the English vocabulary in the Middle and early Modern periods. I shall argue that the account of the etymology and early history of these words given by *OED* (and by other authorities) is in need of amendment. The issues raised by consideration of these two words reflect the need that now exists for a thorough reconsideration of the etymologies and histories of English words with Romance connections, in the light of the very extensive lexicographical work carried out in the various Romance languages since the time of *OED*.

According to *OED*, the word *cabin* was borrowed into Middle English from French, having been in that language the normal descendant of lateL *capanna*. Parallel forms in other Romance languages would be themselves the direct reflexes of the late Latin word:

ME. *cabane*, a. F. *cabane* (= Pr., Pg. *cabana*, Sp. *cabaña*, Cat. *cabanya*, It. *capanna*):- late L. *capanna*, in Isidore, 'tugurium parva casa est; hoc rustici

125

capanna vocant'; in Reichenau glosses 8th cent. *cabanna.*[1]

Romance scholars are, however, inclined to regard F *cabane* as a borrowing of Prov *cabana*:

> Empr. au prov. *cabana* «cabane, chaumière» attesté en 1253 . . ., du b. lat. *capanna* (d'orig. prob. préromane), attesté a) dans le domaine hisp. comme synon. de *casula* par Isidore, XV, 12, 2 . . ., et très fréquemment comme topon. dans le domaine catalan à partir de 854 . . .; b) dans le domaine ital. *ca* 800, utilisé par le scoliaste de Juvénal . . .; la mention du mot dans les *Gloses de Reichenau* (éd. Klein-Labhardt, München, 1968, Glossaire alphabétique, n° 1619, p. 195: *cauanna*) atteste aussi sa présence au VIIIe s. dans la France du Nord.[2]

The earliest evidence for F *cabane* is found in 1387, in the sense 'petite habitation sommaire'.[3] The first examples of ME *caban(e)* in *OED*[4] are of the second half of the fourteenth century, and the *Middle English Dictionary*[5] cites evidence for the word from 1346. The dates of first attestation therefore in no way require us to assume that the English word is a borrowing from French, even if the fact that ME *caban* is attested slightly *earlier* than F *cabane* carries little weight as an argument *against* explaining it as such a borrowing.

If we turn next to the records of Medieval Latin — another language for which we are beginning to see lexicographical words much superior to those formerly available — we find that *capanna* appears from the mid-thirteenth century in the spelling *cabana* in examples cited in the *Dictionary of Medieval Latin from British Sources*.[6] The sense given for those thirteenth-century examples is '(herd housed in) byre or sheep-

---

[1] *OED*, s.v. *Cabin*.

[2] *Trésor de la langue française*, publié sous la direction de Paul Imbs (Paris, 1971 –), s.v. *cabane* [*Étymol. et hist.*]. Other works giving Prov *cabana* as the immediate source of F *cabane* include W. Meyer-Lübke, *Romanisches etymologisches Wörterbuch* (Heidelberg, 3rd edn, 1935), s.v. 1624 *capanna* 1; O. Bloch and W. von Wartburg, *Dictionnaire étymologique de la langue française* (Paris, 6th edn, 1975), s.v. *cabane*; E. Gamillscheg, *Etymologisches Wörterbuch der französischen Sprache* (Heidelberg, 2nd edn, 1969), s.v. *cabane* ('das Wort war wohl auch in Nordfrankreich lebend, vgl. *tugurium-cauanna* in den Reichenauer Glossen 191; dazu in Ortsnamen *Chavannes* in der Ostschweiz u.ä.').

[3] *TLF*, s.v. *cabane*.

[4] S.v. *Cabin*, 3 'A cell', 4 'A natural cave or grotto', 5 'A room or compartment in a vessel for sleeping or eating in'.

[5] S.v. *caban* (d) 'a cabin on a ship'.

[6] *Dictionary of Medieval Latin from British Sources*, prepared by R. E. Latham and D. R. Howlett (1975 –), s.v. *capanna*, b.

cote'. The sense 'cabin, compartment (naut.)' is found associated with the spelling *caban*' from 1342,[7] which again is earlier than the evidence for F *cabane* and close to the earliest date for this sense of ME *caban* according to the *MED* material.[8]

There seems, then, to be reason to doubt the derivation of ME *caban* from F *cabane*, and to consider it at least as likely to have been adopted into English from the Latin of the Middle Ages. The difficulty of deciding between French and Latin as the source of a great many words introduced into Middle English is well known, and we should in any case accept that many words in Middle English have their origins in both French and Latin.

There is a note at the end of the *OED* etymology, that 'Mod.F. has *cabine* from Eng. in sense 5 [*sc.* "A room or compartment in a vessel for sleeping or eating in. An apartment or small room in a ship for officers or passengers"]'. This claim deserves further scrutiny.

The illustrative quotations displayed under the headword *Cabin* in *OED* show considerable variation in the form of the word, most strikingly with regard to the representation of the vowel in the second syllable. A synopsis of the forms is given in the list preceding the etymological section of the entry. Essentially, the situation reported in *OED* is that forms of the type *cabane* (*caban, cabban*) occur from the fourteenth century to the eighteenth century, and forms of the type *cabin* (*cabbin*) from the sixteenth century to the present day. There are also forms *cab(b)on* (fifteenth century to seventeenth century), *cabbaine* (sixteenth century), and *cab(b)en* (sixteenth and seventeenth centuries). From the additional material in *MED*, we can take spellings of the *cabbaine* type back into the fifteenth century.

The occurrence and the dates of introduction of the alternative spellings are not discernibly related to the sense-distinctions set out in *OED*. The impression gained is of a single lexical item, represented by a variety of orthographic forms (and possibly by a variety of phonological forms), and embracing a range of senses.

The unravelling of the development of the vowels of unstressed syllables in late Middle English and early Modern English is a very difficult and often uncertain business. We are all too often unable to assign a phonetic value to a particular spelling with any degree of confidence, it is likely that in many cases the application of straightforward 'sound laws' will not adequately account for the material, and we also have to reckon with a great deal of variation within English as we know it from this period. Nevertheless, what we do know is sufficient to

[7] Ibid., s.v. *capanna*, c.
[8] Cf. fn[5].

show that while it is quite conceivable that ME *cabane* should have become MnE *cabin*, such a development is not a confidently predictable one.[9] We may perhaps note the relatively lengthy overlap of the *cabane*-type spellings with those of the *cabin* type, and also the apparently firmly-established [ɪn] pronunciation of the word in present-day Standard English, as factors justifying doubt as to whether *cabin* is merely an English development of *cabane*.

It is of some interest, in the light of these considerations, to observe that French etymologists are not unanimous in explaining F *cabine* as a borrowing from English. The earliest record of F *cabine* now cited is from 1364, in a Picard text.[10] In context, the word there appears to mean 'room used for gaming'.[11] The sense 'room on a ship' is first attested for the French word (in the form *cabain*) in 1530, in the quotation from Palsgrave's dictionary cited in *OED* (sense 5): 'Cabbyn in a shyppe, *cabain*'. It was argued by von Wartburg[12] that the French word represented by Picard *cabine* in the mid-fourteenth century was the source, rather than a borrowing, of E *cabin*, although he was unable to offer a firm explanation of the origin of F *cabine* itself. The recent etymological discussion in the *Trésor de la langue française*[13] declares the French word to be of obscure origin, although *OED*'s explanation of it as a borrowing from English is judged possible. The suggestion of a Flemish origin, tentatively put forward by von Wartburg,[14] and Gamillscheg's view that F *cabine* represents a reformation of F *cabane* with the suffix *-ine*[15] are not favoured. For the French specialists, therefore, the matter would appear to be unresolved, and the *OED* explanation is at any rate not one on which they are confidently agreed.

The occurrence of an *-ine* form in French as early as 1364 seems to me to make it harder to believe in a wholly English origin for the French word, since forms of the type *cabin* do not begin to appear in English until about two hundred years later. Also, even if we were to assume that *cabin* went unrecorded for a long time as a result of the incompleteness of the written evidence for Middle English, we would need to assume a development *cabane* > *cabin* in English by a relatively early date. While not out of the question, such a development is by no

---

[9] Cf., for example, E. J. Dobson, *English Pronunciation 1500–1700* (Oxford, 2 vols, 2nd edn, 1968), ii. §§ 296ff., 322ff., 336.
[10] Cf. *TLF*, s.v. *cabine* [*Étymol. et hist.*].
[11] Ibid.: 'cabane (où l'on se réunit pour jouer)'.
[12] W. von Wartburg, *Französisches etymologisches Wörterbuch* (Leipzig, 1922–), ii. 13ff., s.v. **cabin*.
[13] *TLF*, s.v. *cabine* [*Étymol et hist.*].
[14] *FEW*, ii. 14/2.
[15] Gamillscheg, *Etymologisches Wörterbuch*, s.v. *cabine*.

means predictable.[16]

It is, of course, possible that the sense-development of F *cabine* at a later date is to be explained wholly or partly as the result of English influence. Since Palsgrave's *cabain* occurs in the very quotation which furnishes *OED*'s earliest example of the English type *cabin* (here, *cabbyn*), we have no clear chronological sequence to guide us. The form *cabine/cabin* seems more likely to have started its existence in French than to be an English development or formation, although the basis for the *-ine* form in French has yet to be determined.

The related word MnE *cabinet* also poses some etymological problems. *OED* gives the following etymology:

> App. Eng. dim. of CABIN, as seen by the earlier forms *cabanet*, *cabonet*, which go with the earlier forms of *cabin*; but in senses 3 – 6 largely influenced by F. *cabinet*, which according to Scheler and Brachet is not a direct derivative of F. *cabane*, but ad. It. *gabinetto* (= Sp. *gabinete*) 'closet, press, chest of drawers', app. a dialectal It. word going back to the same origin as CABIN.[17]

The statements here regarding the interrelationships of the Romance words are no longer in accord with scholarly opinion among the specialists in that field. The main points are conveniently summarized by T. E. Hope:

> There have been wide differences of opinion about the history of Fr. *cabinet*/ It. *gabinetto*. At one time most lexicologists drew the French word from Italian . . . because it appeared at a time and in authors favourable to Italianism (1525; examples in N. du Frail, the *Heptaméron*, Rabelais, translations from Italian) and because of forms with initial *g-* (*gabinet*, R. Estienne, 1549). On the other hand dating and the actual contexts indicate a Fr. > It. loan, and this is now generally accepted. First found in accounts written by Venetians in France (1572, referring to the King's privy chamber in which he received counsellors . . .), it appears in Italian contexts during the 17th century (Tassoni, Davila, Magalotti).[18]

F *cabinet* appears first at the very end of the fifteenth century (1491), in the sense 'small side-room'.[19] Within the first half of the sixteenth

---

[16] Cf. Dobson, *English Pronunciation*, ii. § 293.

[17] *OED*, s.v. *Cabinet*.

[18] T. E. Hope, *Lexical Borrowing in the Romance Languages: A Critical Study of Italianisms in French and Gallicisms in Italian from 1100 to 1900* (Oxford, 2 vols, 1971), i. 332.

[19] *TLF*, s.v. *cabinet*[1] [*Étymol. et hist.*]: 'petite chambre retirée servant d'accessoire à une plus grande pièce'.

century it is found with the senses 'shaded place in a garden', 'room in which valuables are kept', and 'room for private work or study', and also designating an article of furniture.[20] There would therefore be no difficulty in attributing *OED*'s sense 2 ('A summer-house or bower in a garden') to French influence, if not to direct borrowing from French, along with senses 3 – 6 which *OED* itself describes as 'largely influenced by F. *cabinet*'.

As has been seen, however, *OED* explains E *cabinet* as primarily an English formation on *cabin*, citing in support of this explanation 'the earlier forms *cabanet*, *cabonet*, which go with the earlier forms of *cabin*'. In this context, as can readily be seen from the illustrative quotations in the *OED* entry, 'earlier' means not 'preceding the form *cabinet*' but merely 'occurring at an early date'.[21] The *-an-/-on-* forms coexist with the *-in-* forms from the first appearance of the words in the mid-sixteenth century until the earlier part of the seventeenth century, so that date of occurrence of a given form is in itself no guide to priority of introduction.

We may further note that the ordering of senses in *OED* implies a semantic development in English[22] for which we seem to have no firm evidence. The view taken appears to be that the word first meant in English 'a little cabin . . .; a dwelling', and only subsequently acquired the more specialized meanings 'a small chamber or room', 'a case for the safe custody of . . . valuables', etc. Senses such as the latter ones are attested in English, however, on *OED*'s own evidence, even a little earlier than the supposed initial meaning.[23] I wonder whether there is any good reason not to suppose that E *cabinet* was borrowed from French in the mid-sixteenth century, in senses such as those of 'a small chamber or room' (*OED*'s sense 3), 'a summer-house or bower in a garden' (*OED*'s sense 2), and 'a case for the safe custody of jewels, or

---

[20] Ibid.: '1536 «espace ombragé dans un jardin, entouré d'arbrisseaux» . . .; . . . 1542 «pièce où l'on conserve des objets précieux» . . .; . . . 1539 «pièce où l'on se retire pour réfléchir, travailler'; s.v. *cabinet*[2] [*Étymol. et hist.*]: '1528 mobilier'.

[21] For the sixteenth century, *OED*, s.v. *Cabinet*, cites *cabonett* (c1550 [sense 5]) and *Cabbonet* (1572 [sense 1], against *cabinet* (1549 [sense 6], 1565 [sense 3], 1579 [senses 1, 2]).

[22] Cf. *General Explanations*, p. xxxi: 'That sense is placed first which was actually the earliest in the language; the others follow in the order in which they appear to have arisen'.

[23] *OED*'s senses 3 ('A small chamber or room'), 5 ('A case for the safe custody of jewels, or other valuables, letters, documents, etc.'), and 6 ('*fig.* A secret receptacle, treasure-chamber, store-house') are illustrated from 1565, c1550, and 1549 respectively, whereas sense 1 ('A little cabin, hut, soldier's tent') is first recorded by *OED* from 1572.

other valuables, letters, documents, etc.' (*OED*'s sense 5), and that it subsequently — in all likelihood, under the influence of E *caban(e)/ cabin* — acquired the sense 'a little cabin' and also the variant forms *cabanet*, etc.?

There is one respect in which is would be quite convenient to treat E *cabinet* as a loan from French rather than as an English formation. As *OED* comments s.v. *-et*, 'the suffix has been little used as an English formative'. It is true that some formations with *-et*, not all of them diminutives, based on English words are met with in the relevant period. (*OED*'s own example of such a formation from the seventeenth century, *riveret*, is unfortunately chosen. The main entry for this word explains it, as do other works, as a French loanword.) But the suffix appears not to have been very productive in English,[24] and it therefore seems all the more likely that *cabinet* is primarily a borrowing from French.

I have, as is not uncommon in investigations of this kind, raised a number of questions[25] but finally settled none. I hope, however, that the foregoing discussion will have served to illustrate the avenues still open to us for further work in the earlier history of English vocabulary, on the basis of the material in *OED* in combination with other sources, especially in other languages. If it has done so, it will have been, as was intended, entirely in the spirit in which R. W. Burchfield has provided the scholarly world with such a rich extension of that material in his *Supplement*.

---

[24] Cf., e.g., H. Marchand, *The Categories and Types of Present-Day English Word-Formation* (Munich, 2nd edn, 1969), § 4.36.2.
[25] Though not all that might have been asked about this material. For example, I have left untouched the senses of *cabinet* grouped by *OED* under branch II ('In politics'). It would seem that the origin and development of these senses would be likely to repay further examination.

LEXICAL INDETERMINACY

Herbert Pilch

1. The discovery of lexical meaning. It is usually assumed that lexical words have a fairly determinate meaning, witness the meaning of words such as *walk* or *rich*. Some words designate concrete entities (e.g *milk*), some designate abstract entities (e.g. *impenetrability*), still the meaning seems equally determinate in both cases. The lexicographer's job is, then, entirely one of *discovering* the meaning(s) of the particular word in hand. He describes the meaning (in monolingual dictionaries) by either:

(i) paraphrase, e.g. *milk* 'a white or yellowish fluid secreted by the mammary glands of female mammals . . .'. The paraphrase is to circumscribe the denotation class involved;
or:

(ii) relations within a lexical field, e.g. *sober* 'not drunk' (i.e. antonym of *drunk*), *mauve* 'delicate purple' (i.e. hyponym of *purple*, sic![1]). Lexical field relations other than antonymy and hyponymy are hyperonymy (the inverse of hyponymy), e.g. *purple* as a hyperonym of *mauve*, and paronymy ('the relation of being a direct hyponym to a common hyperonym'), e.g. *purple* and *red* as paronyms of *colour*.

Often enough lexicographers disagree among each other about the merits of a particular description. Yet, they take it for granted that the lexicographer can discover a determinate description, if he works patiently and carefully enough.

There are additional complications. As we know, most words are polysemous, i.e. they have more than one meaning. Consequently, lexicographers also disagree how many meanings exactly any given word may have. For instance, is the *foot* of mammals and the *foot* of arthropods one meaning of the word *foot* (this is so in *OED* and in the 2nd edition of Webster's *International Dictionary*), or is it two

---

[1] Are not *purple* and *mauve* paronyms rather than hypo-/hyperonyms? I wonder.

different meanings (this is so in the 3rd edition of the latter dictionary)? Whatever the answer, it is taken for granted that the meaning (or the two meanings) involved can be discovered.

Further disagreement arises whether two given meanings belong to one polysemous word or to two different, but homophonous words. For instance, is *walk* in 'all *walks* of life' (*OED* has it as sense 18 of the substantive *walk*) the same word as 'the *walk* I went for last night'? Or are these two homophonous *walks*? Whatever the answer, it does not detract from the determinacy of the meanings involved.

Lexical determinacy is also taken for granted in theoretical treatises on semantics and lexicology. Witness:

> A denotation class may be an open set, which is not to say that such a set is not *circumscribed*. Conventions are, by definition, operative in setting a *limit* to the potential membership of any given denotation class, in the sense that certain entities may, and others *definitively* may not, belong to that class. Semantic description has as its task the determination and description of these *conventional limitations* such as they are.[2]

John Lyons,[3] in a chapter headed 'reference, sense and denotation' sorts out many different modes of meaning (denotation is just one of them), without, however, questioning their determinacy for any given lexeme:

> By the denotation of a lexeme . . . will be meant the relationship that holds between that lexeme and persons, things, places, properties, processes and activities external to the language-system . . . For example, we will say that the denotatum of 'cow' is *a particular class* of animals . . . There are all sorts of *important logical and philosophical distinctions* lurking behind this liberal and grammatically convenient use of . . . 'denotatum'.

But is lexical meaning as determinate as all that (it would be pointless, at this juncture, to add to the list of authorities)? Contrary to what appears to be the dominant view, we wish to argue in this paper that:

(i) lexical meaning is, in many instances, indeterminate;

---

[2] Sándor Hervey, 'Postulates for axiomatic functionalist semantics', in Jan Mulder and Sándor Hervey, *The Strategy of Linguistics* (Edinburgh, 1980), 203 – 211 (see 206; italics mine!).

[3] *Semantics* (Cambridge, 1977), 207 (italics mine!).

(ii) lexical indeterminacy characteristically arises in the case of SATELLITE WORDS;[4]

(iii) there are specific lexical structures which give rise to satellite words;

(iv) lexical indeterminacy does not necessarily hinge on lexical change in progress, but has been known, in certain cases, to be stable for many centuries.

Before starting, let us rule out contextual (rather than lexical) meanings to make our point. As is well known, any word may, in some specific context, refer to the very opposite of its lexical denotation. This particular type of contextual meaning is generally called IRONY, e.g. the ironic *aren't you clever* 'you are foolish'. Even apart from irony, there is no way of anticipating what any specific word may refer to in some particular context, for instance the moon was 'footing the treetops'.[5] Presumably, the contextual meaning is that the moon 'shone on the treetops'. What is the denotation of the verb *walk* in *a walking dictionary*? The phrase usually denotes a living person (not necessarily one who walks). If we inferred from such examples that 'foolish' is one of the meanings of the word *clever*, 'shine' one of the meanings of the verb *foot*, 'live' one of the meanings of the word *walk*, our list of meanings would forever remain incomplete, and extremely hetero-geneous to boot. Indeed, it would be facile using such heterogeneity to make the case for lexical indeterminacy.

To add one more example, what sort of an 'uncle' is *Uncle Sam* 'the Federal Government of the United States'? Presumably, he is no *uncle* at all. Generalizing on such instances, we assert that any given word can be made plausibly to refer to any denotatum chosen ad hoc. The plausibility hinges just on inventing the suitable context. The extent to which we actually succeed in making up the context in turn depends not on the lexical meaning involved, but on our rhetorical ingenuity. In this sense, we agree with Humpty Dumpty: 'When *I* use a word . . ., it means just what I choose it to mean — neither more nor less'.[6] Humpty Dumpty goes on to describe the 'meaning' of the word *impenetrability*:

---

[4] We owe this notion to Walther von Wartburg, *Einführung in Problematik und Methodik der Sprachwissenschaft* (2nd edn Tübingen, 1962), 145f.; cf. 'Es gibt Begriffe, deren sprachlicher Normalausdruck von ganzen Schwärmen farbig schillernder, gefühlsbetonter Wörter umtanzt werden [sic! emend to *wird*], während andere wiederum fast oder ganz ohne diese Eskorte bleiben'. One of his examples is Fr. *travailler* with its (argot) satellites *bosser, boulonner, bûcher, piocher, trimer, turbiner* (p. 139).

[5] Webster's *Third International Dictionary*, s.v. *foot* v.t. 1b, quoted by Webster from C.E.S.Wood.

[6] *The Annotated Alice by Lewis Carroll*, ed. Martin Gardner (New York, 1960), 269.

'I meant by "impenetrability" that we've had enough of that subject
. . .'. But these are contextual meanings, not the lexical meanings that
the lexicographer is anxious to discover.

2. Synonyms for penal institutions.

An an example of lexical
indeterminacy, consider the three words *prison, jail, penitentiary*. All
three words denote the same type of institution. At first glance, *prison*
appears to be the routine term ('Normalausdruck', cf. fn. 4), *jail* is
connotatively more colourful and expressive, *penitentiary* is technical
for Uncle Sam's *Federal penitentiary*. We should therefore suggest that
jail and *penitentiary* are satellite words to *prison*.

Of course, very few readers will be pleased with this suggestion. Some
will insist on the strict (i.e. determinate) paronymy between *county jail*,
state prison, Federal penitentiary. Others will dismiss this paronymy as
one existing in technical usage at best. Still others will point out that *jail*
is used at least as generally today as *prison* and that, consequently, *jail*
should be accepted as the routine word, *prison* and *penitentiary* as the
satellite words. The latter two have, after all, an official tinge (more
technically, they have a connotation of officialdom). Some will ask for a
statistical investigation, in order to determine the relative frequency of
these words, some for a psycholinguistic investigation to test the
associations they evoke in American undergraduates.

Attention will also be drawn to the incompleteness of the list. Should
not at least *lockup, house of correction, reformatory, dungeon* be
included? Perhaps even paraphrases such as *place of incarceration*,
antonomasias such as *a bridewell*, synecdoches such as *cell block*? In
addition, the authority of dictionaries could be appealed to. Webster's
International Dictionary[7] tells us that (contrary to the technical usage
mentioned above) '*penitentiary* is used of the State prisons and of the
Federal prisons, as distinguished from *reformatory*'. *OED* singles out
'hard labour' as the distinctive feature of the *penitentiary*. This is,
presumably, in addition to the 'confinement' feature which the
penitentiary share with the *prison*; 'In the U.S. the place of punishment
in which convicts sentenced to confinement and hard labour are
confined by the authority of the law'.[8]

Obviously, there is some measure of disagreeement both among
knowledgeable speakers and among standard dictionaries as to 'what

[7] 2nd edn., s.v. *penitentiary* n. 4.
[8] This paraphrase is drawn by *OED* from John Bouvier, *A law dictionary,
adapted to the constitution and laws of the United States of America* (6th edn.,
1843 – 56).

exactly' the meaning of the words is. Actual usage varies widely even to the point of idiosyncracy. This situation is characteristic of the LEXICAL INDETERMINACY which we are arguing for. Even our initial statement to the effect that 'all three words denote the same type of institution' will, inevitably, draw criticism. The (more or less) nice distinctions which we have subsequently proposed are sure to have drawn even sharper criticism, and so has the appropriateness of the list of synonyms designating penal insitutions. The solution we suggest is to model lexical indeterminacy not in terms of nice distinctions within a set of 'synonyms', but in terms of the routine word *prison* (or *jail*) plus an open list of more specialized satellite words with highly variable denotations and connotations.

Is *prison* the routine word, because it is the one used in formal, notably legal language? Or is it *jail*, because it is the routine word of Colloquial English? Frequency counts will not avail us, as the question is one not of frequency, but of stylistic evaluation. From the point of view of formal language, we take it that *jail* is the more colourful satellite of *prison*. From the point of view of Colloquial English, *prison* is a bureaucratic satellite of *jail*. Our choice depends on the style we consider basic. Is formal language a deviation from the basic colloquial routine? Or inversely? Our stylistic tradition chooses the latter alternative. This writer favours the former. There is no very compelling reason for either choice.

There are, we take it, even some open slots in lexical fields, i.e. slots which are not occupied by any particular routine word, but just by a swarm of those elusive satellites. For instance, consider the slot for 'unmarried woman'. It is occupied by satellite words such as *spinster*, *girl*, *maid*, *miss*, *damsel*, *lass*, *Ms.*,[9] but there appears to be no generally accepted routine word in this slot. At the same time, at least some of the satellite words draw the kind of controversy which is so characteristic of lexical indeterminacy: 'The right word is not yours, but mine!'

3. Synonyms for derivatives in -*ness*. Lexical indeterminacy typically arises in morphological paradigms, i.e. paradigms of word derivation, where a morphological derivative occupies the same slot as a previously established lexical term (i.e. one not derived in the paradigm under consideration). Consider, for example, pairs such as *poorness* :

---

[9] Pronounced /mɪz/, to rhyme with *fizz*. The lexicologist's view of the raging controversy is that this word is being recommended as the routine word by one party to the dispute. It appears that this party wishes to relegate all the others to taboo status as 'four-letter-words'.

*poverty, richness : wealth, tangibleness : tangibility, puerileness :
puerility*. There is, in English, a morphological paradigm which derives
abstract nouns in *-ness* from primary adjectives, e.g. *kind → kind-ness*
'the state of being kind', *useful → useful-ness*, *sulphurous →
sulphurous-ness*. Some of the derivatives, inevitably, compete with
existing words, as far as their meaning is concerned. In this way, *poverty*
already occupies the slot for 'the state of being poor', similarly *wealth*
for 'the state of being rich'. It has been claimed, in terms of a
psycholinguistic metaphor, that the morphological derivation is
'blocked' by such preestablished lexical items.[10] This is, however, a half-
truth at best. Words such as *poorness* and *richness* do exist, the blockage
notwithstanding. But their exact meaning is very uncertain, and it
fluctuates regionally, sociolectally, even idiosyncratically. When speaking metaphorically of *rich cheese*, of *poor students*, we would,
presumably, nominalize these attributes as *the richness of the cheese*
(rather than its *wealth*), the *poorness of the students* (rather than their
poverty — which means something else). But how many readers will
agree with us? More than one reader, to be sure, will protest that he, for
one, has other usages. Nor do we propose to argue that they are wrong.
On second thoughts, *the high fat content of the cheese* seems more
appropriate, after all, than its 'richness', *the low standard of the
students* more pertinent than 'their poorness', and we must admit we
have not actually heard anyone talk of 'the richness of the cheese' etc.
Still, the words *richness* and *poorness* do exist. They are, in fact, entered
in the standard dictionaries, and all sorts of highly specialized
'meanings' are listed for them, such as 'leanness or want of vigour
caused by ill feeding', each meaning being supported by a single
quotation. Most of these are probably contextual meanings (in the sense
defined above) rather than lexical meanings. The solution we propose is
to describe *poverty, wealth, tangibility, puerility* as the routine words
for 'the state of being poor' etc., *poorness, richness, tangibleness,
puerileness* as their respective satellite words with the usual lexical
indeterminacy.[11]

4. Disyllabic nouns with different stress. Lexical indeterminacy
abounds equally in other derivational paradigms. For instance, what is

[10] Cf. Laurie Bauer, *English Word Formation* (Cambridge, 1983), 87.
[11] *OED* puts the equality sign = : 'puerileness = puerility'. This is a simpler
way of saying the same thing. Both for *tangibility* and *tangibleness*, *OED* has
the same paraphrase 'the state or quality of being tangible', merely reversing the
order of the nouns *state* and *quality*. But the order is probably not significant in
this instance.

the difference between the nouns *áddress* and *addréss*, *résearch* and *reséarch*, *díspute* and *dispúte*? The morphological paradigm involved is one of disyllabic verbs and nominals (not necessarily of French-Latin etymology), as in *permít* → *pérmit*, *invíte* → *ínvite*, *recáll* → *récall*, *cónflict* → conflíct, *pérfect* → perféct, *tórment* → tormént. In Early Modern English, both the nouns and the verbs concerned had final stress,[12] e.g. *conténts* (Shakespeare, *Son.* 55.3), *protést* (Shakespeare, *TC* 3.2.174), *exíle* Shakespeare, *TGV* 5.4.156). However, Alexander Pope already has initial stress on many nouns involved (as is shown by his metre).[13] By the 18th century, the modern productive paradigm has become established which derives nouns from verbs (and inversely) with stress shift.[14] In fact, I once teamed up with a British computer specialist who routinely used the verb *inpút* (as in *inpút data into the computer*). Doubtless, this verb, however idiosyncratic, is derived from the noun *ínput* within the present morphological paradigm. Inversely, the noun *ínvite* must be a derivative of the verb *invíte* as primary. This goes to show that the derivation works either way in this paradigm.

Now the preestablished lexical nouns with final stress co-exist with the new derivatives with initial stress at least in some cases, and we keep discovering more and more of them. The difference is dialectal for some such pairs, e.g. American English *áddress*, *résearch*, British English *addréss*, *reséarch* (as nouns!). The noun *díspute* is, in my experience, a Scottish peculiarity. But this is just 'in my experience'. The dialectal distribution will, probably, turn out to be somewhat less clearcut once we start studying it in greater detail. At the same time, American English has the noun *addréss* 'speech' (as in *the presidential addréss*) beside the postal *áddress*. Or will even this 'synonymy' turn out to be less than stable once it is investigated beyond 'my experience'? At any rate, as long as the denotation of *áddress* is restricted to the postal address, whilst the *addréss* (of American English) has all sorts of different denotata, the difference of meaning is fairly determinate. We conclude that lexical doublets are not necessarily satellite words, but that determinate differences of dialect, sociolect or meaning evolve in some instances.

[12] Cf. Helge Kökeritz, *Shakespeare's Pronunciation* (New Haven, 1953), 335.
[13] Cf. Cornelia Günthner, *Konversion und Akzentverschiebung im Englischen des 18. Jahrhunderts*, Staatsexamensarbeit (Freiburg, 1978). *OED* does not take note of the stress shift till R. W. Burchfield's *Supplement* (e.g., s.v. *ínvite* sb.).
[14] Oddly, Hans Marchand, *The Categories and Types of Present-Day English Word Formation* (2nd edn, Munich, 1969), 378, misses this paradigm, as he is puzzled by the preestablished lexical nouns with final stress, such as *dismáy*, and by the etymological (!) prefixes involved.

5. The survival of doublets. It has been claimed that this is necessarily so. In other words, doublets do not survive. Either one of them will disappear, or a determinate meaning difference will evolve between them.[15] However, this claim is easy to refute as far as satellite words are concerned. For instance, the earliest *OED* quotation for *poorness* is dated 1275, for *richness* 1338, for *poverty* 1175, for *wealth* 1250. So these doublets have co-existed for at least six centuries (probably longer),[16] and there is no sign yet that either is disappearing or that a determinate meaning difference is evolving. There remains, of course, the indeterminate meaning difference. Its very indeterminacy is the point we are trying to make.

Walther von Wartburg focuses on slang words and dialect words as satellites (cf. fn. 4). Modern English examples would be the engineer's slang term *juice* as a satellite word to *electricity*, Northern *swill* as a satellite word to *wash*, American English *kid* as a satellite to *child*. Certain instances of historical change are documented in which a satellite word takes the place of the routine word. For instance, Lat. *testa* 'piece of pottery' denoted the 'head' in Vulgar Latin metaphorical slang. As French *tête*, it eventually crowded out Lat. *caput*, reducing it to the metaphorical meaning of 'boss' in French *chef*.

Similarly, the Old English words *cnafa* 'boy', *mægden* 'girl' have been replaced by what once must have been their satellite words *boy* and *girl*. The latter show up from nowhere in Middle English (first records in *OED* in 1300 and 1290 respectively). This is typical of slang words which have no etymology by definition, witness modern slang words such as *Yankee* and *G.I.*[17]

As we have seen, the satellite words do not have to be slang words or dialect words, but some are derivatives in productive paradigms of word formation. Even such satellite words have been known eventually to

---

[15] My earliest source for this claim is Hermann Paul, *Prinzipien der Sprachgeschichte* (5th edn, Halle, 1937 [reprint]): '. . . ist die Annahme eines viele Jahrhunderte langen Nebeneinanderbestehens von gleichbedeutenden Doppelformen oder Doppelwörtern aller Erfahrung zuwiderlaufend und muß mit Entschiedenheit als methodologischer Fehler bezeichnet werden' (p. 252).
[16] The denominal paradigm for adjectives in *-ness* was productive in Old English, cf. H. Pilch, *Altenglische Grammatik* (Munich, 1970), section 25.4c.
[17] Cf. H. Pilch, *Empirical Linguistics* (Munich, 1976), 105. Of course, etymologies can be speculated on, and there is no shortage of such speculations. To the etymologies that have been proposed, we could add Irish *buachaill* 'boy' as an etymon for *boy*. But all such etymologies are insufficient, as they just work on chance similarities of sound and meaning, not on similarities that can be generalized on in terms of phonetic laws.

replace established routine words. For instance, EMnE. *ácceptable*[18] has been replaced by its erstwhile satellite *accéptable*, as derived from the verb *accépt* in the morphological paradigm vb. © vb. *-able*. A number of similar doublets survive, such as *ádmirable*, *réfutable*, *préferable* and their satellites *admír-able*, *refút-able*, *prefér-able*. The latter are usually deprecated as ignorant pronunciations (of the three newcomers, only *refútable* is noted by *OED*), but the two sets are different words morphologically, as they are derived in different morphological pàradigms, one set in an Early Modern English paradigm with initial stress, the other set in a currently productive paradigm without stress shift.

The same sort of process accounts for the replacement of OE. *webb-estre*, *bæc-estre* (derived from the verbs with the female agent noun suffix *-estre*) by *weav-er*, *bak-er* (derived with the agent noun suffix *-er*), of OE. *hunt-a* (derived from the verb without an affix)[19] by *hunt-er* (derived with the agent noun suffix *-er*), of OE. *bite* (derived from the verb with the zero-grade stem alternant) by MnE. *bite* (derived from the verb without vowel alternation),[20] of OE. *sund* 'in good health', relegated (as MnE. *sound*) to its metaphorical meaning by *health-y* (derived with the adjectival suffix *-y*, first *OED* record in 1552).

On the other hand, we are focusing on those cases in which both 'synonyms' survive with an indeterminate difference of meaning (if any), such as *wealthy* : *rich*, *wealth* : *rich-ness*, *ádmirable* : *admírable*, *murderer* : *kill-er*, *perceptible* : *perceiv-able*, *in-translatable* : *un-translatable*. One can always set up nice distinctions for such pairs, notably so for their satellite members. However, the wide disagreements that typically arise about them both among lexicographers and ordinary speakers bear out (we take it) our claim that lexical indeterminacy is a more adequate category of description.

[18] Cf. Kökeritz, *Shakespeare's Pronunciation*, 337; this alternant is also noted in *OED*.
[19] Cf. Pilch, *Altenglische Grammatik*, section 25.3.
[20] Cf. Pilch, *Altenglische Grammatik*, section 25.1a. OE. *bite* survives today as *bit* with a new meaning, just as Lat. *caput* survives in French as *chef*.

THE NEW VOCABULARY OF ENGLISH

John Simpson

'Native speakers of English are exposed to about one million words every day of their lives.' This outrageous and rather disconcerting claim was made from the back-benches of a recent lexicographical conference, and was met with a certain amount of ridicule. If it were true, then it would underline what an enormous task lexicographers face each time they prepare a dictionary, and what extensive resources would be necessary to monitor the state of the language from one day to the next even in their own country, let alone in the many other countries of the world where English is spoken as a first or second language.[1] But in terms of a 'ball-park figure',[2] one million words a day turns out to be neither simplistic nor outrageous, but startlingly realistic. There is of course a difference between being exposed to a million words a day, and digesting their contents, but a brief calculation shows that the ball-park is about that size. Suppose you take one of the 'quality' daily papers: by half-past eight in the morning you are in the presence of your first quarter of a million words; radio, television, magazines, reports, correspondence, ordinary conversation, and the additional 'wallpaper' of everyday life probably double the figure, at least, to half a million. The right ball-park, even if it's bush league[3] rather than international-size.

One of the professional duties of lexicographers is to monitor the flow

[1] Recently, lexicographers have made much use of large text corpora through on-line information-retrieval systems. One of the largest of these is NEXIS, 'hosted' by Mead Data Central, of Atlanta, Georgia. Even this (containing some 14 billion words) represents just a tiny proportion of the data needed for a comprehensive examination of the English language, but such systems are having a far-reaching effect upon the editing of both historical and synchronic dictionaries.

[2] An extraordinary figure of speech to use in the present context. It is paralleled only by a seminal use of *nous avons changé tout cela* (Editor's introduction, *A Supplement to the Oxford English Dictionary*, vol. 1 (1972), p. xv.).

[3] See note 2.

of language. No language is static, and within the contents of any newspaper, or in the ordinary conversation of two people, words occur which are not found in any dictionary. Their omission may be for any of a number of reasons: the term may be a chance formation invented for the occasion and not used elsewhere (and therefore not usually acceptable for inclusion in a dictionary); it may be too new to have established itself in the language; it may derive from a technical sphere which is considered too highly-specialized for the dictionary; it may be a proper name (not all dictionaries, especially in Britain, include this category of information). The lexicographer must discover these omitted uses, and decide whether they do in fact deserve inclusion. All decisions are reversible: a term may be too out-of-the-way one year, and yet demand inclusion in the next; editorial policy may change to embrace geographical names or brief encyclopaedic data about particular people.[4] And what lexicographers do decide to include in dictionaries is not the whole picture of linguistic change, but a rigorously examined cross-section of it. A thoroughgoing analysis of the contents of a historical dictionary (whether synchronic or diachronic, or according to some other criteria) provides a useful perspective on how language changes — and will also emphasize that change is just a small part of language development when compared with the mass of linguistic detail which remains constant over time. But then lexical change would be less interesting if it were predictable. If we could establish a universal law which maintained that a certain proportion of intransitive verbs naturally developed transitive senses over a given period, or that suffixation naturally outstripped prefixation as a major ingredient of lexical development, then monitoring the language would be confirmatory rather than exploratory. But fashions in language formation shift without identifiable rules, and diachronic observation is useful to supplement a synchronic linguistic snapshot.

Lexicographers, therefore, are continually adding new vocabulary (in the form of completely new words and new developments of old words) to their dictionaries, and at the same time removing or marking as obsolete items which have fallen out of general currency. The *Supplement to the Oxford English Dictionary* (1972 – 86) augmented the linguistic record of 240,000 headwords in the original *OED* with

---

[4] Inclusion of this category of information is one of the hallmarks of American Collegiate lexicography. However, as dictionaries become available on computer media, it seems likely that the trend will be taken up as strongly in Britain. It is an example of the encyclopaedia-ization of dictionaries, and an acknowledgement that dictionary users expect to find information from many previously-diverse reference sources between the covers or file-markers of their dictionaries.

another 70,000 items deriving mainly from the twentieth century. And yet surprisingly the contents of the *Supplement* are not subjected to analytical scrutiny *en masse*: individual items are continually referred to, but it is impossible to gain more than a subjective picture of the language development recorded by the *Supplement* as it currently exists. It is impossible to establish the percentage of neologisms from, say, Spanish as opposed to Portuguese (or South American Spanish compared with South American Portuguese); it is impossible to compare the rate of terminological proliferation in one scientific discipline over a given period with that of another; there is no way of drawing together all of the words which have to do with birds' names, or chemical elements. No way, that is, except by laborious examination of the printed book.[5]

Dictionaries provide factual information; they also provide organized information. Over twenty years ago the possibility of computerized dictionary databases (or, on a larger scale, knowledge bases) was being considered. The sheer size of dictionaries pushed them from the sharp end of computational development. But the increased memory resources and processing power available on modern computers have caused them to be recalled from the technological wings, and have placed them on centre stage. As the most comprehensive large-scale dictionary of English, the *OED* is suddenly attracting interest from general linguists,[6] computational linguists, artificial intelligence engineers, and other techno-wizards.

The *New OED* project will place the *OED* within the grasp of computational manipulation (and probably mis-manipulation). The

---

[5] One notable example of this is the painstaking, long-term research into Anglo-Norman vocabulary in the *OED* undertaken, but unfortunately never completed, by the late Professor Collas. The arguments for Anglo-Norman (as opposed to mainland French) being responsible for the development of much early English vocabulary in the later medieval period have been excellently expressed by Professor W. Rothwell (see, for example, 'Stratford-atte-Bowe and Paris', *MLR* 50 (1955), 39–54). One of the obstacles to Professor Collas's research was that the *OED* is inconsistent in its codification of Anglo-Norman terms. Even now, much more research is needed to clarify the picture. Some Anglo-Norman material is marked 'Anglo-French' in the *OED* (the term 'Anglo-Norman' is not used), but much more is subsumed under the catch-all term 'OF' (Old French). But see also the General Explanations to the *OED*, p. xxx: 'As a rule, it may be assumed that the original form of every Middle English word of French origin was *identical* with the Anglo-French form; and that, where a gap appears between the earliest known English form of a word and its Old French equivalent, that gap would be filled up by the recovery of the Anglo-French and earliest English form.'

[6] Perhaps a surprising inclusion in this list, and added as an afterthought. General linguists have always used the *OED*, but they have not had to date the ability to use the Dictionary as flexibly as they would have liked.

Supplement brings the original dictionary up to date in terms of linguistic currency, and the Oxford New English Words Series [NEWS][7] makes sure that the dictionary stays up to date. Not all of the questions we would like to ask of the *New OED* database will be answerable straight away: some further (and continual) refinement of the database's contents will be necessary for that. The New English Words Series at present consists of around five thousand vocabulary items new to the Dictionary, mostly from recent years, and information about these terms has been entered on a small database prior to their full publication.[8] From this initial database it is possible to start a preliminary analysis of the new vocabulary of English.

For the purposes of this study, I have limited my investigation to the first thousand new entries, all in the letter A. They represent words, subsenses of words, and phrases neither in the *OED* nor in its *Supplement* — for both of which the earlier letters of the alphabet were edited and published many years before the completion of the full works. It is therefore reasonable to suppose that there are more gaps in the historical record in the first letters of the alphabet than in subsequent letters, when more information (in the form of citation slips) and acquired experience was available to the editor. 'New words' in A may, in fact, be generally older than items currently required to fill gaps later in the alphabetical record.

Firstly, a simple question: in which parts of speech do these new usages cluster? As with the figures given elsewhere in the article, the following table is not intended to be a canonical record of linguistic development, but merely to show what sort of information we might expect to obtain reasonably rapidly from a computerized dictionary. The table begs more questions (in terms of methodology, selection of criteria, etc.) than it answers. I have intentionally glossed over these aspects here, and I hope that more detailed figures, over a much better control sample, will be available as a result of the *New OED* project and the development of other computerized dictionaries.

Table 1, of the one thousand NEWS entries by part of speech, shows the following frequencies of occurrence:

[7] The New English Words Series was started while editorial work on the *Supplement* was drawing to a close. It was clear that a need existed to continue work along the lines laid down by the *Supplement*, in order to embrace the continuing flow of new vocabulary, and the plans for a computerized version of the *OED* made such an undertaking practical.
[8] The data is currently held on an Apricot xi microcomputer, using dbase II software. It is not linked to the main *New OED* IBM configuration, but operates independently, simulating some of the information-retrieval functions planned for the full *New OED* database.

category	percentage
noun	59.7
adjective	19.5
verb	6.3
adverb	5.7
other	8.8

Table 1

A closer look inside these umbrella groupings does clarify the picture slightly. Simple nouns are only two-thirds as frequent as noun phrases, whereas simple adjectives predominate over adjectival phrases at the rate of 20 to 1. Not surprisingly, adverbial phrases fare better: one for every two simple adverbs. The principal subdivision amongst the verbs at this stage is based on transitivity. It seems that a new verb is three times as likely to be transitive as intransitive. From amongst the 'other' category, it is interesting to note that despite the vogue for acronyms in modern linguistic life, straight abbreviations outnumber them by thirty to one in the sample: *AIDS* and *Apex* being the only acronyms, as against a total of sixty-one abbreviations (*AA*, Alcoholics Anonymous; *AAA*, American Automobile Association; *ABC*, Australian Broadcasting Corporation; etc.). It would be fascinating to have detailed charts of this type of information for each period of English in each area of the English-speaking world. The *New OED* database will have to be enhanced before this depth of information is available, but we should be able to extract some general figures now, which can be refined later.

These one thousand items were selected by a careful examination of the Oxford English Dictionaries departmental word-files: they therefore represent a largely objective picture. There is a tendency amongst observers to suppose that nouns and noun phrases are much more heavily represented in new vocabulary: this is because they are much more 'observable'. It is generally more difficult and time-consuming to establish new verbal and adjectival usages by simple observation, as opposed to strict comparison against an existing dictionary and word-file. There are a number of such items which it is hard to miss (*access* and *action* as verbs are two well-known examples), but others less in the public eye are more elusive. This disproportionate weighting in favour of nouns and noun phrases appears in many listings of new words — especially in the addenda of dictionaries. One separate publication which reports on neologisms is the recently-published *Longman/Guardian New Words*,[9] itself a notable work in many ways, and yet

---

[9] S. Mort, *Longman/Guardian New Words* (1986).

still prey to this popular bias. I give its proportion of new items by part of speech, with my own figures again in parentheses (Table 2):

category	percentage
noun	81.0 (59.7)
adjective	8.6 (19.5)
verb	4.3 (6.3)
adverb	0.2 (5.7)
other	5.9 (8.8)

Table 2

Again the sample is from approximately one thousand items. The clustering of items in the noun/noun phrase category is quite clear, at the expense of new adjectives (many of which in this sample simply represent uses of the adjectival component *-friendly*, after the computer jargon *user-friendly*), some verbs, and adverbs (which in this sample are represented by two adverbial phrases).

Figure 1 shows a bar chart representing the influx of this new vocabulary into the language over time.[10] As mentioned above, 'new' means new to the Dictionary, not necessarily new to the language — especially in the earlier letters. Similar charts for letters later in the alphabet would show a growing preponderance of innovation in the recent decades. I have started the chart in 1800. There are 46 items dating from between 1000 and 1799 (the earliest being *ash*, the name of an Old English runic letter, subsequently applied by modern scholars to the Old English *æ* digraph. A surprising 'new' item, and an example of a word which is now included in the Dictionary where the original working policy of the *OED* editorial staff in the 1880s (when the letter A was being prepared) required that it be omitted. Editorial policy does change throughout the lifespan of a large dictionary, and we are now adding this sort of term as well as the 'new' vocabulary of the 1970s and 1980s, in order that the linguistic record can be more complete.

As can be seen from this chart, most of the new words in A already existed when this letter was being prepared for the *Supplement*, the majority having been coined in the preceding two decades. But coinage is one thing, and currency another. Clearly there was insufficient

---

[10] One of the early computational analyses of coinage datings was T. Finkenstaedt et al., *A Chronological English Dictionary* (Heidelberg, 1970), based on material from the *Shorter Oxford English Dictionary*. The trend for providing coinage dating has moved into American lexicography with the inclusion of such information in Webster's *Ninth New Collegiate Dictionary* (1983).

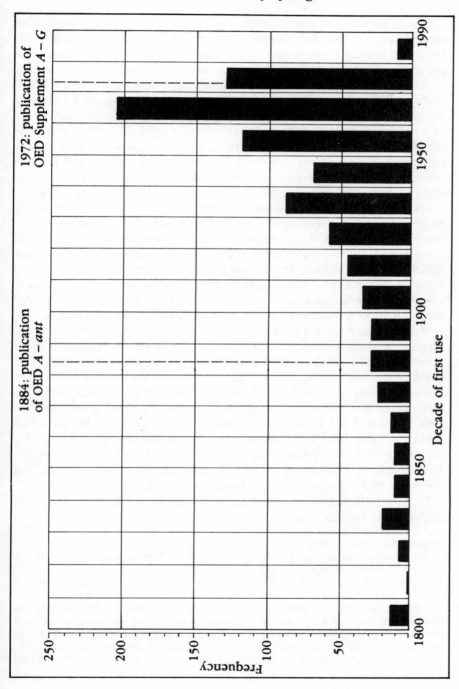

evidence (in terms of citation slips, etc.) in the late 1960s for them to be considered for the *Supplement*. One of the strengths of traditional historical lexicography is that what appears in the 1980s to be a buzz phrase or a vogue word, and hence to merit inclusion in the Dictionary to illustrate the cutting edge of modern linguistic usage, is often easily shown by research to have existed for many years prior to its general acknowledgement and widespread currency. *Acid rain*, for example, is news today, but the term has been around at least since 1859;[11] *artificial intelligence* is state-of-the-art technology, or even state-of-the-future technology, but it seems to have been coined as far back as 1956.[12] The lexicographer who attempts to provide a series of so-called 'new' usages soon finds that he is shooting himself in the foot with his own research.

We have seen one impression of 'when' words come from: perhaps a more interesting question for general lexicographers is 'where' they come from. The following analysis compares results from this *New OED* sample with the results of John Algeo's survey published in *American Speech* (1980).[13] There are substantial differences between the two samples, but many of the figures produced make interesting comparisons. My observations relate to 'new' items introduced into the language between 1900 and the present day. All are, again, from the letter A. The analysis is based on a system for coding the manner in which words are formed, devised for *New OED* new words.[14] The *New OED* sample deals with about 500 items, coded according to a system which differs in detail but not in essence from Algeo's workmanlike framework.

Algeo's survey covers 1000 words taken by random sampling throughout the full alphabetical range in the Barnhart *Dictionary of New English 1963-1972*.[15] The Barnhart material veers in favour of American usage, the *New OED* material covers world English, but with a bias towards (firstly) British usage and (secondly) North American usage. The structural analyses of word formation are at odds in places, but there are more similarities than discrepancies on this score.

Table 3 shows the proportional distribution of word-formation types amongst the two samples:

[11] *Quarterly Jrnl. Chem. Soc.* 11 (1859), 232.
[12] M. L. Minsky, *Heuristic Aspects of the Artificial Intelligence Problem* (M.I.T. Lincoln Lab. Group Rep. 34 – 55), 4.
[13] J. Algeo, 'Where do All the New Words Come From?', *American Speech* 55 (1980), 264 – 77.
[14] I am grateful to Sara Tulloch, of the NEWS editorial team, for devising the coding system, which contains seventy word-formation categories (and additional combinations of these) organized so that reports on individual or related categories can be produced rapidly using a simple outputting program.
[15] C. L. Barnhart et al., *A Dictionary of New English 1963-1972* (New York, 1973).

Type	New OED (%)	Algeo (%)
Functional shift	8.3	6.4
Semantic shift	22.5	7.7
Clipping	2.8	4.5
Abbreviation	11.5	2.2
Back-formation	3.2	1.4
Compounding		
noun (phrases)		
n + n	7.9	14.4
a + n	2.3	6.6
v + n	0.6	1.4
adjective (phrases)		
n + a	0.8	0.8
a + n	0.4	0.1
Composition		
Prefixation	6.0	15.6
Suffixation	19.6	18.5
Blends	1.1	4.8
Loans	6.9	5.7
Unknown origin	0.0	0.5
Others	6.1	9.4
	100.0	100.0

Table 3

The principal differences lie in semantic shifts, in abbreviations, and in prefixation. I know that the *New OED* sample is slightly skewed in favour of abbreviations: that is simply a function of the sorting procedure in operation over this early range of the alphabet. The real discrepancy is between semantic-shift results. I have a tendency to believe my figure here, but with little hope that it reflects the true picture exactly. The sample was selected by careful combing of the word-files, and without the influence of the new-noun(-phrase) pull which I observed earlier. Semantic shift is notoriously difficult to spot without carefully-constructed objective evidence: only a systematic search through the files displays the full degree of linguistic innovation. In simple lexicographical terms, I would find it easier to draw up a list of neologisms formed by compounding or by composition than by semantic shift. The Barnhart dictionary and its sequel are classic lexicographical records, but my suspicion is that they pay slightly less attention to the complexities of semantic shift than they do to simple compounding: this difference is evident in the higher proportions found by Algeo in nouns and noun phrases formed from n + n and a + n in comparison with the Oxford sample. Suffixation and functional shift, on the other hand, show marked similarities over the two samples; clipping, back-formation, blends, etc. are all reasonably similar (taking into account the small size of both samples, differing selection criteria, differences in emphasis and fact between British and American English, and the alternative structural systems employed in the analyses). Prefixation is rather a problem: I tend to put this down to editorial selection or preference (i.e. the degree to which collocations formed on *anti-* or *mega-* are treated), but the question is wide open to argument.

What Sir James Murray and his colleagues would have made of this numerical approach to lexicography is also open to debate. But dictionary-makers are by nature logical, orderly souls, and I think he would have approved of linguistic alphabet-crunching as a component of lexical analysis. It is remarkable how well his framework for the *OED* fits on to the computer. Nowadays there is a requirement for more types of information, but this is a further leap along the same linear path. As computerized dictionaries develop, and as large-scale corpora of both literary and non-literary texts expand, we shall soon be in a position to maintain a constantly-updated mirror of the language — in a way which will undoubtedly make the lexicographer's task harder: the computer will reveal inconsistencies of treatment; it will heighten the general expectation of what can be found in a dictionary; and it will allow statistical analyses to proliferate. None of this will soften the lexicographer's ride, but it may well make the ride more exhilarating. The real work of lexicography will remain in the hands of the dictionary editors, and their editorial and research staff, who discover, verify, and organize the information, but it would be dangerous to disregard the effect that computers will have in re-organizing lexicographers' work.

THE PERSISTENCE OF SHAKESPEARE IN MODERN DICTIONARIES

Marvin Spevack

The quintessential lexicographer was Sisyphus. Even Dr. Johnson, only immodestly a self-styled 'harmless drudge', was well aware of the monumentality and yet ultimate hopelessness of his task. For, as printed book, a dictionary is questionable in its conception and outdated at its appearance. In the Preface to his *Dictionary of the English Language* (1755) Johnson admitted that 'there never can be wanting some . . . who will consider that no dictionary of a living tongue ever can be perfect, since while it is hastening to publication, some words are budding, and some falling away' (p. C2ᵛ). More than two hundred years later R. W. Burchfield in the Preface to the first volume of his *Supplement to the Oxford English Dictionary* (1972) shows a similar awareness: in the selection 'we have kept constantly before us the opposing concepts of permanence and ephemerality, retaining vocabulary that seemed likely to be of interest now and to future generations, and rejecting only those words, phrases, and senses that seemed transitory or too narrowly restricted in currency' (p. vi). Both — indeed all — lexicographers know their Shakespeare well enough to sense the appropriateness to lexicography of Ulysses's dictum on Time:

> Time hath, my lord, a wallet at his back,
> Wherein he puts alms for oblivion,
> A great-siz'd monster of ingratitudes.
> Those scraps are good deeds past, which are devour'd
> As fast as they are made, forgot as soon
> As done.
>
> (TRO 3.3.146 – 50)

Perseverance, Ulysses's recipe, has from the beginning been the cardinal virtue of lexicographers. Today computers, making updating immediate and fluid, help provide the 'instant way' Ulysses goes on to prescribe as essential to keep 'honor bright', for 'to have done is to hang / Quite out of fashion, like a rusty mail / In monumental mockery' (150 – 3).

The criteria for the continuum of adding and deleting — a process not unlike refuelling planes in mid-air — have been various but not substantially varied. They all revolve about authority, and they all involve a subjective determination of that authority. A bibliography containing the canon which mirrors the cultural totality and not simply the sources of the lexicon is normally neglected, partial, or unexplained — or most often it is replaced by prefatory and perfunctory references to the latest or last-minute developments. Developments do develop and styles do change, persons and personalities come and go: the concept of authority remains, the determinant of the fitness and thus legitimacy for lexical existence. But it is increasingly elusive.

The concept and the concrete, however, would seem to merge in Shakespeare. Although almost four centuries have elapsed since his death, although the language and the language-makers have undergone sea-changes, his presence in modern, eminently utilitarian — if not egalitarian — dictionaries is not unexpected. Even Webster's *Third International* (1961), which tends to substitute Eisenhower and Sinatra for Milton and Pope, concedes the inevitability of Shakespeare. Not untypically, however, it does not know for sure the extent to which Shakespeare is represented in its pages.[1] Assessing the influence of Shakespeare with some degree of exactitude — the present aim — is one way of measuring the power of the greatest writer of the language on the language as it is presented in dictionaries and so on the process of selection — adding and deleting — which is the major occupation of lexicographers.

Recent research makes possible the identification of the Shakespearean vocabulary within the development of English to the present day.[2]

---

[1] Philip B. Gove, 'Shakespeare's language in today's dictionary', *Texas Studies in Literature and Language* 7 (1965 – 66) states that there are 'two thousand acknowledged quotations and a few hundred obsolete and archaic words or senses entered in the Third Edition chiefly because Shakespeare used them' and finds 'more fascinating . . . the unacknowledged evidence for the pervasive influence of Shakespeare's language' (132) but finally admits that his 'entire study is made up of just examples' (136).

[2] For example, *A Chronological English Dictionary*, ed. T. Finkenstaedt, E. Leisi, and D. Wolff (Heidelberg, 1970); M. Spevack, H. J. Neuhaus, and T. Finkenstaedt, 'SHAD: a Shakespeare dictionary', in *Computers in the Humanities*, ed. J. L. Mitchell (Edinburgh, 1974), 111 – 23 (SHAD employs a Computer Dictionary, an extract of the lemmata and pertinent data derived from the *Shorter Oxford English Dictionary* with certain supplementary material from the *OED* and other sources); Thomas Finkenstaedt and Dieter Wolff, *Ordered Profusion* (Heidelberg, 1973). The data of all these works have been used in one way or another.

By 1613, for example, Shakespeare's vocabulary represented slightly more than 41 per cent of the total words recorded in the *Shorter Oxford English Dictionary*: of the 42,689 lemmata in English to 1613, 17,671 are to be found in Shakespeare.[3] As the English vocabulary increased, Shakespeare's share, of course, decreased: by the middle of the twentieth century there were more than 80,000 lemmata in the *SOED*, the overlap being only about 22 per cent. This general orientation says little about Shakespeare's contribution since of course Shakespeare was writing English and overlap is to be expected. Nor does a similar superimposition, however startling on the surface, of the Shakespeare vocabulary upon the restricted vocabulary of a modern, medium-sized dictionary designed for the educated native speaker, the *Advanced Learner's Dictionary of Current English*[4]: 10,375 of Shakespeare's words account for some 35 per cent of the total of about 30,000 in *ALD²*. But sharper focuses are possible.

Since the great majority of words in Shakespeare were already firmly established in the language before his time — and are today normally unmarked, i.e., they belong to what James Murray called 'a nucleus or central mass of many thousand . . . "common" words, in which literary and colloquial usage meet' (*OED*, p. x) — one such focus would be the words which are recorded by the *SOED* as first appearing in the period from, say, 1580 to 1613, a span which would cover Shakespeare's career, plus the earlier decade from 1580 to 1590 to allow a certain flexibility for earlier datings of his works as well as for his employment of very new words. Of the 9475 lemmata which are recorded as having their first appearance in this period, 1628 are to be found in Shakespeare. In other words, Shakespeare would seem to fulfill the general observation that his vocabulary is 'modern' and 'progressive'.

---

[3] The statistics derive from the SHAD project. For this essay, foreign words and proper names in Shakespeare have not been included. The counts may vary slightly from those in my earlier publications, for the data are continuously being refined. Statistically, the differences are slight and insignificant. The problems connected with the dates of first occurrences are too complex for discussion here. (See Finkenstaedt and Wolff, *Ordered Profusion*, pp. 44 – 54.) They do not substantially affect the main points of this essay, however.

[4] The second edition, edited by A. S. Hornby, E. V. Gatenby, and H. Wakefield (1963), has been used because it was incorporated into the data for the *CED* and then for SHAD. The abbreviation *ALD²* also includes the 2000 most frequent English words plus about 1900 derivatives found in *A General Service List of English Words*, ed. M. West (rev. edn. 1953). In general, the matching of vocabularies is on the basis of lemmata (although 'word' is often used for the sake of simplicity). Shifts in semantics are, as a rule, not observed when the lemma remains the same. A semantic investigation, certainly essential, is far beyond the scope of this brief essay.

This view cannot be taken at face value, of course, since there is no comparable evidence to show that 17 per cent of a total vocabulary is enough to support such a conclusion. Indeed, Shakespeare's share may be less if works not selected or noticed by the *SOED* are considered. Or the percentage may even be higher if an adjustment is made for the special attention given to important works which happen to have appeared in the same period: it is no accident that by far the largest number of words (844) is recorded for 1611, the year in which the King James Bible was published. Since absolute numbers can be misleading, a closer analysis of the possible presence of Shakespeare in *ALD²* by means of certain information available from the *SOED* and other sources for words whose first occurrence is recorded as between 1580 and 1613 is necessary.

Only 15 such lemmata are marked by the *SOED* as being other than of 'common' usage (as opposed to well over 800 so marked which do not appear in *ALD²*): *affright, back-sword, punk, unaneled, zany*, and *zounds* are considered archaic or obsolete; *dickens* and *youngster* are colloquial; *changeful, illume*, and *viewless* 'chiefly poetical'; *flapjack* is 'in dialect use' or 'in the English of the U.S.A.'; *homo* and *toga* are 'alien or not naturalized'; and *beetle* (vb.) is considered a nonce-word. This brief list illustrates several features of lexicographical practice. For one thing, the fluidity of classification according to usage is apparent in *ALD²*'s unmarking of *back-sword, dickens, youngster, changeful, flapjack, toga*, and *beetle*, although both dictionaries appeared within a few years of each other. Interestingly enough, the changes go the other way too: the preposition *midst*, 'common' in the *SOED*, is marked 'literary or archaic' in *ALD²*. *ALD²*'s successor, the *Oxford Advanced Learner's Dictionary* (1974), appearing only some ten years later, considers *dickens* once again 'colloquial'. Second, the fluidity of inclusion/exclusion is evident in the *OALD*'s exclusion altogether of *affright, back-sword*, and *changeful*, as in Dr. Johnson's exclusion of *zounds, flapjack*, and *homo* some two hundred years earlier. Dr. Johnson, in fact, has no entry at all for dozens of Shakespearean words found in *ALD²*, even if allowance is made for different lexicographical principles (like the definition of the lemma) or text of Shakespeare. Nor is this situation to be explained simply by, say, Johnson's prudishness (he may exclude *zounds* but does include *punk*) or his avowed regard for only the best of the 'best authours' (he may exclude the interjections *faugh, pah, pooh, whoa*, and *zounds*, but does include *halloo, hollo* [holla, 'now vitiously written *hollo* by the best authors'], *hist, pish*, and *wo*).

This lexicographical lability makes it difficult to assess Shakespeare's influence in the persistence of words in his vocabulary appearing for the first time between 1580 and 1613, especially since all but 15 — i.e., some 782 — are regarded as 'common'. To be sure, some assistance is provided at times by the quotations used to illustrate meaning. In a dictionary of some 40,000 words, Dr. Johnson, for example, quotes Shakespeare 8694 times in the first volume (A – K) alone.[5] But the practice is not uniform or even predictable, since lexicographers are admittedly torn between their admiration for Shakespeare and their duty to find first appearances or illustrations representative of a wide spectrum of authors and fields. Still, certain words seem inseparable from Shakespeare's works. *Hamlet* is almost automatically evoked by *beetle* (vb.), *cerement*, *heyday*, *out-Herod*, *palmy*, *primal*, *unaneled*, *unhand*; *Macbeth* by *assassination*, *multitudinous*, *unsex*; *Romeo* by *duellist*, *hist*, *inauspicious*, *lady-bird*. For all, as if to confirm one's 'prophetic soul', the *SOED* gives Shakespeare as the first or only citation. But very soon the automatic association becomes difficult or is apparent perhaps only in the first element of well-known collocations, like *unvarnished* tale (*Othello* 1.3.90), *viewless* winds (*Measure for Measure* 3.1.123), *seamy* side (*Othello* 4.2.146), *unlicked* whelp (cub) (*3 Henry VI* 3.2.161). It may well be that the association with Shakespeare is due to or is connected with the fact that all but one of these words occur but once or only in one play.

Indeed, the distribution of all these lemmata according to frequency may lend support to the influence of Shakespeare. Although the occurrences of individual lemmata range from one to forty-nine, the 382 occurring but once make up more than 47 per cent of the total. If the 154 lemmata which occur twice are added, two-thirds of the total is achieved. It is of course impossible to establish a direct causal connection between Shakespeare's vocabulary and its inclusion in dictionaries, much less the transmission of single lemmata from dictionary to dictionary. Even his being cited is at most circumstantial evidence. But the preponderance of lemmata occurring but once makes it tempting to try to establish a motivation, if not relationship. This tendency is strengthened by the fact that at least a third of the lemmata which occur once have only one definition in the *SOED* and thus, very restricted in range, would seem to derive from one particular source.

---

[5] The statistics for Volume I are from Lewis Freed, 'The sources of Johnson's Dictionary', Diss. Cornell 1939, quoted in Theodore Stenberg, 'Quotations from Pope in Johnson's Dictionary', *Texas Studies in English* 24 (1944), 203. Gove, 'Shakespeare's language', mentions 2000 'acknowledged' quotations in Webster's *Third*.

At the other end of the scale, the 14 lemmata which occur twenty or more times — *frown* (n.) and *parley* (n.) 20, *affright* 23, *torture* (vb.) 24, *discontent* (n.) 26, *split* (vb.) 27, *zounds* 29, *mettle* 30, *design* (n.) and *share* (vb.) 31, *admire* (vb.) 34, *effect* (vb.) 35, *act* (vb.) 42, *disgrace* (n.) 49 — are all recorded in the 1580's (if the *SOED* dating of Shakespeare's plays is observed). Further, with the exception of *affright* and *zounds* (not surprisingly, deemed 'archaic' by the *SOED*), all have anywhere from two to eleven definitions in the *SOED* and consequently more citations through the centuries, an indication of the elasticity of the lemmata and militating against the direct influence of Shakespeare on lexicographers. But, undeniably, that they are so few lends greater weight to the lemmata which occur infrequently.

It is also interesting to note that of these higher frequency lemmata all but *admire*, *affright*, *mettle*, *split*, and *zounds* are examples of noun-verb or verb-noun conversions in Shakespeare, one word-class of which is considerably earlier than Shakespeare (with the exception of the verb *split*, whose noun form follows in 1597). This situation introduces the possibility that the Shakespearean contribution to dictionaries, if not the distinctiveness of his vocabulary as a whole, may be at least partially attributable to the distribution and nature of word-classes in the corpus. If the relatively few adverbs among these 797 lemmata between 1580 and 1613 are omitted because of the uncertainty and inconsistency of the treatment of adverbs in the *SOED*, as well as minimal totals for the so-called 'minor' word-classes, there remain 215 adjectives, 290 nouns, and 219 verbs. The distribution in percentage of the three major word-classes is unusual: adjectives account for almost 27 per cent, as against a bit more than 22 per cent for adjectives in the entire corpus; nouns for more than 36 per cent, as against almost 47 per cent for the corpus; and verbs for a bit over 27 per cent, as against slightly more than 22 per cent for the corpus. The increase in adjectives and verbs, as well as the decrease in nouns, suggests something about both Shakespeare's creativity and lexicographers' selectivity, as well as their interaction. The abundance of adjectives may be attributed to their relatively small representation before 1580: 41.3 per cent of all the adjectives in Shakespeare are recorded as appearing between 1580 and 1613. Since Shakespeare's share is consistent with the overall growth in the English of his time, it is not surprising that the lexicographer should reflect both simultaneously. It is also possible to begin to detect the contours of the Shakespearean idiolect, and so perhaps the direct influence of Shake-speare on the *ALD*[2] lexicographer, in, *inter alia*, the fairly large number of adjectives formed by the addition to a noun of the suffix -*y*, although unlike the modern constructions not chiefly to concrete mass nouns: *batty*, *bosky*, *brassy*, *bristly*, *bulky*, *choppy*, *doughy*, *flaky*, *gloomy*, *gusty, inky, leaky, nervy, palmy, seamy, shiny, stealthy, tiny, wiry,* and *yeasty.*[6]

The productive noun-to-verb and verb-to-noun conversions are suggestive in a similar way. Shakespeare practiced these principal forms, favouring the former. In the more than 200 homograph pairs of nouns and verbs in his work with one word-class occurring for the first time before 1580 and the other between 1580 and 1613, about two-thirds are verbs converted from nouns without the addition of an affix. Although the number of those appearing in *ALD²* is of course less, it is still proportionately higher than the percentage of the overall selection. As with the other phenomena it is admittedly difficult to attribute these instances to Shakespeare: after all, conversion is common and comparative statistics are not yet available. Still, although Shakespeare is not always cited, his authority would seem to account for a good number of entries in a modern dictionary. Granted, nouns first appearing between 1580 – 1613 may disappear even when the verb is now common, like *accept, accuse, expect, knit, supervise, swagger, thwart, vary, vouch —* for many of which the *SOED* gives a first or only citation from Shakespeare. Similarly, among verbs not given in *ALD²* are *barber, blanket, casket, companion, kitchen, monster, palate, scandal, shark.* But a few fairly unusual nouns connected with Shakespeare survive, like *botch, caparison,* and *gabble,* as do verbs like *champion, cudgel, dower, gibbet, sliver, usher.*

It is likewise difficult not to connect certain groups of words retained in *ALD²* with their early use by Shakespeare. Two are especially numerous and compact; both have something special about them. The first consists of the large representation of a minor word-class, interjections: *faugh, halloo, hist, hollo, pah, pish, pooh, whoa, wo, zounds.* The second consists of compounds made up of an adjective or adverb plus the *-ed* (*-en*) participle, a process (although in itself not unusual) often discussed in connection with Shakespeare's creativity:[7] *barefaced, base-born, cold-blooded, cold-hearted, foul-mouthed, full-*

---

[6] Affixation has always been of interest in discussions of Shakespeare's language. See, for example, George Gordon, *Shakespeare's English*, Society for Pure English, Tract 29 (1928), esp. 269 ff., and my 'Shakespeare's language' in *William Shakespeare: his World, his Work, his Influence*, ed. John F. Andrews (3 vols., New York, 1985), ii. 343 – 361, esp. 355 – 358. It is perhaps interesting to note that of the 620 adjectives in the contemporary *Table Alphabeticall* of Robert Cawdrey (1604) not one is composed of a noun plus *-y* suffix.

[7] For example, Bernard Groom, *The Formation and Use of Compound Epithets in English Poetry From 1579*, Society for Pure English, Tract 49 (1937), 300 – 304.

grown, *high-pitched*, *hot-blooded*, *ill-starred*, *ill-tempered*, *long-winded*, *low-spirited*, *noble-minded*, *open-eyed*, *raw-boned*, *short-lived*, *smooth-faced*, *soft-hearted*, *still-born*, *well-chosen*. Strikingly, for all but one of these, the *SOED* gives a Shakespeare quotation, citation, or date. Only *full-grown* has none — but that is because it is erroneously first-dated 1667.

Ironically enough, the lemmata not appearing in *ALD²* may be the best evidence for the recognition of Shakespeare in the English lexicographical tradition. . That Shakespeare has been favored by all English lexicographers is not to be disputed. If his contemporaries are sometimes quoted instead — for whatever reason — it must be conceded that Shakespeare cannot have been ignored. The omissions appear to be conscious and deliberate acts by dictionary-makers, of which the *ALD²* selection is but one, not untypical, instance. On the surface at least, certain groups of omitted lemmata are explainable on the basis of Shakespeare's practice or lexicographical policy or both. Some general criteria for the selection are obvious enough. For one thing, proper names and foreign words, which account in Shakespeare for 1766 and 644 lemmata respectively, play only a very minor role in dictionaries (although the amount of encyclopedic information has been increasing of late): the *SOED*, for example, has a not very considerable 2632 names. Similarly, since dictionaries are essentially prose-oriented, they tend to ignore euphonic devices, just as they give relatively little attention to dialect. Of more importance is the fact that the definition of the lemma or the headword is not fixed, as is evident, for example, in the *SOED*'s uneven treatment of adverbs or its employment of sub-entries and differing typefaces, thus making it difficult to accommodate or recognize numerous lemmata. As a result of these and other considerations one of the major forms of Shakespeare's creativity receives — *a priori* — slight acceptance: his mouth-filling, experience-spanning compounding. As a complement to the 20 adjectives formed from adjective or adverb plus the *-ed* participle given above, the more than 400 compounds between 1580 – 1613 which find no place in *ALD²* and normally no headword in the *SOED* will suffice to illustrate a major disparity between Shakespearean and lexicographical practice. The simple listing of such compounds beginning with the letter B should indicate what has been lost: *bald-pated*, *bare-armed*, *bare-boned*, *bare-grown*, *bare-picked*, *bare-ribbed*, *barren-spirited*, *big-boned*, *big-looked*, *big-swollen*, *black-browed*, *black-cornered*, *black-eyed*, *black-faced*, *bloody-faced*, *bloody-minded*, *bloody-sceptred*, *blue-eyed*, *blue-veined*, *blunt-witted*, *bold-faced*, *broad-fronted*, *burly-boned*. Similarly, complementing the earlier list, the following adjectives formed by the addition to a noun of the suffix *-y* are not represented in *ALD²*:

barky, beachy, brisky, corky, cursitory, finny, mothy, primy, rheumy, rooky, shelvy, skyey, sphery, spleeny, womby.

Compared to these omissions and other important morphological examples, the instances of normal or natural attrition — be they grammatical or semantic — are of relatively less interest since they are more restricted in their consequences or at least less immediately Shakespeare-related. In this connection it may be well to point out that frequency of occurrence in Shakespeare plays a relatively unimportant role in the retention of the lemmata in *ALD²*: 382 of the 797 lemmata occur but once, 154 but twice; only 14 lemmata occur 20 or more times, the most frequent being the verb *disgrace*. And, not surprisingly, the inherent or even popular interest of a work may well play a role. For 1602, the date generally assigned to lemmata first recorded and largely present in *All's Well That Ends Well*, 15 lemmata survive in *ALD²*, 66 do not. But then again only some 30 of about 125 lemmata mainly from *Hamlet* survive. Obviously, this hypothesis would have to be tested in detail before it could be treated as anything more than speculation.

Despite the numerous and apparently unmistakable glimmers of his vocabulary, it is undeniably difficult to assess Shakespeare's presence in modern dictionaries. The overall contours are imprecise, for much of the evidence presented is admittedly incomplete and circumstantial. For many the 'real' Shakespeare is in the more than 7000 of his words which are not to be found in *ALD²* and not in the 10,000 or so 'worn-down' ones which are. Against the 797 words first recorded between 1580 and 1613 which appear in *ALD²* stand some 3000 which do not. They are striking in ways too numerous for discussion here: in length, in morphological complexity, in the whole range of unencumbered linguistic inventiveness. Be that as it may, what is indisputable is that Shakespeare is subject to the tradition of lexicographical transmission, as dictionaries manipulate those dictionaries which have preceded them, in these days of computer tapes a process amounting to lexicographical cloning. In this respect, Sisyphus's rolling stone gathers a bit of moss. But Shakespeare is dominated even more by the lexicographer, whose aim has changed since Dr. Johnson sought to preserve the language through the 'chief glory of every people . . . its authours' (p. C2ᵛ) and whose authority is today diminished by the lack of clearly defined theoretical criteria and official sanction, on the one hand, and the pluralism if not fractionation of national languages, on the other. The greatest power over Shakespeare, to return to Ulysses, is of course exercised by the unvanquishable: 'envious and calumniating Time'. Or if the figure seems overly dramatic, then Shakespeare provides Ulysses with an even more chilling domestic image to describe the fate of his vocabulary:

Words

Time is like a fashionable host
That slightly shakes his parting guest by the hand,
And with his arms outstretched as he would fly,
Grasps in the comer. The welcome ever smiles,
And farewell goes out sighing.

(165 – 169)

WORDS FROM *A SUPPLEMENT TO DR. HARRIS'S DICTIONARY OF ARTS AND SCIENCES, 1744*

E. G. Stanley

The Oxford English Dictionary made little use of John Harris's *Lexicon Technicum: or an Universal English Dictionary of Arts and Sciences, explaining not only the Terms of Art, but the Arts themselves*, the first edition of which was published in London in 1704. It was augmented in several editions,[1] and especially in *A Supplement to Dr. Harris's Dictionary of Arts and Sciences. By a Society of Gentlemen* (London, 1744). Of course, the *Supplement* to Harris was able to make use of works of reference as well as more original writings which might now be called monographs. Thus, in spite of protests in the *Supplement* that, among others, Nathan Bailey in his dictionaries and Ephraim Chambers in his cyclopaedia had freely made use of Harris, the *Supplement* in turn made frequent use especially of Chambers's *Cyclopaedia, or an Universal Dictionary of Arts and Sciences*, the first edition of which was published in 1728. It is a commonplace that works of reference feed on each other,[2] *cannibalize* them — though that word is too savage to use for so gentle a craft as lexicography.

Harris was early in the field among English lexicographers to give for many of his articles the sources from which he had derived his information or which he had quoted, and the *Supplement* followed his example. One reason why it is often unnecessary for a dictionary like *OED* — or *A Supplement to the Oxford English Dictionary*, to the editor of which, ROBERT BURCHFIELD, we wish to do homage and honour in this volume — to refer explicitly to Harris's *Lexicon* and the *Supplement* to it is precisely because, so alerted, the modern dictionary can take its quotation direct from the source itself. The title-page of the *Supplement*

---

[1] See R. C. Alston, *A Bibliography of the English Language from the Invention of Printing to the Year 1800* (reprint, Ilkley, 1974), iii, 123 – 4, nos 528 – 33; *Supplement*, iii, 125, no. 534.
[2] Cf. De W. T. Starnes and G. E. Noyes, *The English Dictionary from Cawdrey to Johnson 1604 – 1755* (Chapel Hill, 1946), ch. XI.

has the significant words: '*N.B.* Those Subjects in which Dr. *Harris* is any way deficient are here perfected; no trifling and insignificant Words inserted, but only such as may convey some useful and entertaining Knowledge to the Reader; for whose further Benefit and Satisfaction, all the Authors made use of in this Work are quoted.' In fact, the *Supplement* is so dependent on the work of others, both of original scholarship and lexicographical compilations, that even for the small number of examples I give and for which I have not provided a source it is likely that there is a source. Because entry in the *Supplement* is evidence of earlier use noted by the 'Society of Gentlemen' who compiled it, and not evidence of original, scholarly usage of 1744, it is probably not to be regarded as a record of living usage: in short, when it comes to supplementing *OED*, the *Supplement* to Harris is valuable for antedatings but not for postdatings of *OED*.

For the lexicographer wishing to use the *Supplement* as a short cut further help is provided by its anonymous editors, as they say (p. iv): 'Those Articles mark'd with an Asterism, of which there are above ELEVEN HUNDRED, are entire new ones, and not to be found in any Performance of the like Nature.'

With so large a number of new articles it is clearly impossible in the space available to do more than give a few examples which seemed to me of interest. It should be noted that the *Supplement* — like Toller's to Bosworth-Toller,[3] but unlike Robert Burchfield's to *OED* — is much fuller at the beginning of the alphabet than at the end, perhaps because the beginning was more in need of augmentation, or more probably because patient diligence or resources waned. Thus A and C have just over 200 pages each; B 74; P and S just over 60 each; M 45 and D just over; E and T 36 each; F, G and I (that is, I and J) between 24 and 28 each; H, L, N, O, R, V (that is, U and V) and W between 11 and 19 each; and the rest, K, Q, X, Y and Z 5 or less each. That *OED* made, as far as I know, so little use of the *Supplement* to Harris may be, to some extent, related to the distribution of entries in the *Supplement* to Harris. At the beginning of the alphabet, when it is at its fullest, *OED* was less well in command of the earlier lexicographical material than towards the end of the alphabet when the *Supplement* to Harris is at its scantiest.

The following quotations from entries in the *Supplement* to Harris have been chosen to illustrate several characteristics. First, the *Supplement* at its best provides good earlier uses than the earliest in *OED* or Robert Burchfield's *Supplement* to *OED*. Secondly, the references given in the *Supplement* lead to an earlier use which *OED* might have used

[3] *An Anglo-Saxon Dictionary based on the Manuscript Collections of the late Joseph Bosworth — Supplement*, by T. Northcote Toller (Oxford, 1908 – 21).

without necessarily quoting or referring to the *Supplement* to Harris that should have led to it. Thirdly, definitions in the *Supplement* to Harris are often derived from some earlier work, especially some earlier work of reference, though that debt is not always acknowledged. Obviously it is likely that as a result of more extensive reading than mine of earlier technical literature much more of the *Supplement* will be found to be indebted to earlier writings. The *Supplement* is not a great and original creator of authoritative definitions; and that is not merely a reason for my suspicion that when I regard it as being first in the field with a word it is only apparently so, that is, it is only so because I have not found where it gets it from, but it is also a reason for thinking that *OED* was not gravely at fault in its ignoring the *Supplement* to Harris in the following examples.

ACCENTOR [not in *OED*], one of the three Singers in Parts, or the Person that sings the predominant Part in a Trio.
Supplement refers to GRASSINEAU's *Musical Dict.*[4]

CACOPHONY [*OED*, 3. *Med.* no quotation, only a reference to Mayne *Exp. Lex.*[5]]. *Cacophony* is also an immusical Tone of the Voice, arising from the ill Constitution of its Organs.

CANTO [*OED*, 3. *a*1789 Burney —] in *Musick*, is the Treble, or at least the higher Part of a piece. When it is marked with a C, it is the upper Bass: But the Word *Canto* more properly signifies the first Treble, unless the Word *Secondo* for the Second, or *Ripieno* for the Treble of the Grand Chorus be added.
Supplement gives further *Canto Concertante*, *Canto figurato*; as well as: *Canto fermo* [*OED*, *a*1789 Burney —], or *Semplice*, is what they call the plain Song; such was Pope *Gregory*'s Church-Music. The *Italians* call every Part a *Canto fermo*, whether plain or figured, if it be the subject of any Counterpoint.

CARTULARY [*OED*, this sense no quotation before 1848]. *Cartularies* are Papers wherein Contracts, Sales, Exchanges, Privileges, Immunities, Exemptions, and other Acts that belong to the Church and Monasteries, are collected, the better to preserve the antient Deeds, being much later than the Facts mentioned in them. The Compilers of

---

[4] J. Grassineau, *A Musical Dictionary* (London, 1740), 2; the same wording.
[5] R. G. Mayne, *Expository Lexicon of the Terms . . . in Medical and General Science* (London, 1853 – 60), *Cacophonia: Pathol.* Old term for a harsh, grating or discordant state of voice: cacopho'ny.

these *Cartilaries* [*sic*] have not been always very faithful to their Trust; for we find an immense Number of Pieces manifestly false.

Supplement gives a reference to R. SIMON's *Traite de Benefic.*,[6] where (1684 edition, pp. 63 – 4; 1703 edition, p. 49) *cartulaire* has the sense taken over in the *Supplement* to Harris:

> Il est fait mention dans le Traité des matieres Beneficiales, atribué au P. Paul, d'une forme de Contract nommé *precaria*, qui a apporté de grandes richesses aux Monasteres. Les vieux Cartulaires sont remplis de ces sortes d'Actes, qui consistoient en une donation que les particuliers faisoient de leurs biens aux Eglises; puis ils obtenoient des mesmes Eglises par des Lettres qu'ils appelloient *precarias* ou *precatorias*, les mesmes biens, pour les posseder par une espece de Bail Emphytheotique . . . J'ai mesme trouvé dans des Cartulaires anciens, des Formules de *precaires*.

CHERUBICAL-HYMN [cf. *OED*, s.v. *Cherubic*, 1876 only], an *Hymn* of great Note in the antient Christian Church. The original Form of it, as it stands in the *Constitution*, was in these words; *Holy, Holy, Holy Lord God of Hosts; Heaven and Earth are full of thy Glory, who art blessed for ever. Amen*.

Among references given in *Supplement* is BINGHAM *Orig. Eccles.*, B. xiv. c. 2.[7] Bingham writes:

> A third Hymn [following 'the lesser Doxology' and 'the Angelical Hymn, or Great Doxology'] of great Note in the Church was the Cherubical Hymn, or the *Trisagion*, as it was called, because of the thrice repeating, *Holy, Holy, Holy, Lord God of Hosts*, in Imitation of the Seraphims in the Vision of *Isaiah*. The Original Form of this Hymn was in these Words, *Holy, Holy, Holy, Lord God of Hosts, Heaven and Earth are full of thy Glory, who art Blessed for ever.* Amen. Thus it is in the Constitution, and frequently in St. Chrysostom, who says always, that it was in the same words that the Seraphims sung it in *Isaiah*.

CRITICISM [cf. *OED*, 2.a., 1674 Dryden—; and for *literary criticism* Robert Burchfield's *Supplement*, s.v. *literary*, 3b., 1876 George

---

[6] That is 'Jerome à Costa', *Histoire de l'Origine & du Progrés des Revenus Ecclesiastiques* . . . (Frankfurt, 1684), which has a good account of the false documentation in cartularies to substantiate claims to benefices, privileges, etc.

The term *cartulaire* has no Italian cognate in the underlying *Trattato della Materie . . . Beneficiarie* ('Mirandola' [i.e. Venice?], 1676), by 'Father Paul', that is (Fra) Pietro Sarpi, where it should occur at p. 71; nor is it to be found in the English translation of the *Trattato*, viz. *The Treatise of Beneficiary Matters* (Westminster, 1727), where the corresponding passage is at p. 60.

[7] J. Bingham, *The Works*, i (London, 1726), 672, *Origines Ecclesiasticae*, Bk XIV, ch. II, sect. iii.

Eliot—], the Art of judging . . . We may distinguish divers Sorts or Branches of this Art; viz. Philosophical, Sacred, Political and Dramatical *Criticism*, *Criticism* of Antiquities, *&c*. But the ordinary Use of the Word is restrained to Literary, which however is of great Extent as it takes in the Art of judging of Facts, a Branch of *Criticism*, which regards not only History, but also the Discernment of the real Works of an Author, the true Authors of a Work, the genuine reading of a Text; the Art of discovering suppositious[8] Monuments, Charters, interpolated Passages, *&c*. The other Parts of Literary *Criticism* are the Art of Judging of Works of Genius, their Excellencies and Defects, to explain what was most beautiful, most solid, and most remarkable, and to assign Reasons for their Judgment, *&c*.

Chambers (1738 edition), has s.v. CRITICISM:

> *Literary* CRITICISM, which, however, is of great extent, as it takes in the art of judging of facts: a branch of *criticism*, which regards not only history, but also the discernment of the real works of an author, the real author of a work, the genuine reading of a text, and the art of discovering supposititious monuments, *&c*. The other parts of *literary criticism*, are, the art of judging of works of genius, their excellencies and defects.

DIVIL [*OED* and Robert Burchfield's *Supplement*, s.v. *devil*, 8. A name of various instruments or mechanical contrivances, *esp.* such as work with sharp teeth or spikes, or do destructive work, but also applied, with more or less obvious allusion to others. 1831—]. DIVIL *on the Neck*, a tormenting Engine formerly used among the prosecuting Papists, straitening and pressing a Man by the Neck, especially whenever he stirred.

Supplement has a reference to FOX's *Acts, sub. R.H.S.*, that is, to Fox's *Book of Martyrs*, 'The Story of John Porter, cruelly martyred for reading the Bible in Paul's', A.D. 1541. The second edition, 1570, ii, page 537 (sig. Yy4[r]) has:[9]

---

[8] *Sic*, but see Chambers's definition, given next, with the correct reading 'supposititious'.

[9] John Fox(e), *The Second Volume of the Ecclesiasticall history, conteyning the Actes & Monumentes of Martyrs* (London, Iohn Daye, 1570). The full account of the martyrdom of John Porter is first given in this edition, 'Newly recognised and inlarged by the Author. I. Foxe'. It is not in the first edition (London, Iohn Day, 1563), at p. 621, which has a much shorter account of John Porter's martyrdom. For a modern edition, fully indexed, see that by G. Townsend: J. Fox(e), *The Acts and Monuments* . . .(London, 1843 – 9; reprinted New York, 1965), v, 452.

It is signified to vs by credible information, that the same night before hee was found dead, they that dwelt neere to the same place of the prison where Porter lay, did heare him pitiously to groan and make a lamentable noyse, where some suppose that he was put in certaine strait irons which bee there in the house, called, *The Diuell on the necke*, being after an horrible sort deuised, straining and winching the necke of a man with his legs together, in such sort, as the more he stirred in it the straiter it presseth him, so that within three or foure houres it breaketh and crusheth a mans backe and body in pieces. Jn which diuelish torment whether John Porter was slaine or no it is not certaine.

EXPECTORANTS [*OED*, s.v. *Expectorant*, B., *sb.*, 1782—], such Medicines as expel, through the *Larynx*, the morbose Matter that hangs in the *Bronchia*.

NAULUM [*OED*, —1677], *Charon*'s Fare.

OPERA [*OED*, 2. (usually *the opera*) As a branch of dramatic art. (Cf. *the drama*, *tragedy*, *comedy*, etc.); 1759 Goldsmith —]. These musical Interludes, interrupted by performing the several Acts in the principal Pieces, afforded a formal and pompous Show; and if they had been separated from Pastoral, or Tragi-Comedy, to which they were annexed, they wanted nothing but a Name to denounce them a Species of Representations quite differnt from Tragedy or Comedy. The *Italian* Writers are at a great deal of Pains to settle the precise Time in which the *Opera* began . . . Formerly, the *Opera* comprehended all Subjects, but, since the Machinery has been laid aside, it deals no longer in Fables, Divinities, Music, Pastoral, and the like, but confines itself entirely to History.

In fact, Chambers (1738 edition) is close, but less explicit:

While the English and French comic and tragic theatres were forming, the Venetians invented the *opera*.

THORACICS [*OED*, s.v. *Thoracic*, B. 1; 1710], those Medicines come under this Denomination, which promote either Respiration, or the propelling of the Blood into the left Ventricle of the Heart. There is scarce any such Thing as a Specific *Thoracic*, properly so called; all that have obtained this Name, act in the same Manner together as other Medicines, by attenuating, inspissating, stimulating, *&c.* and then they are to be accounted *Thoracics*, when the venal Blood is so viscid as not to be able to flow thro' the Lungs. But if anything is to be accounted a true *Thoracic*, it must be the Air itself, so far as being impregnated with some Vapours, it is received into the Lungs.

The *Supplement* to Harris is, as we have seen, not a primary source, but it provides clues to primary sources, and is, therefore, a short cut to something better than itself. It cannot be said of it, in the pompous terms familiar from book-reviews, that lexicographers ignore it at their peril. At most we can say that, not infrequently, the result of ignoring the *Supplement* leads to a greater expenditure of time when the history of a word in the scholarly usage of the earlier eighteenth century is to be established. Very occasionally, the *Supplement* may guide the lexicographer to a word not recorded in *OED*, and since the *Supplement* is unoriginal it is likely that there is an earlier use whether the entry has a reference to a source or not. *The New Oxford English Dictionary* would do well to make full use of Dr Harris's *Lexicon Technicum* and the anonymous *Supplement* to it.

ON EDITING A USAGE GUIDE

Edmund Weiner

What are we to make of that neglected genre, the Usage Guide? In the course of distinguishing the sense 'prescriptive grammar' from other senses of the term *grammar*, the authors of *A Comprehensive Grammar of the English Language* made passing mention of it:

> Authorities on *usage* . . . primarily deal with *disputed usage*, a relatively small number of syntactic and lexical items that are controversial within the standard varieties . . . Over the last two centuries prescriptive rules have accumulated into a general prescriptive tradition for formal writing that is embodied (with some variation) in school textbooks and student reference handbooks, and in usage guides for the general public.[1]

A year later, the last volume of the *OED Supplement* listed *usage guide* as an undefined italic headword, supported by two quotations; one, from 1972, spoke of

> the 'usage guides' which editorial offices and printeries use in order to impose a consistency of style.

The other, from 1980, remarked

> Readers of these usage guides too often take them as gospel truth.[2]

Do Grammar and Dictionary, senior siblings to the usage guide, agree in supporting a rather low view of the genre: a genre with a limited scope and an appeal chiefly to the less sophisticated? True, the usage guide

[1] R. Quirk, S. Greenbaum, G. Leech, J. Svartvik, *A Comprehensive Grammar of the English Language* (London, 1985), p. 14.
[2] R. W. Burchfield, *A Supplement to the Oxford English Dictionary* (Oxford, 1986), s.v. *usage* sb.

171

genre has had a fairly short independent lifespan (less than a century) but its antenatal existence, as an aspect of the English Grammar before modern linguistics had arisen, was long. It comprises only a small number of works, but some of the classic ones of a former generation were written by authors who were notable for their other achievements. None, to my knowledge, have set down their thoughts on the practice of usage guide writing: the scope of the genre, the selection of subject-matter, the use of evidence, the principles of guidance, and the organization of the material. This is my excuse, as one who has attempted the genre, for putting down my thoughts on the subject here.

The writing of a usage guide involves two presuppositions:

(1) there is a set of linguistic habits available to the speaker of a language, which is acquired, not automatically — through growing up among speakers of the language — but through a conscious educational process:

(2) it is reasonable and feasible to provide people with a short cut to the acquisition of these habits.

I grant that some people would regard such a body of linguistic usage as a factitious entity and the desire for it as a delusion. I do not propose to make a direct approach to this controversy; I hope, however, that the points which emerge below may make some contribution to it.[3] I want instead to consider how in practice the usage guide writer views his material as he proceeds with his task. I turn first to its scope.

---

[3] A sensible and thoughtful discussion of the issue, including an authoritative discussion of the wider subject of style, has recently been presented by Dr Walter Nash in *English Usage: a guide to first principles* (London, 1986). On pp. 154ff. he asks 'what do we look for in the government of usage?' and of the two sets of requirements he describes, I find the 'more liberal' one to be close, in some of its details, to several points made in the present essay:
    (a) A need for discussion, explanation, evaluation, of disputed points in usage.
    (b) A disposition to accept some changes more readily than others, but not to feel that changes are destroying the language.
    (c) A wish to feel that there are alternatives in usage and style, the choice of which is dictated by context and function.
    (d) A tendency to regard the 'standard' style as a convenient fiction or abstraction, and to perceive, in reality, various *styles*.
(Nash, pp. 154 – 155).

The scope of a usage guide

Coverage of the language

In one dimension, the scope of a usage guide is as broad as the English language, covering spelling, punctuation, phonology, morphology, syntax, and lexis, and involving sociolinguistic considerations. But obviously a usage guide does not describe the whole language. It takes for granted the bulk of it, and it assumes that its audience are native speakers or advanced learners. It has nothing to say about some of the central facts of the language, while going into great detail about others.

Variation in the language

The usage guide addresses itself to a tiny fragment of the language, or rather to a number of tiny fragments, for the subjects it treats are not inherently linked together, as the phenomena explored in a grammar are interconnected by being part of an overall system. What holds the parts together is an external function. The characteristic function of a usage guide gives rulings and makes recommendations, in its best forms presenting explanations and arguments to support them. Its purpose is to enable its user to make choices between linguistic features that can be functionally equivalent in a given context. This is so whether the subject is spelling (e.g. *alright* versus *all right*), pronunciation ('grievious' versus 'grievous'), lexis (*infer* versus *imply*), or grammar (*unlike my mother and I/me*). The issue in usage is which of two or more alternatives to choose, while the status of the alternatives and the factors influencing the choice differ from case to case.

The usage guide resembles a work of grammar for foreign learners, which not only describes the structure of the language but also lays down what is grammatical and rules out what is not. But a distinction, not absolutely clear-cut but nevertheless useful, can also be drawn. The foreign learner is trying to master choices between the English and the non-English, where frequently the non-English alternatives may be many. The usage guide user is trying to decide between alternatives that, from a descriptive point of view, co-exist within the ambit of English, even if some are thought less English than others.

This statement may be considered somewhat surprising. Is every dilemma that a usage guide claims to resolve an affair of two (or more) alternatives, each of which is part of the language even if disowned by some language users? Clearly this is true of some of the old chestnuts of usage: con*trov*ersy is admitted to be English even by the champions of *con*troversy; it is acknowledged that people actually say 'he is older than me' whether it is 'right' or 'wrong'. But what about some of the less familiar corners of this variegated linguistic zone? Reflection shows that it must be true. For a usage guide to discountenance linguistic alternatives that were never likely to occur within the speech-community would be pointless. Rightly or wrongly, usage guides can only evaluate alternatives that actually occur somewhere in the speech-community. For any item of usage they treat, usage guide writers ought in principle to be able to cite evidence of its actual use — evidence of the less acceptable just as much as of the more.[4]

The diachronic aspect

The third dimension of the usage guide's scope is time. Grammarians and lexicographers can, if they choose, largely ignore the diachronic aspect of language. The usage guide writer is acutely aware of linguistic change; it is the force that underlies, overtly or by implication, much of his subject-matter, and in fact without linguistic change there would be nothing much for him to write about. This is an aspect to which I shall return.

The selection of material

The usage guide writer's subject-matter is drawn from every department of the language, but selected on the basis that variation or optionality is involved, and considered both synchronically and diachronically. The grammarian and the lexicographer deal with one aspect of the language exhaustively; while the usage guide writer deals with every aspect of the language selectively. Since a usage guide concerns itself with only fragments of the total linguistic stock, it is important to ask how the usage guide writer selects his subject-matter. It is not enough merely to say that he directs his attention to areas where variation exists, for there

[4] The part played by linguistic evidence in the construction of a usage guide is central. This idea, once stated, seems a truism, but it is often obscured by the way usage guidance is presented. Especially in the more concise guides, rulings are often made very baldly, and if examples are given they are unattributed and give the impression of being invented. However, it is not on the presentation of real evidence, important though that is, that I want to lay stress, but on the use of it in the construction of the guide.

are many variations about which usage guides have nothing to say. Few are concerned with choices between, for example, *somebody* and *someone* or *he isn't* and *he's not*. The reason must be that they cause no difficulty and arouse no controversies.

It seems to be generally supposed that usage guide writers are mainly attracted to controversial variations in usage — the old chestnuts which recur in all usage guides. Or, as the next best thing, they will 'discover' a previously unremarked point of usage in which there is variation and, by coming down in favour of one variant and against the other, they will generate a new controversy around which other students of usage will eagerly gather — and so a new issue will have been added to the stock. This is to make out that their chief motivation is a taste for controversy and polemic.

I would rather suggest that their dominant motivation is genuinely educational. It relates to both the research and the pedagogic aspects of education. As regards the former, I would suggest that usage guide writers have an alertness about linguistic matters that leads them to notice curious and noteworthy phenomena of usage. If these have passed unnoticed before, it may be that they are relatively new phenomena, but not necessarily. The fact that usage guide writers keep on drawing attention to peculiar variations of usage can be attributed as easily to the constructive instincts that motivate any respectable research as to a perverse desire to arouse sociolinguistic strife.

A recent parliamentary report in *The Times* was headed 'Action sought on lethal catapaults': the spelling was repeated throughout.[5] Is such a form evidence that *-ult-* under low stress is merging with *-alt-*? This is typical of what arouses the curiosity of usage guide writers. They are curious about what the past participle of *to stride* is or whether the *t* of *bayoneted* is doubled by those who stress the final syllable of the root.

As regards the second aspect of education, usage guide writers clearly desire not only to bring the phenomena of usage which have aroused their curiosity to the attention of other interested parties, but also to summarize the principles involved and arrive at some kind of recommendation. The acceptability of the idea of making such recommendations may be debatable but there is no doubt that a real demand exists for them. This is not an entrepreneurial point — that there is a market for usage guides (though it is true). Rather, I believe that the demand exists within the usage guide writer himself. Being aware of a variation in usage is not satisfactory: the usage guide writer wants to know what to do about it. He frames the recommendation primarily to satisfy himself.

[5] *The Times*, 25 July 1986, p. 6.

This means that the choice of material will be guided by the repeated question 'which are the questions of usage that bother *me*?'

The things on which usage guide writers focus, in the first place, are or involve instances of linguistic variation; the variation is of a kind that, on examination, raises questions or problems in the mind of the observer — questions both of the pure 'why?', 'how?', and 'when?' variety (which he attempts to answer) and of the applied kind: 'which variant shall I choose?'

The mechanism of linguistic change, like that of biological evolution, involves the selection of a particular variant from among a range. A range of linguistic alternatives may remain static for generations, but equally, where two variants co-exist in the same context, one may be growing dominant and the other undergoing eclipse. Examples from contemporary British English might be the competition between *should* and *would* with the first person in conditional sentences, between original *hoofs* and analogical *hooves*, between *fewer* and *less* in plural noun phrases, and between lexical items like *enormity* and *enormousness*. Focusing on linguistic variation is thus tantamount to focusing on contemporary linguistic change. Willy-nilly, the usage guide writer is committed to the diachronic study of the present-day language. This puts the profession of the usage guide writer closer to that of the lexicographer, or at least the commercial lexicographer, who, if he wants his work to retain maximum usefulness, must constantly monitor changes in meaning, construction, pronunciation, and spelling, than to that of the grammarian, for whom the use of a synchronic cross-section of the language amounts to a kind of laboratory condition.

The use of evidence

Evidence is as indispensable to the usage guide writer as it is to the grammarian or lexicographer. Once the usage guide writer has selected the material for study, he can make no worthwhile observations about it until he has collected a body of examples. (Of course, this is an oversimplification. The identification of noteworthy linguistic phenomena and the recording of occurrences of them are almost always two parts of the same activity.) There is a close resemblance between the research of the usage guide writer and that of the lexicographer, especially the historical lexicographer. The usage guide writer will assemble a file of examples of each usage phenomenon which interests him. Reading and excerpting from the whole range of written literature will obviously be a major source for this. He will use concordances and textual corpora and, if he has access to them, on-line databases. For certain kinds of usage question, the last-mentioned can often provide rough-and-ready statistical information. An enquiry to DIALOG, the database of scientific abstracts, concerning the spelling of *f(o)etus*, yielded the expected confirmation that 95.9% of occurrences were spelt with *-e-* not *-oe-*. An enquiry to LEXIS/NEXIS concerning the *-ing* derivative of *stymie* yielded 28 examples with a preterminal *-y-* as against 17 with *-ie-*.

The usage guide writer can benefit enormously by working in a centre for lexicography containing files of linguistic material. Yet, because he aims to discover rather different things than the lexicographers, he will frequently be disappointed in his searches. He will also turn to resources that they would not use so much. Examples of spoken usage will be of greater value to him than they are to the conventional historical lexicographer. In particular, he will draw on English linguistic studies to an extent that non-ELT lexicographers would not. He will try to discover how the usage phenomena with which he is concerned have been described within the disciplines of grammar and phonology. It is grammatical scholarship which draws his attention to ambiguities arising from the clash of different constructions, such as 'the most important thing for Argentina is that Britain recognize(s) her sovereignty over the Falklands'[6] or 'I wondered whether, when I was cross-examined, I should admit that I knew the defendant'.[7]

The usage guide writer will use the linguistic principles established within existing descriptions of the language to explain and describe features which have not yet received specific attention. He is not tied to a particular model, but can draw on any source that sheds light on his preoccupations. Popular approaches to language and usage are as much grist to his mill as scholarly ones. A twenty-year-old article from a Sunday colour supplement criticizing innovations in pronunciation or solecisms in grammar, found at the back of a drawer, can be valuable evidence for usage at the date of the article and for the attitudes behind linguistic criticism.

The principles of guidance

Discussion within a usage guide can be organized in many different ways. The choice of presentation, for most usage guide writers, is likely to be governed by the availability of space. It would be pointless to present comprehensive, objective arguments for and against rulings on

[6] *The Oxford Guide to English Usage* [*OGEU*] (Oxford, 1983), p. 179.
[7] *OGEU*, p. 174.

matters where it can be assumed that most would agree to be bound by an arbitrary convention: for example, in the principles of punctuation or in the main areas of spelling. There will therefore always be subjects on which unsupported dogmatic statements are made. But even in some quite conventional subjects, the usage guide writer may decide that it is worth while explaining the reasons for the convention, if any, on the sound educational ground that understood principles are remembered and used better.

In the fields of grammar and vocabulary, and pronunciation to some extent, recommendations require supporting arguments. The usage guide writer can give them without support, but if so he weakens their authority. A good usage guide entry requires three things: exemplification, explanation, and recommendation. The examples identify and contrast the competing linguistic forms or constructions. The explanation is the heart of the entry: it defines the linguistic feature under consideration, describes its context, function, and meaning, and tries to show how that feature has come to be realized in two (or more) competing forms. Inevitably, the explanation merges into the recommendation, or the latter grows out of the former; for as the parallels and analogies are adduced, the context (register, region, currency) is described, and the intended meaning is clarified, the ground is prepared for an argument in favour of one of the rival forms.

The theoretical arguments on which recommendations are based can be classified under six headings: structural, logical, statistical, historical, social, and aesthetic. Structural arguments involve relating the linguistic feature being considered to others that are similar or parallel to it; appealing, in short, to the principle of analogy. An example would be the argument against using *hopefully* as a sentence adverb on the grounds that other sentence adverbs, such as *regrettably*, can be converted to *it is regrettable*, etc., *that*, but *hopefully* cannot be converted to *it is hopeful that*.

Logical arguments are closely allied, but generally bring in the referents of the linguistic items; they propose one of the structures to be the more congruent with the intended meaning. An example of this is the objection to *someone called it to my attention* used in place of the more logical *someone called my attention to it*.

Statistical arguments consider the relative frequency of different usages (including whether they really occur). For example, many authorities object to the use of *disinterested* in place of *uninterested*; yet of the (structurally) related nouns, *disinterest* (= 'lack of interest') is quite common, whereas *uninterest* is rare.

Historical arguments make use of the facts concerning the origin and development of a given form for or against it. This is perhaps the commonest kind of argument employed: an example would be the preference for using *decimate* in a sense approximating to its etymological meaning, e.g. 'to destroy by a large proportion of' rather than in a transferred sense 'defeat utterly'.

'Social' is a rather inadequate label for a category of argument based upon the incidence of a given linguistic form among different groups of language users, who may be classified by region, nation, cultural affinity, education, or even (dare one say) class. For example one could appeal to the usage of many 'good writers' in support of *self-deprecating* in the sense of 'self-disparaging'.

The aesthetic argument compares the relative amount of pleasure given by each of the rival linguistic forms. It is highly subjective, but there may be grounds (phonetic, for instance) on which a consensus is attainable: for example, a recommendation to avoid jingling adverbs like *scholarlily*.

These six kinds of argument overlap a good deal. Two or three of them may be combined: statistical evidence, especially, may be combined with other kinds of evidence in support of a recommendation. More significantly, one kind of argument may indicate the opposite conclusion to another. This poses an interesting problem for the usage guide writer. By what criterion does he decide? There is, of course, no simple answer. I should like to suggest, however, that he is swayed by more weighty considerations than mere caprice or blind dogma. A usage guide writer is a linguist, like a lexicographer or a grammarian. The facts of language are his primary concern: to try to argue them away would be to go against his own calling. But in many issues of usage there are telling facts on both sides. It may be that one variant is used in speech by the majority, but its rival is strongly felt to be more appropriate in formal (especially written) English by most people for whom careful writing is a regular occupation. What weight can be assigned to each side? Is mere force of numbers to decide which to follow? Or is the likelihood that the majority usage will eventually oust the other a clinching argument? It is surely rash to predict the outcome of linguistic change, and to base present practice on what it may be in the future seems philosophically dubious. In such circumstances it is often wisest for the usage guide writer to state the facts — the widespread instinctive employment of one variant, beside the strongly held conscious preference for the other — and leave it for the reader to decide.

A particularly important tool of the usage guide writer in this situation is the concept of register. Some linguistic variations occur only within a given variety, or pervade all varieties. But many can be accounted for in terms of the variety in which they are at home and appropriate. A large part of the usage guide writer's purpose is to describe a variety of linguistic behaviour that is appropriate for formal occasions and for an audience that transcends regional, class, and even national boundaries. He will therefore depend particularly on the distinction between 'formal' and 'informal' usage — the latter being, roughly, what comes naturally in familiar communication, the former, a variety we cultivate.

The organization of the material

A usage guide can be organized like a textbook, with chapters devoted to broad subjects such as 'Principles of Composition'. Such works are generally conceived as handbooks to the wider topic of style, which includes usage but should be clearly distinguished from it. An outstanding example would be 'Strunk and White'.[8] But even following a relatively belletristic model, it is hard for the usage guide writer to avoid enumerating things in lists. In the work just referred to, for example, the fourth chapter, 'Words and Expressions Commonly Misused', comprises a series of small entries, virtually unrelated to each other, dealing with *all right*, *as to whether*, *data*, and so on.

'Fowler' still concerns itself pre-eminently with good style, but turns its structure the other way about. Though many entries are discursive, each is an item in an alphabetical list. Because there is no overall structure enabling the reader to locate them by logical position, the entries are all assigned identificatory titles, with varying success. *Latin plurals* and *Subjunctives* handle expected subjects under guessable headings, but the unlikelihood of our ever expecting to find an entry *Out of the frying pan*, or of guessing what it might be about, has often been observed. Such a work, as was recognized in the first edition, contains two kinds of entry: 'general articles', and 'those on individual words'.[9] Achieving the right balance between the two is one of the usage guide writer's greatest difficulties. In an expansive book like *Modern English Usage* it perhaps does not matter that the plural of *forceps* receives two lines of discussion under *forceps*, eleven under *Latin plurals*, and four more under *Singular -s*, all making the same recommendation. But if one has less space at one's disposal, where does one place such a topic? Does *forceps* get an entry to itself, for ease of reference, or does it join a collection of other Latin-derived nouns whose plurals can cause uncertainty?

Clearly, the most economical approach is to collect together whatever can be grouped by a common feature, and to give separate treatment to

[8] W. Strunk and E. B. White, *The Elements of Style* (3rd edn, New York, 1979).
[9] H. W. Fowler, *A Dictionary of Modern English Usage* (Oxford, 1926), p. v.

everything else. Questions of grammar have generally to be treated under general headings; conversely, topics in the lexis call for separate handling (though from time to time two or more words can be discussed together, as for example *thankfully* alongside *hopefully*). Spelling and pronunciation require both approaches: the many general rules, or tendencies, have to be set forth, but there are also large numbers of individual cases that conform to no rule and must be listed one by one.

The advantages of the collective entry are great. First of all, a saving of space is achieved if an explanation and recommendation have only to be presented once for a number of similar items. Then there is the pedagogic argument: the user is likely to grasp and remember a generalization that can be applied to a number of linguistic phenomena better than isolated statements about individual cases. If one is reminding oneself whether to write *i* or *y* in *siphon*, it is useful to be given the complete list of words in which the variation between *i* and *y* poses difficulty for many people — *cider*, *cipher*, *gypsy*, *sibyl*, and all the rest. But the pedagogic argument is part of a deeper principle. To know only that there is a variation between two alternative forms or constructions, and to be aware of the recommended alternative, is not very interesting; it is the lowest level of knowledge. To know that there exists a whole range of parallel sets of alternatives is knowledge of a higher order: a pattern is observable; intellectual interest is aroused. If the usage guide writer not only reveals the existence of a pattern, but also goes on to advance possible reasons or to infer some kind of general law or tendency, he progresses to a third degree of instruction. This is no longer the black-and-white statement of the classroom, but is akin to serious academic discourse, even though it lacks the context and presentation associated with the latter. At this point the motivation of the usage guide writer — which I have suggested above is educational rather than polemical — and the practicalities of organization on the page, merge. The usage guide writer is by nature an observer and analyst of linguistic patterns; by presenting his observations and his analysis (it may be, in a glibber, cruder way than would satisfy academic standards) he both fulfils his scholarly aims and also achieves a large measure of economy, memorability, and interest in his published pages.

The gathering of related phenomena under common headings gives rise to a problem of reference. *Forceps* no longer has an entry to itself; the user has to look for it under *-s*, or, better, *plurals*, or perhaps *Latin plurals*. This places an increased burden on the user. The most satisfactory way to ease this burden seems to be threefold: the use of the clearest possible entry headings, the provision of copious cross-references, and the adding of a detailed index covering both subjects and forms, including endings like *-s*. One has to part with the ideal of the user's always finding what he wants in one shot; but that ideal has never been completely realized. For example, it is difficult to furnish many grammatical topics with adequate and simple descriptive labels, and even harder for the user to describe the topic he is seeking. Some topics have well-known labels, such as *split infinitive* or *hanging participle*, but, convenient as they are, these contain an already-implied summary of and judgement on the topic — that the *to* and stem of an infinitive are an indissoluble unit, and so forth. The question whether a relative word is required in a construction like 'if he would take it in the sense (in which) he meant it' is rather difficult to encapsulate in a brief, readily recognizable heading (*adverbial relative clauses*, perhaps?). This seems an inevitable problem, and if its only solution is to require users to do a little extra reading and learning, perhaps they are the better for it.

The value of the usage guide

The subject matter of the usage guide is a collection of scattered topics; it would be easy to impute weakness to the genre on this account. Is it merely a ragbag, or can it have a coherent and distinctive purpose?

As has been said, the scattered topics gathered by the usage guide are related by an external function. They all involve variation, uncertainty, and in some cases controversy, and the immediate purpose of the compilation is to facilitate choice. This, it may be argued, has its own value. But the collecting of data on this basis is valuable in other ways. Let me suggest three.

Firstly, the usage guide has a valuable function with regard to established, accepted rules. By setting out to catalogue in full the known principles it is able to investigate and settle the less well-known and marginal cases. Lexicographers are likely to decide between *mateyness* and *matiness* on the basis of their evidence for those two words alone: the usage guide writer will consider the choice in the context of his evidence for all the adjectives in *-ey*.[10] The usage guide is the only authority making such rulings on a systematic basis, and it is a useful, if unspectacular, function.

Secondly, the usage guide has the potential to enlighten the obscurity which controversy both draws attention to and tends to increase. For example, we know of the rivalry between lexical items like *anticipate* and *expect*, *depreciate* and *deprecate*, *different from* and *different than*;

[10] *Cagey* and *clayey* seem usually to keep the *-ey* before *-ness*, whereas *phoney* and *wheyey* change it to *-i-*, as they all do before *-ly* (see *OGEU*, p. 33).

but is it just a case, as some claim, of the usurpation by B of a function proper to A, or has a new function that did not exist in A or B before been evolved by B?

Thirdly, the usage guide has the potential to document linguistic trends or features that might otherwise be overlooked. For example, the mere listing of words exhibiting contemporary variation and change in pronunciation like *abdomen*, *decorous*, *sonorous*, *subsidence*, and so on, might be criticized as barren in itself. But when we consider them together, as three-syllabled words, we begin to reflect on the causes of the variation and that may possibly lead to insights into English phonology. Even a consideration of why some variation is controversial while the rest is not could yield valuable sociolinguistic understanding. The icebergs of disputed usage can offer insights into the linguistic glacier that they broke off.

I am far from claiming that the usage guide governs a linguistic province over which Dictionaries and Grammars have no jurisdiction, or that the others wilfully ignore the topics which usage guides consider important. Lexicography and Grammar are concerned with the same territory as usage guides, and they map many of the same localities, but they are working on a vast scale and must inevitably miss some details. The usage guide does not rival but complements its older siblings. By concentrating on the fine details of linguistic variation, scattered, apparently without pattern, far and wide over the surface of the English Language, the usage guide, in its best embodiments, may be able to pick up trails that the other disciplines, from their loftier vantage points, do not spot.

PROVENANCE AND PERSISTENCE OF STANDARD AND LITERARY FORMS IN ENGLISH REGIONAL DIALECTS*

J. D. A. Widdowson

In recent years, the historical study of English regional dialects in the diachronic perspective has been the target of considerable criticism. In the rest of Europe and in North America, however, dialectology and sociolinguistics have moved steadily ahead on parallel and mutually supportive paths, no fundamental dichotomy being perceived between them. Not only has this enabled dialectologists in these countries to benefit from new techniques of analysis but it has also maintained an awareness of the importance of the historical dimension in language study. In England, on the other hand, there has been demonstrable impatience with the work of so-called 'traditional' dialectologists, whose techniques are often regarded as outmoded, inadequate and wrongheaded.[1] However, criticism of the *Survey of English Dialects*[2] seems to have ignored the fact that its fieldwork techniques were not only advanced and sophisticated for their time, but eminently successful in eliciting a massive body of data, the richness of which has been as yet only partially revealed, much less exploited. It is also necessary to point out that the Dieth-Orton division of their material into the four analytical levels of phonology, lexis, morphology and syntax was in step with, if not in advance of, the use of these categories by the structural linguists of the early 1950s. We need to remind ourselves that the preliminary work of Harold Orton and Eugen Dieth on the *SED*

---

* An earlier version of this paper was presented at the Third Historical Linguistics Conference, University of Sheffield, March 30th, 1983.
[1] For a discussion of such criticisms see Stewart Sanderson and J. D. A. Widdowson, 'Linguistic Geography in England: Progress and Prospects', in J. M. Kirk et al., eds, *Studies in Linguistic Geography* (London, 1985), 34 – 50.
[2] H. Orton et al., *Survey of English Dialects (B): The Basic Material* (4 vols, each in 3 parts, Leeds, 1962 – 71). For a discussion of critical comment see Kirk et al., *Linguistic Geography*, 40ff.

preceded that of such pioneers of structuralism as Trager and Smith,[3] Fries,[3] and that redoubtable and lucid populariser of the structuralist gospel, James Sledd.[4] It is all very well to say that the *SED*'s sample was restricted as regards age-group and rurality, but one needs to bear in mind that, with deliberate and purposeful endeavour, Orton resolved to record for posterity the full range of the usage of the oldest stratum of the rural English population at that time before it disappeared for ever. Even he could not have been fully aware how timely this survey was. Happily, it was undertaken in what are now recognised as the final decades when a representative sample of what George Ewart Evans has called 'the old rural pattern' or 'the old prior culture'[6] survived in sufficient numbers throughout rural England for such a study to be carried out. It is all too easy to be critical of Orton and Dieth with the benefit of hindsight. Their work, however, needs to be set in its historical perspective where it is seen not only as pioneering and extraordinarily farsighted, but also as furnishing a wealth of unique data whose depth and breadth are only now being revealed some thirty years later. Hampered by lack of funds and staff, the enormous task of analysing and presenting the data is inevitably a slow process. Moreover, the analysis and presentation, while taking account of new techniques wherever possible, must perforce reflect and respect the aims and methodology of the Survey itself. The *SED* database is of course too extensive and significant to be ignored, and it is salutory to note that its published material has been drawn on very freely by scholars, and not least by those who have criticised it.[7] What is more, the collected data, including the original fieldwork notebooks and recordings, is available for further study, analysis and alternative interpretation. Even so, it seems that no English sociolinguists have availed themselves of these opportunities, perhaps suspecting that this might involve them in years of painstaking study of a kind undertaken by Harold Orton, his colleagues and students over more than three decades.

Among many other potential opportunities for exploration, the *SED* Basic Material provides ample evidence of the survival of forms from earlier stages of the language. Regional dialects are in many respects

---

[3] George L. Trager and Henry Lee Smith Jr., *An Outline of English Structure*, Studies in Linguistics, Occasional Papers No. 3 (Norman, Oklahoma, 1951).
[4] Charles Carpenter Fries, *The Structure of English* (New York, 1952).
[5] James Sledd, *A Short Introduction to English Grammar* (Glenview, Illinois, 1959).
[6] See George Ewart Evans, *Where Beards Wag All* (London, 1970), 17ff.
[7] See, for example, J. C. Wells, *Accents of English* (3 vols, Cambridge, 1982); Peter Trudgill, *On Dialect: Social and Geographical Perspectives* (Oxford, 1983).

living exemplifications of earlier usage — a commonplace which incidentally deserves more specific investigation. While it is obvious that the overwhelming majority of regional dialect forms are simply older usages retained, often with some nonstandard modification, in current speech, there is still a tendency, especially among educators, purists and pedants, to stigmatise them as the language of the ignorant or the uneducated, or at least of the unsophisticated. These attitudes, founded on the prestige of Standard English, itself a comparatively recent phenomenon, echo such eighteenth-century branding as Johnson's *vulgar*, not to mention Wyld's 1930s use of *provincial*,[8] and even the *OED*'s magisterial labels *dial.* and *colloq.* which often prove ill-advised because of the tendency of words to change status, often over a very short period of time.

The *Basic Material* of the *SED* reveals a number of regional dialect forms which are the modern equivalents of older regional variants, and also forms which were originally to be found in standard and/or literary English. While it is universally recognised that the study of regional dialects yields valuable information about earlier dialectal usage, and indeed this is central to the justification of the diachronic approach to them, little attention has been paid to the provenance and retention of standard and literary usage in regional speech. Philologists, for instance, have been primarily concerned with the development of the standard language, and have taken little account of dialect variation. Dialectologists themselves seem largely to have ignored the subject, especially in recent years. One of the earliest and undoubtedly one of the most detailed and significant studies is that of Elizabeth Mary Wright, written over seventy years ago, in which she draws on the rich resources of her husband's *English Dialect Dictionary*, and demonstrates the scope and potential of the topic.[9]

Using the Basic Material of the *SED* as a starting point, and drawing on more recent fieldwork of my own, the intention here is to draw attention again to this field of enquiry, to point out how the record might be revised and updated from evidence made available since the turn of the century, and to suggest some possible ways in which the retention of such forms in English regional dialects might be investigated further. One might begin by noting that such retention occurs at all analytical levels — phonological, lexical, grammatical and syntactical. The provenance of a given form, however, is frequently difficult to

---

[8] H. C. Wyld, *The Best English: A Claim for the Superiority of Received Standard English*, S.P.E. Tract No. XXXIX (Oxford, 1934).
[9] Elizabeth Mary Wright, *Rustic Speech and Folk-Lore* (London, 1913), esp. Chapters V, VI and VIII.

establish, not least because of the lack of spoken evidence before the advent of electronic sound recording. Like the philologists, we are therefore once again obliged to rely on written evidence, filtered through the uncertain conventions of spelling and printing, to identify a historical basis for comparison. In establishing provenance, the work of certain writers — diarists, novelists and others who are keen-eared listeners to 'the real language of men', is generally more reliable in its representation of spoken usage. Paradoxically, however, it is often the relatively static and stultified poetic diction of eighteenth-century writers which may constitute the most fruitful basis for comparison, since their language tends towards a selfconscious standardisation and rectitude, which makes for relatively easy identification of standard and literary words and phrases which have persisted in the regional dialects of twentieth-century English but have been lost or become obsolescent or archaic in the standard language. At the same time, those colloquial and slang expressions employed on occasion by eighteenth-century writers are clearly distinguished as such by virtue of their being strongly contrasted with the literary register typical of the period, thus polarising formal and informal usage in the literature of the time and implying that the former is the perceived and accepted norm and the latter merely a diverting and amusingly racy variation.

Unfortunately, since philologists have singularly failed to take due note of dialectal and analogical influence on Standard English, they typically attribute any apparent anomaly to 'mistakes' or 'exceptions' which they see as deviations from a perceived norm. Behind the difficulties of provenance there also lurks the much more fundamental problem of the definition of the terms *standard* and *dialect*, especially when attempting to compare their constituent forms over various timespans. The retention in regional speech of usages formerly in the standard language is also characteristically capricious and haphazard. Why is it, for example, that according to the *SED*, the standard botanical name *convolvulus* is used for *bindweed* in four widely-separated areas of Northern England, rather than one of the fourteen or so other dialectal forms recorded: *bear-bind, bell-bind, bethy-wind, bind, corn-bind, wave-wind, with-wind, withy-wind, bell-vine, devil's gut, ground-ivy, lap-love, wheat-vine* and *bindweed* itself?[10] Some interesting patterns of variation and distribution emerge from an analysis of such forms and offer useful clues as to how the sideways slippage from standard to dialect might occur.

[10] See Harold Orton, Stewart Sanderson and John Widdowson, eds, *The Linguistic Atlas of England* [*LAE*] (London, 1978), Maps L11a, 11b.

The study of standard or literary survivals in regional dialects is full of surprises. Among many examples at the phonological level, for instance, the dialects continue to offer solid evidence for an arbitrary division midway between Cardinal Vowels 4 and 5 for the 'normal' development of /ɑ:/ to /ɔ:/ (*stān* to *stoon*) in the course of Middle English on the one hand and the non-breaking forms of Scottish and Northern English regional speech on the other, the complex present-day diphthongal realisations constituting shibboleths for the differentiation of standard and nonstandard speech. More paradoxically, fieldwork reveals such apparent anomalies as the unexpected Chaucerian East Midland pronunciation of the medial vowel in *yis* /jɪs/ for Standard English *yes* in East Yorkshire, for example, which immediately raises questions as to how these seemingly identical pronunciations are replicated over time and space. Even more intriguing is the semi-malapropistic alteration of phonemes in the process of their sideways movement, e.g. the very common *obstropolous/obstrocolous* variants of *obstreperous* which are well attested in the various glossaries published by the English Dialect Society.[11] Also of interest is the omission of final consonants in such words as *give*, *in*, *of*, *with*, which was of course normal in Elizabethan English, both written and spoken, and is a common feature in some regional dialects today, as is the reduction and/or omission of the definite article *the*. Medial /v/, typically omitted in such forms as *o'er* in literature until the nineteenth century, is also lost in many dialects. Thus the Sheffield *gi' o'er*[12] would have been perfectly acceptable in Shakespeare's day, and poets of the eighteenth and nineteenth centuries would naturally also have found it quite unexceptional, though whether they would have interpreted it as meaning 'to stop, desist' remains open to question; certainly this sense is rare in current standard English, if indeed it occurs at all. The same is true of dialectal *e'er* and *ne'er* whose medial /v/ was commonly lost in literary English from the sixteenth to the nineteenth centuries. The retention of /r/ finally in syllables, finely discriminated into several regional variants, of course remains one of the most obvious features distinguishing dialectal pronunciation from the standard, as does the typical omission of initial /h/, and the realisation of final /ŋ/ as /n/ in words ending in *-ing*. This latter example is particularly significant in that such pronunciations as *huntin'*, *shootin'*, *fishin'*, until recently stereotypical of the upper classes, are now virtually confined to regional dialect speakers. Among

[11] This invaluable series of glossaries, which appeared regularly from 1873 to the turn of the century, is a testament to the vigour of dialect studies at that time — a vigour which was unfortunately not sustained.
[12] Data drawn from The Survey of Sheffield Usage [SSU], Department of English Language, University of Sheffield.

other notable retentions of older pronunciations one might mention the medial plosive in /'fadə, 'mʊdə, 'brʊdə/, the continued use of /s/ for /ʃ/ in *ash* in Northern and West Midland counties, and the preservation of variants which are in some ways more akin to the earlier pronunciation of words borrowed from other languages than the current standard forms, e.g. /'nɛvɪ/ for *nephew* in many *SED* citations from the Northern Counties, and occasionally reported from the East and West Midlands and the Southern Counties.

At the grammatical level regional dialects also retain a remarkable number of older features of standard and literary usage. The complexity of forms exhibited by auxiliary and modal verbs is perhaps the most fruitful ground to explore, regional dialects often being distinguished by these forms alone, not to mention the retention of second person inflections consequent on the continuing presence of the pronouns *thee*, *thou*, *ye* and their variants in many dialects today. The dialectal paradigms of the verbs *be*, *have*, *do*, *shall*, *will*, *ought*, *must*, *may*, *can*, *dare*, *get* especially repay investigation, in their positive, negative and interrogative realisations. The retention of the older past tense forms, e.g. *spake*, *eat*, *goed*, *catched* and such past participles as *gotten*, *putten*, *setten* is of course also well known.

Occasionally the researcher is rewarded by following a trail which leads all the way back to Old English. A memorable example of this occurred in my fieldwork in East Yorkshire in 1960. A man describing the infestation of a wooden jetty with rats commented: 'Aye, it was forwadden wi' rats was piles.' Fresh from an undergraduate course in which Old English was a dominant element I 'translated' the word *forwadden* almost without realising it, and its meaning was obvious from the context anyway. Remarkably, it is not listed in any of the major dictionaries, and yet has remained in the dialect for over a thousand years. Its meaning is, of course, transparent, preserving the intensifying force of the prefix and having the sense of 'completely walked through'.

Numerous archaic inflections persist in nouns. Plurals include *bellowses* /'bɛləsɪz/, *gallowses* (i.e. trouser braces) /'galəsɪz/. /'poustəz/ (posts), *childer* (children), and the possessive inflection is frequently omitted, e.g. *my sister son*. Regional dialects also tend to preserve the *-s* inflection in *forwards*, *towards*, *besides*, *backwards* etc. and final /st/ in *whilst*, *alongst*, *amongst*, *betwixt*, this latter word, now archaic in standard English, being recorded in several *SED* localities in the North and Midlands, though clearly in retreat. Dialectal reflexives tend to mirror the form of personal pronouns, omitting *self/selves* and/or preserving archaic recensions of *self/selven* as *-sel/-sen*.

The retention of older syntactical features is least evident, but interesting examples include the postpositional adjective in: 'Times many I've told you not to do that',[13] variation in the placement of negators and of direct and indirect object: *Give it me/Give me it*,[14] not to mention the well-known alternatives *We put the light on/We put on the light*,[15] *Twenty five to three/Five and twenty to three*,[16] and the variations of *On Friday week* (*Friday week, next Friday, next Friday week, a week on Friday, a week next Friday, a week come Friday, a week Friday*),[17] which are remarkably complex in their patterns of distribution.

As might be expected, the most significant retention of earlier standard and literary forms is found at the lexical level. Just as proverbial expressions such as *With might and main* and *Mony a mickle maks a muckle* preserve forms no longer otherwise extant in Standard English, so also do the regional dialects. Examples are so numerous that it must suffice here simply to present a limited selection of items to give some idea of their range and to note some of their general characteristics. These include the following:

1. It is important to recognise that most of the notions (keywords) in the *SED* questionnaire, i.e. the standard forms for which dialectal variants are to be elicited, themselves appear as regionally distributed responses, and thus become part of the regionally distributed patterns of lexical choice. This obviously constitutes a fundamental problem in the analysis of the data and in the quantification of variants. Ignoring for the moment those keywords which are used to elicit phonological, morphological and syntactical variation, it is abundantly clear that such keywords as *ants, freckles, brew, donkey, dregs, hens, slide, trim* etc. appear as regionally-distributed responses along with other forms which might be more properly defined as truly dialectal.

2. Several of these standard keywords are now archaic, obsolescent or specialised. This is especially true of certain agricultural and domestic terms, many of which have fallen victim to advancing technology and other changes in lifestyle and modes of reference. Typical examples are: *ash-hole, ash-midden, bait* (feed horses), *beestings, breeches, chemise, coulter, crane* (device to suspend cooking utensils over fire), *fellies, flitch, gridiron, knee-straps, pilch, plash, ridgel, whelp, wright*. Also now archaic are most of the keywords referring to pre-decimal coinage.

---

[13] SSU.
[14] See *LAE*, Map S1.
[15] *Ibid.*, Map S2.
[16] *Ibid.*, Map S7.
[17] *Ibid.*, Map S8.

3. A number of *SED* keywords and phrases are now used mainly or exclusively in formal or literary contexts, e.g. *aftermath* (in its literal sense), *to bring forth* (= to bear young), *rivulet, in spate*.

4. A number of *SED* responses, e.g. *brimming over/flowing over, marshy/swampy, rise/incline/slant*, can hardly be regarded as dialectal, even though they are regionally distributed. Others are simply synonyms, with full accredited status in the standard language, e.g. *pantry/larder, sitting-room/parlour, rubbish/garbage/refuse, brew/mash/infuse, steep/soak*.

5. Some responses indicate a lack of discrimination on the part of the respondent, the fieldworker, or both, e.g. the apparent confusion in references to certain items which would normally be distinguished in standard English — *lice/nits, threshold/weatherboard, quilt/counterpane, brush/broom*. This may of course be due in part to the form of the question and the respondent's understanding of it.

6. Colloquialisms abound which are difficult to group on a regional basis, e.g. such baby-talk forms and pet names as *pinny* (pinafore), *shimmy* (chemise), *taddy* (tadpole), *sweety* (sweet).

7. Euphemism is at work in regional dialects as well as in standard English, e.g. *entire* (*horse*) for stallion, *to tread* (by cockerel), *chemise, backside/behind/bottom/bum, stomach* (belly). On the other hand, the dialects retain four-letter words now considered impolite but once standard: e.g., *arse, fart, piss, shit*.

Drawing on the *SED*, again supplemented by other recent fieldwork in England, it is possible to identify, among many other examples of the retention of older lexical forms, the following words and phrases presented in alphabetical order for ease of reference. Very few examples are to be found in Books I – III of the questionnaire (concerning the farm, farming, animals), but examples are progressively more frequent in Books IV – VIII.

ABEAR = endure (Q. *bear*)[18]
ABIDE   *"*   *"*
ADDLE (Q *earn*)

---

[18] Examples drawn from *SED* are followed by the relevant keyword from the Survey's Questionnaire [Q].

(A)FEARED (Q. *afraid*)
ATTERCOP (Q. *spider*)
AUGHT (Q. *anything*)
AYE (Q. *yes*)
BAIRN (Q. *child*)
BEVER = shiver, tremble
BIDE (Q. *stay at home*)
BLACKGUARDING (Q. *cursing*)
BOGGART, BOGGIN, BOGLE (Q. *bogey*); BUGA-BO, BO-BOY
BRAT (Q. *apron*)
BROCK (Q. *badger*)
CHEMISE (Q. *chemise*)
CLOUT = cloth (Q. *dishcloth*)
COTTED (Q. *tangled*)
EMMETS (Q. *ants*) OE *æmete*
ENOW = even now, next
FAIN (Q. *glad*)
FALL (Q. *autumn*)
to FAVOUR (Q. *resemble*)
FIT (Q. *ready*)
FLESHER = butcher
FLESHMEAT (Q. *meat*)
FLIPE (Q. *brim* (of hat))
FOWLS (Q. *chickens*)
GREITHER (Q. *cobbler*)
HINDMOST (Q. *last*)
KEEK (Q. *peep*)
KEN (Q. *know*)
KINK-COUGH (Q. *whooping-cough*)
KIRK (Q. *church*)
LAP (v) (Q. *wrap*)
LATHE (Q *barn*)
LEARN = teach
LISK (Q. *groin*)
(A) LITE (Q. *a few*)
I'd as LIVE = I'd rather. OE *leof*
MAIDS (Q. *girls*)
MIND (Q. *remember*)
NAUGHT (Q. *nothing*)
OXTER (Q. *armpit*)
PACE-EGGS (Q. *Easter eggs*)
PADDOCK (Q. *frog*)
PARSON'S ACRE (Q. *churchyard*)

193

RIGHT (intens.) = very (Q. *very glad to see you*)
RIME (Q. *hoar-frost*)
SARK (Q. *chemise/shirt*)
SCALLION (Q. *spring onion*)
SOMEWHAT (Q. *something*)
STITHY (Q. *anvil*)
SUPPING (Q. *drinking*)
SURRY/SORRY/SIRRAG[19] (cp. Shakespearian *sirrah* = sir: respectful term of address to a man)
THRONG (Q. *busy*)
TUNDISH (Q. *funnel*)
WARK (Q. *ache*)
WED(DED) (Q. *married*)
WENCHES (Q. *girls*)
WETSHOD[20] = having wet feet
WICK (Q. *active*)
WICKS (Q. *mouth corners*)[21]
WROUGHT (Q. *earned*)
YONDER (Q. *those over there*)

This restricted and random sample can do little more than hint at the wealth of lexical items once standard or literary which have been retained in English regional dialects over several centuries and are still spoken today. The Basic Material of the *SED* is indeed a rich and unexploited source for the identification and study of such survivals. They offer us a unique opportunity to investigate not only the pronunciation, form and function of numerous items no longer in standard or literary usage, but also to discover how and why such words are modified, decline or disappear.

In order to open up this subject for further study it is necessary for a systematic and detailed survey to be made, not only of the full range of the Basic and Incidental Materials of the *SED* but also of all other research data on regional dialects collected in this century, whether published or unpublished. As a first step, the extensive materials collected in the recent dialect surveys in Scotland, Wales, Northern Ireland and the Irish Republic,[22] as well as in sociolinguistic surveys of

[19] SSU.
[20] SSU.
[21] Cp. J. R. R. Tolkien and E. V. Gordon, eds, *Sir Gawin and the Green Knight* (Oxford 1925), 49; 1.1572.
[22] The Linguistic Survey of Scotland, The Survey of Anglo-Welsh Dialects, The Tape-recorded Survey of Hiberno-English Speech and The Linguistic Survey of Anglo-Irish.

urban dialects[23] should be examined, firstly to ascertain whether a comparable degree of retention is found in towns and cities as in more rural areas, and secondly to establish a norm of current usage against which the continuity and change of the relevant data can be measured over time. Such an investigation might then be followed up by a study of all other available databases, especially the many unpublished dissertations and monographs available in those universities, polytechnics and other higher educational institutions in which dialects have been a focus of attention in teaching and research.[24] Furthermore, the material collected during the first (onomasiological) phase of the *Atlas Linguarum Europae* remains virtually unexplored[25] and, since the localities investigated were selected from the network established for the *SED*, the data would provide valuable comparative evidence for developments over the last thirty years or so. Nor should we neglect the numerous studies and glossaries which have appeared in the publications of the various regional dialect societies,[26] and in the work of individual scholars.

The primary source for future investigation, however, remains the *SED* itself, and the lexical data for such a study will become more readily accessible with the publication of the *Dictionary of the Traditional Dialect of England*.[27] Far from being an outworn or irrelevant database, the *SED* constitutes the only nationwide regional dialect survey conducted in this country — and conducted contemporaneously with the most significant watershed between the language of age-old agrarian England and its modern technological counterpart. Whatever its

[23] See, for example, J. Cheshire, *Variation in an English Dialect* (Cambridge, 1982); C. D. Heath, *The Pronunciation of English in Cannock, Staffordshire: A Sociolinguistic Survey of an Urban Speech Community* (Oxford, Philological Society, 1980); Caroline Macafee, *Glasgow*, Varieties of English Around the World, gen. ed. Manfred Görlach, Text Series vol. 3 (Amsterdam/Philadelphia, 1983); K. M. Petyt, *Dialect and Accent in Industrial West Yorkshire*, Varieties of English Around the World, gen. ed. Manfred Görlach, General Series, vol. 6 (Amsterdam/Philadelphia, 1985); P. Trudgill, *The Social Differentiation of English in Norwich*, Cambridge Studies in Linguistics 13 (Cambridge, 1974).

[24] Notable among these are the Universities of Edinburgh, Leeds, Newcastle, Reading and Sheffield, and the University Colleges of Wales at Bangor and Swansea.

[25] Photocopies of the questionnaire responses and the accompanying tape-recordings for the England and Wales section of the Atlas are deposited in the archives of the Centre for English Cultural Tradition and Language at the University of Sheffield, where the fieldwork for the *ALE* was co-cordinated.

[26] For a current list of the major societies see Clive Upton, Stewart Sanderson and John Widdowson, *Word Maps* (London, 1987).

[27] C. S. Upton, Stewart Sanderson and J. D. A. Widdowson, *Dictionary of the Traditional Dialect of England* (in progress).

limitations, the Survey provides a massive and homogeneous body of data which will furnish scholars with research materials for many years to come. When the current overriding preoccupation with synchronic studies begins to lack credibility and we once again come to realise that the language of today is firmly rooted in the past, the Survey's potential for diachronic analysis, if nothing else, will at last be recognized. The study of the retention of older linguistic features in English dialects is merely one aspect of that potential which is worthy of scholarly investigation.

TABULA GRATULATORIA

A.J. Aitken, *Edinburgh*
Dr Richard Allsopp, *University of the West Indies*
Ashley Crandell Amos, *Dictionary of Old English*
Richard W. Bailey, *University of Michigan*
Clarence L. Barnhart, *Bronxville, USA*
Professor Janet Bately, *King's College, London*
Professor Michael Benskin, *Universitetet i Oslo*
N.F. Blake, *University of Sheffield*
Dr Jean Branford, *Dictionary of South African English*
Avril Bruten, *St Hugh's College, Oxford*
Professor J.A. Burrow, *University of Bristol*
Frederic G. Cassidy, *Chief Editor, Dictionary of American Regional English*
Professor Peter Clemoes, *Emmanuel College, Cambridge*
J.E. Cross, *University of Liverpool*
Anna Morpurgo Davies, *Somerville College, Oxford*
D.M. Davin, *Oxford*
Department of English, Victoria University of Wellington, New Zealand
Professor R.D. Eagleson, *University of Sydney*
The English Faculty Library, Oxford
Denton Fox, *University of Toronto*
Professor Roberta Frank, *University of Toronto*
Professor Helmut Gneuss, *Universität München*
Professor Douglas Gray, *Lady Margaret Hall, Oxford*
Richard Hamer, *Christ Church, Oxford*
Antonette diPaolo Healey, *Dictionary of Old English*
T.F. Hoad, *St Peter's College, Oxford*
Dennis Horgan, *St Catherine's College, Oxford*
Anne Hudson, *Lady Margaret Hall, Oxford*
A.M. Hughes, *The Oxford Dictionaries*
Nicolas Jacobs, *Jesus College, Oxford*
John F. Kiteley, *Hertford College, Oxford*
Professor em. Dr Martin Lehnert, *Berlin*
Bernard Levin, *London*

Professor Robert E. Lewis, *Middle English Dictionary*
The Master and Fellows of St Peter's College, Oxford
Bruce Mitchell, *St Edmund Hall, Oxford*
The New Oxford English Dictionary Department
Marguerite Y. Offord, *Oxford*
The Oxford English Dictionaries
Professor Dr Herbert Pilch, *Albert-Ludwigs-Universität Freiburg*
Eddie Playfair, *London*
John C. Pope, *Yale University*
Sir Randolph Quirk, *President, The British Academy*
Dr William Ramson, *Australian National University*
Jane Roberts, *King's College, London*
Fred C. Robinson, *Yale University*
Emeritus Professor H.L. Rogers, *Sydney*
Vivian Salmon, *Oxford*
John Simpson, *The New Oxford English Dictionary*
Celia Sisam, *St Mary's, Isles of Scilly*
Professor Dr Marvin Spevack, *Westfälische Wilhelms-Universität Münster*
Professor E.G. Stanley, *Pembroke College, Oxford*
G.M. Story, *Memorial University of Newfoundland*
Professor Yoshio Terasawa, *University of Tokyo*
Dr Felicien de Tollenaere, *Warmond, The Netherlands*
Professor J.B. Trapp, *The Warburg Institute, London*
Francis Warner, *St Peter's College, Oxford*
Edmund Weiner, *The New Oxford English Dictionary*
Professor J.D.A. Widdowson, *University of Sheffield*